NEW WORLD EMPIRE

NEW WORLD EMPIRE

Civil Islam, Terrorism, and the Making of Neoglobalism

William H. Thornton

JZ
1480
·A55
N49
2005
West

ROWMAN & LITTLEFIELD PUBLISHERS, INC.

Lanham • Boulder • New York • Toronto • Oxford

ROWMAN & LITTLEFIELD PUBLISHERS, INC.

Published in the United States of America
by Rowman & Littlefield Publishers, Inc.
A wholly owned subsidary of The Rowman & Littlefield Publishing Group, Inc.
4501 Forbes Boulevard, Suite 200, Lanham, Maryland 20706
www.rowmanlittlefield.com

P.O. Box 317, Oxford OX2 9RU, UK

Copyright © 2005 by Rowman & Littlefield Publishers, Inc.

All rights reserved. No part of this publication may be reproduced, stored in a retrieval
system, or transmitted in any form or by any means, electronic, mechanical,
photocopying, recording, or otherwise, without the prior permission of the publisher.

British Library Cataloguing in Publication Information Available

Library of Congress Cataloging-in-Publication Data

Thornton, William H., 1950–
  New world empire : civil Islam, terrorism, and the making of neoglobalism / William
H. Thornton.
    p. cm.
  Includes bibliographical references and index.
  ISBN 0-7425-2940-1 (cloth : alk. paper) — ISBN 0-7425-2941-X (pbk. : alk. paper)
  1. United States—Foreign relations—Islamic countries. 2. Islamic countries—Foreign
relations—United States. 3. United States—Foreign relations—2001– 4. Islamic
countries—Foreign relations. 5. Terrorism—Government policy—United States.
6. Islam and politics. I. Title.
  JZ1480.A55N49 2005
  327.73017'67—dc22
                                                                              2005009155

Printed in the United States of America

∞™ The paper used in this publication meets the minimum requirements of American
National Standard for Information Sciences—Permanence of Paper for Printed Library
Materials, ANSI/NISO Z39.48-1992.

For my father, Harry Thornton,
and his soul-daughter, Songok

Contents

Introduction: Islamic Terrorism as Power Politics

Cold War II

SEPTEMBER 10, 2001, was the last day of a religious era: the age of the gospel according to neoliberal globalism. That unalloyed faith in capitalism as a global solution came crashing down the next morning. Finally it dawned on the world's sole superpower that its Cold War victory was not the end of history. Washington Consensus economism had proved as useless as geography or military supremacy for fending off the enemy that struck on 9/11.

Cheered on by the New Economy, neoliberalism had considered itself the final victor in the ideological wars of the twentieth century. It had won its case for world peace and harmony through "free trade." Even tough-minded realists had begun rating economic power over geopolitics as the chief guarantor of security. This mentality worked its way into the post–Cold War security debate, such that to deny the seriousness of the terrorist threat was to tacitly affirm the liberal capitalist vision of globalization. Too late it sank in that neoliberalism had missed at least half the story: the same global processes that unite disparate worlds can put them on a collision course. Little wonder that Huntington's *The Clash of Civilizations* and Barber's *Jihad vs. McWorld* were back on the charts after 9/11, while Fukuyama's "end of history" thesis seemed almost as dated as the Berlin Wall.[1] It too was "history" now—the fading icon of post–Cold War triumphalism.

The marvel is that the defense establishment manages to miss the qualitative thrust of these new insecurities. More attentive to its own quantitative desire than to the present danger, it tries *at all costs* to regenerate the power and glory of its Cold War mission—the Pentagon equivalent of *Happy Days*. As Jack Beatty notes, the military "is using the war on terror to binge on Cold War weapons, including a missile-defense system that is to our imminent peril what the Maginot Line was to the Nazi blitzkrieg. . . . Every dollar spent on yesterday's threat is a dollar subtracted from today's."[2]

This fixation on Cold War ways and means is matched, in terms of realist counterpoise, by an even greater security risk: the post–Cold War conception of the world as a market ripe for picking. Throughout the 1990s this globalist agenda sidelined geopolitics while reducing noncapitalist cultures to the status of developmental refuse—a myopic combination that precluded any awareness of mounting geopolitical pressures outside the globalist sphere. When Thomas Friedman (who found a home at the *New York Times* as Francis Fukuyama lite) asserted that two nations with McDonald's golden arches cannot make war, he clearly meant two fully globalized nations. Few imagined that the rest of the world mattered much, so no one thought to plant the golden arches in, say, Kabul. But after 9/11 the global periphery took on geopolitical weight. Power politics had come back with a vengeance, effectively putting an end to the "end of history."

Two questions became paramount for what remained of the New World Order: how the United States would react to the new geoterrorism, and how other powers would react to the U.S. reaction. How long, for example, would Europe tolerate its role as Washington's faithful spear carrier? A good test case would be the European response to coming resource wars, and especially to U.S. intransigence concerning Iraq. It is the Islamic response, however, that will most decide the course of power politics for years to come. Prior to the U.S. invasion in 2003, Salman Rushdie warned that precipitate action against Iraq could draw Iran in on the side of its erstwhile enemy and forge the united Islamic front that was bin Laden's supreme goal. President Bush and his advisors would then have fulfilled al Qaeda's supreme objective.[3]

Clearly America is reverting to its Cold War habits, but without the restraint that Soviet competition had imposed. This geopolitical recidivism prompted the Bush administration's renewal of aid to Indonesia's military,[4] its anti-terrorist accord with ASEAN (August 1, 2002), and its new "great game" engagement in Central Asia—e.g., its unabashed support for post-Soviet tyrants such as Turkmenistan's Saparmurat Niyazov, Uzbekistan's Islam Karimov, and Kazakhstan's Nursultan Nazarbayev. In short, Cold War anti-communism has been replaced by anti-terrorism, in what can fairly be described as Cold War II.

If the Afghan "war on terror" was the "first front" of this new Cold War, its prelude was Desert Storm. Some celebrity interpretations of the Gulf War border on comedy in their effort to press events into ponderous theoretical packages. While Jean Baudrillard saw the whole thing as a media fabrication, in keeping with his theory of boundless hyperreality, Immanuel Wallerstein thought the war ended in a draw,[5] in keeping with his thesis of the powerlessness of the world's lone superpower. These perspectives collide head-on, since part of what made the war fictional for Baudrillard was its very nonfictional military asymmetry. As he saw it, the war was over before it started, the rest being mere theater. He was not entirely wrong: the victory was never in doubt, though casualties were a great concern, and few imagined the larger price of victory in terms of later "blowback." If this was theater, the Islamic world was not enjoying the show. America's patent preponderance of power—economic and cultural as well as military—made it the perfect lightning rod for anti-globalist reaction. And the gross abuse of that power, as Gore Vidal admonishes, invites a perpetual terroristic response.

Seeing themselves as the benefactors of the world's underprivileged (a hyperreal stretch worthy of Baudrillard), neoliberal globalists failed to notice the storm clouds gathering outside their commercial orbit. So too their blanket economism caused them to prematurely retire other forms of global damage control, such as a healthy balance of power. The geopolitics that survived neoliberalization was stripped of the anarchic element that had always kept Hobbes in the realist game, and at times made him seem more contemporary than Woodrow Wilson. From the vantage of the new Washington Consensus, American power had transcended nationalism to become the chief agent of a universal good—namely, globalization. As suggested by its glittering label, "Operation Enduring Freedom," America's attack on Afghanistan of October 2001 was seen as so unimpeachably benign that no countervailing coalition against the United States was conceivable. The "end of history" spelled, therefore, the end of realist logic.

Without that geopolitical brake, U.S.-directed globalization comes to see itself as a new and improved manifest destiny. Not even 9/11 could alter this delusion, for the Islamic resistance that gave us that horrific jolt was interpreted as evil personified—a case of anti-globalist criminality rather than geopolitical opposition. Muslims who say "no" to globalization are treated much as American Indians were when they refused to stay on the reservation: not as armies of resistance, but as loathsome heathens who had the gall to obstruct manifest destiny. In this unipolar spirit, Stephen Brooks and William Wohlforth drop any Clintonian attempt to paper over raw power. They conclude, with undisguised satisfaction, that "no global challenge to the United States is likely to emerge for the foreseeable future. No country or group of countries wants to maneuver itself into a situation in which it will have to contend with the focused enmity of the U.S."[6]

That assessment holds true, however, only within the bounds of traditional statist geopolitics. Outside those bounds a new kind of realism is taking shape.

Much as some American Indians chose death over surrender to white man's ways, some Muslims see globalization as a fate worse than death. The difference is that the resistance, this time, is well armed and globally connected. The main reason it was not on the geopolitical map long before 9/11 is that the Pentagon as well as the CIA and FBI were of the opinion, like the French at Dien Bien Phu, that they were dealing with cultural if not racial inferiors. Nor did this attitude evaporate after 9/11. It lives on in the American refusal to treat captive Taliban soldiers—who by necessity are usually irregulars without uniforms—as legal prisoners of war.

Has European thinking gained a better grasp of post–Cold War realities? Yes and no. The New World Order is fraying at the edges as America's European allies—partly out of distrust of U.S. unipolar motives, and partly because many see 9/11 as America's problem, not theirs—attempt their own break with "history." That quixotic enterprise notwithstanding, they realize better than most Americans that more is at stake in the Islamic resistance than organized crime. It is wishful thinking to equate bin Laden with Al Capone.[7] That would make him and the whole al Qaeda phenomenon far less dangerous than they are. The fact that al Qaeda was essentially an NGO and 9/11 a distinctly nonstate action did not dent their geopolitical status. Rather it marked the countervailing reaction that realism had long predicted, albeit in the form of a statist alliance, not jihad.

Gilles Kepel explores some of the less visited sources of jihad: (1) the failure of Muslim postcolonial nationalism in the mid-Cold War period, (2) the oil politics that artificially inflated the theological status of Riyadh's ultraconservative Wahhabism, (3) the Iranian Revolution of 1979, which raised the status of fundamentalist politics in general, and (4) the Afghan veterans' shift from Saudi Sheikism to jihadic salafism (*salaf* in Arabic meaning the devout traditions that modernity polluted). Being outside the control of any state, these jihadists became the "free electrons" of radical Islamism.[8] Nonetheless it was foreordained that America would take the place of the Soviets as the primary target of Islamic resistance. The spectacle of Allied forces massing on Saudi soil during the Gulf War finally lit the pan-Islamic fuse; and the continued presence of 6,000 U.S. troops on that soil has kept jihadic passions stoked ever since. The occupation of Iraq, and the shocking revelations of torture and sexual abuse in American military prisons, put the final nail in this coffin.

Kepel, however, refuses to surrender his belief that the jihadic firestorm reached its zenith long before, with the Soviet expulsion from Afghanistan in 1989. From this perspective radical Islamism was already in a rearguard slide by the early 1990s, its most infamous terrorist feats of that decade—the 1993 World Trade Center bombing, the 1996 attack on U.S. troops in Saudi Arabia, the 1998 embassy bombings in Kenya and Tanzania, and the 2000 bombing of the USS *Cole* in Yemen—being born of sheer desperation. Hence jihad is on the wane.

That optimism—a latter-day variant of end-of-history globalism—runs aground on the counterglobalist dialectic of Benjamin Barber and Gore Vidal. Simply put, brutal, hegemonic actions will sooner or later evoke hostile reactions. In the absence of civil anti-globalism,[9] uncivil resistance is bound to erupt. Lee Harris makes a good case for jihad's grand theatrics,[10] but that is small comfort unless there is reasonable certainty that 9/11 was a one-act play. That hope vanishes when the internal dynamics of Islamism are set within the external dialectic of globalization and its enemies.[11]

For Michael Klare this larger drama is not centered in Afghanistan, Kuwait, or any of the so-called "Axis of Evil" states, but in America's own sandbox, Saudi Arabia. Since the time of the Carter Doctrine—which obligated America to safeguard the Persian Gulf against all outside aggression—the Al Saud family enterprise has enjoyed formal U.S. protection against invasion and (given Reagan's input) insurrection as well.[12] It hardly matters to the U.S. power elite, and the Bush energy elite in particular, that in Saudi terms the mildest liberal criticism counts as insurrection. Shortly before Vice President Cheney lectured veterans on the need for the forceful democratization of Iraq, the president was having lunch at his ranch with his Saudi friend, Prince Bandar, the one who engineered the expeditious departure of Osama bin Laden's relatives from the United States after 9/11. The Arab world is fully aware of the hypocrisy whereby America, in Maureen Dowd's words, supports "a corrupt, repressive dictatorship that sponsors terrorism" while simultaneously condemning another "corrupt, repressive dictatorship that sponsors terrorism. . . ."[13]

Secure pipelines are obviously more important than human rights in the globalist scheme of things. That is why jihadic militancy, the only real threat to stable oil politics, is today's substitute for communist insurgency. By the same token, anti-terrorism is taking up where anti-communism left off. The fact that this polarity is a military mismatch does not reduce its geopolitical potency, for the dramatic force of random terrorism compensates all too well—in the Sorelian sense of mythic empowerment—for jihad's lesser firepower.

That much must be granted after 9/11: patently this is a world-scale contest. What jihad lacks in military hardware it compensates for in nebulosity and sheer determination. Its weakest point may be its moral TINAism,[14] for the power politics of jihad ultimately rests on its claim to being the only credible sword of anti-globalist justice. The best way to combat jihad, therefore, is not with cruise missiles, cluster bombs, or special operations forays,[15] but with a better moral sword. To that extent Joseph Nye is perfectly on track with his concept of "soft power."[16] Unfortunately the Bush administration understands this as the need for better propaganda, as if the problem of anti-Americanism is one of packaging rather than substance. Thus we get Charlotte Beers, formerly the public relations guru for Uncle Ben's rice, as the undersecretary of state for public diplomacy and public affairs. What we won't get is the only power politics that would work in the world of jihad: a geopolitics of hope.

Rolling Back History

Viewed in terms of power politics, 9/11 could be seen as a geopolitical blessing in disguise for the United States. Granted, the sole superpower seemed at first to have been rendered far less "exceptional" on that day. But normalization on the side of defensive vulnerability soon redounded to abnormalization on the side of offensive reaction. Two ages were simultaneously born: one of ubiquitous insecurity, certainly, but also one of awesome unipolarity. America was at once the winner and loser in a much revised New World Order. There was no separating the two, since to be on top of the global heap was to be the prime target of global resistance. After 9/11 the New World Order was exposed for what it is: a Washington-directed New World Empire.

The full price of this global paramountcy did not immediately sink in, for most countries were inclined to condone America's post-9/11 war dance. This martial consensus signaled the end of the globalist "end of history" and the advent of a highly bellicose *neoglobalism*. International relations were taken off automatic pilot. In the relatively placid 1990s it had been assumed that peace and prosperity could be purchased in a neoliberal two-for-one sale. Despite the Gulf War and a host of lesser interventions, the belief had persisted that the New World Order was the natural state of things to come. Minor tune-ups might be required, but no major overhauls were anticipated. Pockets of disorder were expected to fade away by economic attrition.

9/11 changed all that in a flash. The 1990s turned out to have been at best a respite between two warring ages. It was made abundantly clear that order would not simply unfold, but would have to be imposed. In the White House this revelation was so far from bad news that the challenge was not smiling too broadly in front of the cameras. At home and abroad, security took full priority over all the things the administration wanted to dispose of anyway. Securitization also enhanced the comparative advantage of America's military supremacy—this at a time when its economic supremacy was flagging.

That gain in hard power was not offset by any major loss in soft power, since America was still swimming with the global tide. Just to make a point, however, Washington let the fact be known that it could go it alone or even swim against the tide if need be. NATO responded to 9/11 by invoking for the first time a provision of its founding treaty that construes an attack on any member as an attack on all. But, as if to put multilateralism in mothballs, Deputy Defense Secretary Paul Wolfowitz curtly vetoed that collective action, saying that if the United States needed help, it would ask for it.

Soon, of course, it had to do just that.[17] In neither Afghanistan nor Iraq was much thought given to the aftermath of war. But Americans hardly registered these glaring setbacks. Bush Inc. found its salvation in the new security imperative. Before 9/11 the administration had faced not only prolonged recession and declining public trust in capitalist institutions, but growing awareness of the president's habit of wading maladroitly in the corporate mire. The war of retribution against the Afghan Taliban helped get his public image out of the muck, but it ended (as the Gulf War had for his father) far too soon for reelection purposes. Worse yet, the chief culprit got away cold. This was no minor setback, since by most accounts the whole affair had been justified as a "get Osama" operation.

Another Islamic demon would have to be targeted without delay. The war on terrorism's "second front" in Southeast Asia, as treated in chapter 3, held some promise, but it would be hard keeping such a simmering engagement on the front pages. The solution advanced by neoconservative hawks such as Wolfowitz and Vice President Dick Cheney was a preemptive strike on Bush Senior's old nemesis, Saddam Hussein. Saddam was the perfect inflatable target, given his penchant for sword rattling and his petulant defiance of UN weapons inspections, as if he had much to hide. But to justify a full-scale invasion, two obligatory threats—which Wolfowitz conflated as one—had to be fairly well established: that Saddam had an ample WMD stockpile and/or solid links with Osama's al Qaeda network. Norman Mailer well describes the improbability of these two trusting each other. Saddam saw bin Laden as a religious zealot, while bin Laden saw Saddam as an irreligious brute. The two, moreover, were locked in competition for control of the Muslim world.[18]

All credible intelligence services had their doubts concerning both White House allegations. This was not an insurmountable obstacle, however, since the necessary intelligence could be obtained by other means. If Enron could make billions through "creative accounting," the Bush administration could make war through creative intelligence. It was simply a matter of setting up new intelligence operations for this precise purpose. This was not without precedent. Proto-neocons, including Wolfowitz, had used this "B-team" device in 1976 when the CIA failed to deliver a sufficiently frightful estimate of Soviet military strength. Now a special intelligence operation was set up inside the Pentagon to counter the CIA's cautious assessments. And to bring the

CIA itself around, Secretary of Defense Rumsfeld began openly discussing the merits of positioning a special undersecretary for intelligence within the Defense Department. That did it. Saddam was soon being cast not only as a nationalistic butcher, which he was, but as the mother of all global hazards. The Bush administration got its perfect target: an enemy that could be dependably blown away, even as the real enemy, al Qaeda, enjoyed the game from the sidelines.

It was a clear case of kill or be killed: get Saddam or follow in Dad's one-term footsteps. The Iraq invasion afforded a double diversion: a timely escape from real problems at home and real enemies abroad. That dual opportunity made the cover charge (a grossly underestimated $100 billion) seem like a bargain. This promised to be the best historical remake ever aired: a Middle Eastern version of the "good war" that brought liberal capitalism to Germany and Japan. With Saddam out and the mullahs muffled (which turned out to be the harder task), regional politics would flow on a river of oil in Washington's direction.

But to sell this corporate bonanza back home, to families that would be paying for it in blood and taxes, it would be necessary to put Saddam high on the WMD wanted list. This was not an easy task, given the obstinate integrity of Hans Blix (formerly the top UN weapons inspector) and the *initial* intractability of the CIA. Political pressure on the CIA was getting results as early as March 2002, when CIA Director George Tenet spoke before the Senate Armed Services Committee. Already the gap between classified and unclassified CIA reports had begun to take on Bushian/Enronian proportions. By definition, creative intelligence is not discomfited by mere facts. Call it designer information. This was the art form in which Bush Junior, after years of professional bungling, finally found his niche. Clinton, of course, was a master of the same craft, but he had wasted much of his talent on personal designs. Bush Junior's fabrications were more "presidential," and therefore far more dangerous.

The good news, from a neoconservative perspective, was that "history" was here to stay, wars and all. The globalist dream of a history-less future would have cut deeply into military-industrial profits. The Iraq invasion, conversely, was an act of military-corporate redemption, rolling history back into a comforting "good war" narrative, complete with its own salvation drama (saving Private Lynch). Assuming it all went well, this would be a much better draw come Election Day than a shadow war on al Qaeda could ever be.

This daring operation—setting Saddam up so as to knock him down— would require reality reconstruction on an Orwellian scale. The choice of targets was a matter of geopolitical surety: better to have a sure outcome (Saddam as sitting duck) in an unnecessary war than the indeterminate war on terrorism that issued from 9/11. In opting for certainty, the Bush administration implicitly chose a modernist narrative with a fixed location and a suitably progressive ending (democracy promotion, say, or anything but *oil*) over a postmodern nightmare. Casting Saddam over Osama in the lead villain role of the good war on terrorism was a stroke of neoconservative genius, if also a dangerous case of geopolitical denial. In that real-world respect, it was born of the same gentleman's 'C' mentality that made the president think global warming would go away if he ignored it hard enough.

This was not the first time that resistance to postmodern contingency entered into the analysis of terrorism. The lure of certainty was evident, for example, in the pre-9/11 analysis of the RAND Corporation's terrorism guru, Bruce Hoffman, who put an untimely cap on America's anxiety toward (and hence vigilance toward) al Qaeda. Speaking at a conference on terrorism in April 2000, Hoffman dismissed the alarmist school that predicted a "new face of terrorism" in years to come. Especially he disputed the growing fixation on Osama bin Laden, who in his view could never effect "any fundamental political change in American foreign or domestic policy."[19]

Comforting as that "old face" of terrorism might be, it ran the risk that attends any Orwellian rewrite: putting reality perilously on hold. Saddam Hussein, the devil we knew, was the best "old face" around. As Mailer puts it, this dream opponent "had a tough rep, but not much was left to him inside."[20] Like Bush himself, or Enron's Ken Lay, Saddam was image all the way down. This fits the new American dream (and dream target): a world without certifiable facts, where history can be scripted, and wars made good (at least for Bechtel, Halliburton, and the Carlyle Group).[21] The idea is to roll history back, but not too far: back to World War II, not to the hard lessons of previous decades, when even Theodore Roosevelt came to realize that imperialism breeds more resistance than it is ever worth.[22]

Notes

I wish to express special appreciation to three people for their invaluable input throughout the course of this project. They are Susan McEachern at Rowman & Littlefield, Raff Carmen at the University of Manchester, and my wife, Dr. Songok Han Thornton. In addition I wish to thank Hans Theunissen at *EJOS*, Kira Brunner and Gina Neff at *Radical Society*, Ros Whitehead at *Antipode*, and Sunil Sharma at *Dissident Voice* for their tremendous help and encouragement.

1. See Samuel P. Huntington, *The Clash of Civilizations and the Remaking of World Order* (New York: Simon and Schuster, 1996); Benjamin R. Barber, *Jihad vs. McWorld*

(New York: Ballantine Books, 1995); and Francis Fukuyama, *The End of History and the Last Man* (New York: Avon Books, 1992).

2. Jack Beatty, "The Expulsion from the Magic Kingdom," *The Atlantic Online* (June 5, 2002), <www.theatlantic.com/cgi-bin/send.cgi?page=http%3A//www.theatlantic.com/unboun>.

3. Salman Rushdie, "Double Standards Make Enemies," *Washington Post* (August 28, 2002): A23.

4. Raymond Bonner and Jane Perlez, "White House Seeks to Review Aiding Indonesia's Army," *New York Times* International (June 29, 2002), <www.nytimes.com/2002/06/29/interview/asia/29INDO.html>; and Todd S. Purdam, "U.S. to Resume Aid to Train Indonesia's Military Forces," *New York Times* International (August 3, 2002), <www.nytimes.com/2002/08/03/international/asia/03POWE.html>.

5. See Immanuel Wallerstein, "The Eagle Has Landed," *Foreign Policy* (July/August 2002), <www.foreignpolicy.com/issue_julyaug_2002/wallerstein.html>.

6. Stephen G. Brooks and William C. Wohlforth, "American Primacy in Perspective," *Foreign Affairs* (July/August 2002), <www.foreignaffairs.org/Search/printable_fulltext.asp?I=20020701FAEssay8517.xml>.

7. Nonetheless there are interesting parallels between the 1930s "war on crime" and today's war on terrorism. See Bryan Burrough, "How the Feds Got Their Men," *New York Times* (May 14, 2004), <www.nytimes.com/2004/05/14/opinion/14BURR.html>.

8. Gilles Kepel, *Jihad: The Trail of Political Islam*, trans. by Anthony F. Roberts (Cambridge, MA: Belknap Press of Harvard University Press, 2002), 219.

9. See William H. Thornton, "Civil Antiglobalism and the Question of Class," *Social Analysis: The International Journal of Cultural and Social Practice* 46, no. 2 (2002): 123–30.

10. Lee Harris, "Al Qaeda's Fantasy Ideology," *Policy Review* (August 2002), <www.policyreview.org/AUG02/harris_print.html>.

11. Kepel could be right so far as those internal dynamics are concerned, but this only underscores the importance of the externals (most notably globalization) that he effectively brackets. There is no necessary contradiction between Kepel's internal and Barber's external causalities.

12. Michael T. Klare, "The Geopolitics of War," *Wagingpeace.org* (originally published in the November 5, 2001, issue of *The Nation*), <www.wagingpeace.org/articles/01.11/011105klareprint.htm>.

13. Maureen Dowd, "I'm with Dick! Let's Make War!" *New York Times* Opinion (August 28, 2002), <www/nytimes.com/2002/08/opinion/28DOWD.html>. Both the Clinton and Bush administrations have obstructed investigations into the Saudi money trail that leads all too pointedly to known terrorists. Likewise there has been a systematic blackout of the historical facts surrounding the $7 billion that Saudi Arabia funneled into Saddam Hussein's nuclear program. See Greg Palast, "See No Evil: What Bush Didn't (Want To) Know about 9/11," *Tom Paine.com* (March 1, 2003), <www.tompaine.com/scontent/ 7310.html>.

14. TINAism is the doctrine that "there is no alternative" to the present expansion of neoliberal globalization. Jihadism ironically supports this myth, giving itself as the sole exception to the rule.

15. Not to mention the growing paramilitary network of clandestine prisons in America's global gulag. See Stephen Gray, "America's Gulag," *New Stateman* (May 17, 2004), <www.newstatesman.co/nscoverstory.htm>.

16. See Joseph S. Nye Jr., *The Paradox of American Power: Why the World's Only Superpower Can't Go It Alone* (New York: Oxford University Press, 2002).

17. A 5,000-member International Security and Assistance Force (ISAF) would be required to maintain a semblance of order in Kabul, and in August 2003 NATO assumed command of the operation. Another 10,000 such troops will be needed if a modicum of order is to be achieved outside the capital. Mounting chaos forced the UN to suspend all aid activities in the south, America's 9,000 troops being too occupied hunting Taliban and al Qaeda insurgents to give much time to ordinary policing. See Amy Waldman, "NATO Takes Control of Peace Force in Kabul," *New York Times* (August 12, 2003), <www.nytimes.com/2003/08/12/international/asia/12AFGH.html>; and "NATO's New Role," *The Christian Science Monitor* (August 13, 2003), <www.csmonitor.com/2003/0813/p08s03-comv.htm>.

18. Norman Mailer, "Only in America," *New York Review of Books* 50, no. 5 (March 27, 2003): 49 (49–53).

19. Hoffman did better on other matters. Against the grain of his stated optimism, he accurately noted the shift of terroristic organizations from small, pyramidal hierarchies to today's more amorphous command systems. See Bruce Hoffman, "Change and Continuity in Terrorism," a speech delivered at the "Terrorism and Beyond: The 21st Century" Conference, cosponsored by the Oklahoma City National Memorial Institute for the Prevention of Terrorism and the RAND Corporation, April 17, 2000, 4–5 of 18, <www/mipt.org/hoffman-ctb.html>.

20. Norman Mailer, "The White Man Unburdened," *New York Review of Books* 50, no. 1 (July 17, 2003), <www.nybooks.com/articles/16470>.

21. In April 2003 Bechtel (with former Secretary of State George Schultz on its board) won the State Department's largest contract, for up to $680 million over an eighteen-month period. Another big contract winner is Halliburton (whose CEO from 1995 to 2000 was Vice President Cheney), which will get most of the nearly $500 million that Bush is requesting from Congress for restoring Iraq's oil flow. See Mark Gongloff, "Bechtel Wins Iraq Contract," *CNN Money* (April 17, 2003), <money.cnn.com/2003/04/17/news/companies/Bechtel>; and Mark Gongloff, "Iraq Rebuilding Contracts Awarded," (March 25, 2003), <money.cnn.com/2003/03/25/news/companies/war_contracts>.

22. See John B. Judis, "History Lesson: What Woodrow Wilson Can Teach Today's Imperialists," *The New Republic* (June 9, 2003), <www.tnr.com/doc.mhtml?pt=9aNIN97FJx83cfpk2gpKZA%3D%3D>.

1

Apartheid without Borders: The New Globalism and Its Enemies

The New Global Apartheid

THE ERA OF UNALLOYED GLOBALIZATION LASTED roughly a decade, from the end of the Cold War to September 11, 2001. Never before had world affairs been entrusted so completely to "free market" forces. With power politics sidelined, or relegated to the erstwhile Third World, the Treasury and Commerce Departments won out over State and Defense as the chief power brokers for an emerging "Washington Consensus."[1] Even those who saw through the myth of globalization as a ticket to universal peace and prosperity were often taken in by the lesser god of TINA, which grants that "there is no alternative" to current globalization. Clearly there were, however, alternative globalizations.[2] While Europe took the high road of cosmopolitanism, purging foreign policy of power itself,[3] America took the all too effective low road of *power economics*.[4]

That road proved even less amenable to the needs of the global South than geopolitical realism was at the height of the Cold War. The change was in the works long before the full Soviet collapse. During the Reagan years it took a rock concert to draw attention to mass starvation in Africa, and still the issue was left to fester. Not even the 1990s economic boom could stir a more generous attitude, thanks in part to the global application of domestic "trickle down" theory. The plight of the South got little more than passing reference at economic summits.[5]

Now, with roughly a billion people living somehow on less than $1 per day, and billions more losing their grip on yesterday's global promise, the dream of universal modernization is collapsing into a postmodern nightmare. At best globalization offers a limited number of luxuriously furnished lifeboats, with lifeboat ethics to match. From any more egalitarian perspective the "win-win" formula of early globalism has joined the twentieth century's long line of failed ideologies. Globalization was supposed to replace the old economic ladder with an elevator. Instead, as William Greider puts it, the world's working classes got more of a seesaw: many must fall for some to rise. Only the capitalist classes won on both sides, and even within their ranks the price of survival was the surrender of all competing loyalties. In the lingo of anti-globalist protest, power economics (which is to say actually existing globalization) works by putting "profits over people"—and over nations, indigenous cultures, ecosystems, and every trace of nonmaterialist values.

Few know how low this reaches. The vaunted information revolution, as dissected by Manuel Castells, caters to a criminal economy that includes child prostitution (slavery, pure and simple) and a genocidal drug trade which by the mid-1990s was grossing more than the global trade in oil. Meanwhile a massive traffic in weapons supplies the needs of criminal and terrorist organizations, which are also gaining access to nuclear materials.[6] We can rest assured, however, that the same information economy that services this global firestorm also makes a better fire engine: America's "new face of war," to borrow Bruce Berkowitz's title. Clearly globalism is a double agent, being at once the arsonist *and* the firefighter.

The success of neoliberalism's public relations lies in what is omitted from its mission statement. Many globalist enterprises disappear from view. These unmentionables include a burgeoning trade in bodies, dead or alive: the transport of illegal immigrants—netting $1 billion a year in Mexico alone— as well as assorted body parts. Cases of literal slavery are emerging across the United States, especially in immigrant farmwork, where the standard remuneration is about $150 a week. Other growth industries include money laundering and rogue banking, the privatization of water supplies,[7] and all kinds of subemployment: the use of workers as literal industrial fodder, without contracts, minimal safety standards, union representation, or the most limited health care. China, for example, has become a major supplier of manufactured exports, but the workers making those goods suffer much the same disease and abuse that plagued early industrial workers.[8]

This is not to suggest that sweatshop horrors are absent from today's America. When student protests recently exposed the global network linking overseas sweatshops to on-campus stores, attention was also drawn to a startling amount of sweatshop production in American cities. While giant agricorporations rake in massive subsidies, family farms are passing out of existence, victims of the same rural impoverishment that is hitting the Third

World. Regardless of location, the global system encourages bare subsistence wages, inhuman hours, abysmal working conditions, and draconian action against workers who dare to question the system.[9]

It is also not mentioned how pharmaceutical companies block access to generic medicines in impoverished regions, or how double trade standards allow America and Europe to flood less developed countries with highly subsidized agricultural products, undercutting the subsistence incomes of small farmers throughout the world.[10] Then there is "structural adjustment" (euphemistically termed economic "reform" by the World Bank), which indentures the future production of developing nations. On the same moral plane there is the environmental holocaust perpetrated by multinationals, often with direct funding from the World Bank and other global institutions.[11] And finally there is the general cultural onslaught of consumerism. Postmodern culture critics write this off as a commendable exercise in "hybridity," but those being hybridized may have a radically different opinion. What they lack is a means of collective resistance—unless of course they are Muslim.

Although the vast majority of Americans—especially those in the "red state" zones that gave President Bush a second term—see the Muslim world as the aggressor in our current civilizational clash, Islamism is patently on the defensive. Coral Bell reminds us that until recently Islam and the West shared a rich religious heritage—one, we may add, that took on new meaning in the face of Soviet-enforced secularization during the Cold War. Islamic societies survived that challenge only to be slammed harder than ever by their former theistic allies. Western secularization removed Christian nations from this common ground, setting the stage for the present East/West culture clash.[12] When the West, emboldened by its Cold War victory, launched its full assault on the non-secular East in the name of globalization, Islamic resistance was inevitable.

Islamism may be, as Bryan Turner suggests, the only surviving alternative to Western capitalist hegemony.[13] Whether it alone can hold the fort is uncertain, but soon it may get some help. Little as CNN viewers would know it, another global firestorm is building in the South. Neoliberalism reserves its most deafening silence for the neocolonial dynamic whereby the world is put on the capitalist auction block. There is nothing TINAesque about this geocorporate power grab, which has more to do with purchased political decisions than with inexorable economic forces. But the end result, in terms of both class and culture, is every bit as grievous as the colonialism that led to war in 1914.

A clue to what is happening is provided by the ironic plight of South Africa's poor after the official end of apartheid in 1994. By 1996, as Arundhati Roy comments, 10 million people out of a population of 44 million had had their water and electricity cut off, and the old economic power structure was more secure than ever behind its new shield of "democracy."[14] Robert Mukolo charges that while the old racist apartheid set white against black in his country, a new corporate hegemony sets rich against poor. This would be bad enough if it were unique to South Africa, but regretfully it is but a chapter in the new *global apartheid.*

Even the United States is not exempt. The 1990s saw the victory, as Thomas Frank puts it, of one America over another.[15] But America's place at the top of the global food chain gave this corporate takeover a much broader sweep, constituting the victory of one world over many. Today's global ethnocide and cultural homogenization trace in part to America's own cultural implosion, beneath its rhetoric of multicultural difference. There are signs, however, that a pluralist counterlogic is starting to take shape. Castells points out that except for a small "globapolitan" elite, world opinion deplores the loss of local and national control that attends globalization.[16]

Making Democracy Safe for Empire

So far, though, those who have the power to implement change are the least likely to want any. That is why, as Bruce Scott recognizes, it hardly matters that the economic resources to remedy this eco-social crisis exist; for the political will does not[17]—not, at least, within the reigning Washington Consensus. And grassroots efforts carry their own risks. One danger is that homegrown resistance can take a highly reactionary form, fueling the kind of militia or "underground man" mentality that inspired Timothy McVeigh,[18] Theodore Kaczynski, and (allegedly) Erich Rudolf. Globalists who railed against anti-WTO protesters in Seattle might reconsider the matter if they knew more about the new social movements waiting in the wings.

Neoconservatism has absorbed much of this ultra-Right disaffection, including a good deal of its anti-government animus, but that linkage is strictly opportunistic. The neocon commitment to Empire ultimately ties it to bigger and more intrusive government, in both a geopolitical and "law and order" sense. The welfare state may be under siege, but a new mode of statism—prone to use more stick and less carrot—is under production. This ultimately puts neoconservatives at odds with anarcho-rightists as well as cosmopolitan globalists.

There is an organic accord, however, between neoconservatism and neoliberalism, both being factories for cultural homogenization. Both are shamelessly at ease with the deepening divide between global haves and have-nots. It is only when an antiseptic view of globalization is contrasted with a noxious view of Empire that a diametrical opposition is obtained. Even in the sphere of geopolitics, where the two seem most at odds, the seeds of Empire were deeply planted within neoliberal globalization. The cardinal feature of Empire's foreign policy—its "for us or against us" binaryism—has long been a feature of the globalist outlook on the non-globalized world.

For those outcast regions the end of the Cold War signaled the dawn of an even colder peace. Washington served notice on them that nonaligned strategies would no longer be tolerated. The message they got was sink or swim, join or starve. The old realist restraints—which had the accidental effect of curbing imperialist ambitions—were cast off. So too the Cold War's sometimes generous (albeit strategically motivated) developmental assistance was suspended. Ingeniously this was all done in the name of the greater good. It had been a postwar cliché that what was good for General Motors was good for America. Now it was ordained that what was good for Unocal was good for the world.[19] Nor was this geocorporate conceit advanced on economic grounds alone. Like Islamic jihad it was packaged as a moral and civilizational injunction. And like communism before it was looked to as a blueprint for world domination with a clean conscience.

That moral wrapping allowed Francis Fukuyama to declare this the best of all possible world orders, and hence the "end of history." But unlike his vast globalist following, Fukuyama comprehended the banality of posthistorical security. He worried that the sheer boredom of it all could drag humanity back into the "historical" abyss. If that concern seems overdrawn after 9/11, it is because we know with perfect hindsight that history will soon enough come to us. Fukuyama is nevertheless on target with his recognition that mainstream politics has moved beyond the bigger questions that once animated it. He understands, as his imitators rarely do, that this seeming concord has its darker side. As we enter the new millennium, it is hard not to see that something is sorely missing in the globalist concept of "democracy": *actual political options.*

To be posthistorical, it turns out, is to be postpolitical. This is the grating contradiction at the heart of neoliberalism and cosmopolitanism alike. The end of ideology that was falsely proclaimed in the late 1950s is here at last, as the liberal/conservative tug-of-war that once energized democratic politics slips into "history." On both sides of the Atlantic, all that is ideologically off center melts into air, putting real political difference out of business. Few in establishment circles seem to realize or much care that this "Third Way" circumvention of Left and Right brooks no opposition. Democratic resistance becomes a relic of the past.

Spearheaded by the Democratic Leadership Council (DLC), the neoliberalization of the Democratic Party took (and continues to take)[20] the "politics" out of American liberalism. But even more profoundly an absence of liberal opposition has allowed for the Republican transfer of power from "paleocon-servatives" to neoconservatives. So it was that the neocons could all but dic-tate the nation's response to 9/11. Even if America's Afghan incursion was un-avoidable—and in chapter 5 I argue that it was entirely avoidable—America's "second front" in Southeast Asia, and especially its preemptive strike on Iraq, would have been unthinkable without this illiberal power shift.

This was the hard Right turn that Sheldon Wolin dubs "inverted totalitar-ianism," with reference to Nazi totalism and expansionism. But unlike the Nazis, who strictly subordinated corporations to political control, the neo-cons (being neoliberals with the last vestiges of progressive liberalism re-moved) corporatize the state. And against the Nazi goal of full and continu-ous social mobilization, the new Right depends upon the sheer apathy that comes with wall-to-wall consumerism. The president brilliantly played this hand, shortly after 9/11, by exhorting the public to "Unite, consume and fly!" Visit Disneyland.

Globalization exports that consumerist ethos in the name of "democracy," and Empire does the same on its neoliberal side. Yet, like Cold War realism, Empire is less guarded in its security trade-offs, such as its blatant funding of dictators like Pakistan's Musharraf.[21] In its 2002 annual report on human rights abuses, Amnesty International charged President Bush's security agenda with sheltering some of the world's worst regimes. So too Thomas Carothers blames the administration for sorely neglecting democratization. He is right so far as the more capacious meaning of democracy is concerned, but misses the utility that pro forma democracy has for the new power elite. Without this fig leaf, Empire would be naked imperialism.

So it is that Paula Dobriansky, undersecretary of state for global affairs, was only half lying when she rebutted Carothers by adducing the Bush adminis-tration's record of "democracy" promotion.[22] The trick is in what counts as democracy. The administration supports an overlay of largely procedural re-forms for the same reason that corporate globalists have: Not only do "free" elections provide good public relations for authoritarian regimes and their corporate cronies, but they offer an effective inoculation against more sub-stantive democracy, which is always unpredictable and often anti-American. For these reasons the new Empire builders tend to be more "democratically" engaged than traditional conservatives, and far more so than traditional real-ists. Such "instrumental" democracy, as Carothers terms it,[23] permits Empire to seize the moral high ground while tending the geocorporate bottom line.

Far from contesting globalization, as Tom Nairn would have it, Empire im-bibes all the tenets of earlier globalism except one: the neoliberal promise to keep geopolitics out of sight, if not always out of mind. The resulting hybrid—let us call it *neoglobalism*—is all about power economics, but sees power politics as the best route to that end. The problem is that power corrupts, and without opposition it usually dictates. After the global fall of communism and liberalism alike, the New World Empire is immune to systemic criticism from the Left. That critical default means that only the neoconservative Right is in a position to forcefully contest market fundamentalism, and even they must do so by way of a globalist sleight of hand. In the name of rescuing corporate globalization, the neocons deftly implant their own vision of a world made safe for *democracy without politics.*

The Fourth Way

With "history" and oppositional politics out of the way, all that remains is the mopping-up operation known as "development": the final solution for regions that have the right stuff (preferably oil or cheap labor) to offer in exchange for global connectivity.[24] This insuperable rage to globalize has been for neoliberals what the unfolding of communism was for the Old Left: a crude but functional teleology that just needs an extra kick now and then. What revolution was for the Old Left, so economic restructuration became for globalists. Otherwise the system rolled on its own. Or so it was imagined in the days before "Osama" became a household word.

Fukuyama himself did not yield a single footnote of his core thesis after 9/11.[25] But the rift between America and Europe over Iraq was not so easily dismissed. With the West "cracking" and the United States not much caring, Fukuyama's "end of history" paradigm was clearly at risk.[26] Less vested neoliberals had long since abandoned his triumphalism, having seen that much more is needed than an extra kick here and there to keep the capitalist wheels spinning.

That is where "Empire" steps in, subsuming globalization in order to save it, by force of arms if necessary. While Empire promises to keep the wheels spinning (well oiled, as it were), it also explodes a cardinal tenet of globalist foreign policy: the myth that the new economism can all but supplant the old geopolitics. Empire keeps all the major features of globalization, plus one: it stands ready to enforce market privileges the old-fashioned way. Neoliberalism hereby drops its Third Way vestments to join neoconservatism within the American fortress state. Call it the *Fourth Way.* After 9/11 this iron-fist globalism could also drop its multilateral guise. Washington's war on Iraq consummated its unilateral drift and, equally, its turn from 1990s economism. Emphatically, however, power economics did not surrender the field to resurgent power politics. Rather the two joined forces in the common cause of Empire.

This melding of neoliberal and neoconservative strategies translates as $billions in new Pentagon contracts—not that the Pentagon had ever suffered for lack of funds. Even after the Cold War its budget held steady at around $300 billion a year. With the promise of a post–Cold War "peace dividend" forgotten, military-industrialism is more than spared the axe. It looks forward to a major role in post-9/11 globalism, whose basic operating assumption is perpetual war between "us" and "them," as President Bush would have it.

There is no easy exit from the vicious circle of terror whereby Empire generates the enemy it requires, and vice versa. This self-sustaining dialectic may be the most novel feature of neoglobalist foreign relations. Armed globalism had its trial run in the Gulf War but only got its permanent marching orders after 9/11. Despite a litany of denials from Washington, the subsequent war on terrorism is in fact the war on Islamism that Margaret Thatcher and Italian Prime Minister Silvio Berlusconi prescribed. U.S. authorities filled that prescription by detaining hundreds of Muslim suspects, usually on flimsy evidence and with dubious constitutional authority.[27] Such policies unwittingly generate further support for militant jihad, all in the name of homeland security.

But it is neoconservative foreign policy that poses the greatest danger, sowing seeds of jihadic unrest in relatively stable regions such as Southeast Asia. While the Pentagon is pleased to find itself welcome once more in its old stomping ground, the price of this welcome mat is exorbitant. After the 1997–98 Asian Crash torpedoed the legitimacy of the region's authoritarian regimes, local reformists could at last challenge the developmental tactics of generals and technocrats. They got rare international backing from the U.S. Congress, in the form of the Leahy Amendment's ban on military support for repressive regimes. But this promising commitment is now in jeopardy. Even as the attacks of 9/11 entrenched the power of neocons in Washington, they dealt a possibly fatal blow to Asian reformism.

In the Philippines, for example, the United States once more serves as a guarantor for an embattled presidency. A simple quid pro quo has been struck: while Manila gets internal security, America gets better geopolitical footing in the region.[28] So too Singapore's ruling party has good reason to support the U.S. regional strategy. Having been the hub of "Asian values" during the region's "miracle" years, and having successfully peddled these values under the globalization label (a real miracle, given the neoliberal claim that globalization is all about liberal democracy), the PAP (People's Action Party) needs post-Crash legitimacy as well as geopolitical backup. Under cover of securitization, Singapore can now dance with Washington without fear of offending China, which has moved in the same direction so far as "terrorism" is concerned.[29] This is a remarkable shift from the Chinese attitude shown as late as April 2001, during the spy plane stalemate on Hainan Island.

Likewise, U.S. cooperation with Indonesia's military—suspended, in compliance with Leahy, after the East Timor debacle—has been quietly reestablished, while Malaysia walks a tightrope between Washington and domestic Islamism. In his final days in office, Mahathir Mohamad reached a timely understanding with President Bush at the October 2001 APEC meeting in Shanghai, as the two effectively bought each other's silence. The Bush administration would mute U.S. criticism of the Anwar Ibrahim affair and the whole array of abuses associated with Malaysia's Internal Security Act, while Mahathir would tone down his rants about America's war on Islamism.[30]

Securitization thus affords a geopolitical solvent as well as an implicit pledge on Washington's part to accept a vastly expanded definition of terrorism—one that includes not only secessionism, as in Aceh, but any radical activism on behalf of opposition politics, human rights, or social justice.[31] What we are watching, Alan Dupont discerns, is a generational rethink of the Asian security agenda. Whereas Chinese communism was the prime mover behind the last such rethink, back in the 1950s, the new revolutionary cadres operate out of Washington. What most distinguishes their foreign policy is their lockstep commitment to military solutions. In place of the neoliberal commercialism that prevailed in the 1990s, neocons put security over everything—albeit on the assumption that profits will follow. Whereas traditional realism sought a favorable balance of power, Empire seeks a favorable *im*balance. The "shock and awe" tactics employed in Iraq were not aimed merely at the Iraqi Republican Guards, but at the world. Indeed, America's ostensive indifference to world opinion was part of the show. On both levels unipolarity was on full and awesome display.

After Iraq, Empire needs no clear and present danger to justify its decisions. Any perceived *future* threat is sufficient ground for preemption. This shoot-first mentality has moved from the neoconservative fringe to the editorial pages of a once "liberal" press. The basic elements of Empire, however, were always latent in U.S.-directed globalization. Power politics went undercover during the neoliberal glory years of the 1990s. But even then the Pentagon was drawing new life from an emerging New World Disorder, and it found veritable salvation in 9/11. Likewise the nation state did not wither away, as earlier globalism predicted, but rather got new work in the service of Empire.

It may be that developed nations serve more as means of globalist enforcement than as ends in themselves, but they are capable of reclaiming their Westphalian status in times of crisis. What seriously challenges that status is not corporate globalization, as conventional wisdom of the 1990s had it, but rather the paramountcy of *one* nation state. American hegemony is turning globalization on its head by openly embracing power politics. In effect it enforces neoliberal ends by geopolitical means. Unfortunately, Empire easily becomes an end in itself. After 9/11 the neocon Right grabbed up the globalist shield of TINA. Accordingly, any opposition worthy of the name must begin by proving that other alternatives do exist. Isolationism, however, is clearly not an alternative for either Left or Right (e.g., Chomsky or Huntington). The best available alternative, I shall argue, is culturally informed moral realism.

Moral Realism

9/11 not only exposed a strategic vulnerability, but a cultural one as well: a solipsism so thick that cultural difference can be registered only by way of world-class violence. Joan Didion relates how for one brief moment American readers tried to break out of this cultural incarceration, such that by the end of September 12, 2001, the shelves were emptied of books on Islam and associated foreign policy. But by late October or early November that curiosity had faded under a barrage of accusations.[32]

By no means was this closure the monopoly of the Right. Cultural Leftists, as Richard Rorty calls them, have long served the globalist power structure by leaving vital issues untouched or twisted beyond recognition, as when Jean Baudrillard effervesces about the twin towers on 9/11 "responding to the suicide of the suicide jets with their own suicide," or when Fredric Jameson describes Osama bin Laden as "the very prototype of the accumulation of money in the hands of private individuals."[33] But the prize goes to Gayatri Spivak's treatment of suicide bombing as "a confrontation between oneself and oneself, the extreme end of autoeroticism."[34] If that is the best cultural studies can do with the subject of terrorism, geopolitical realists should be forgiven for bracketing culture from their analysis throughout the Cold War.

Fortunately there are alternatives to such cultural inanity. One is the new moral realism, as I term it,[35] which confronts the twin axes of global conflict after the Cold War: the East/West civilizational clash that Huntington paradoxically shares with Osama, and the global class divide that has returned, like the new wave of tuberculosis, more lethal than ever. This North/South chasm grabbed world attention with the election of Brazil's new leftist president, Luiz Inácio Lula da Silva; but the ultimate neoliberal nightmare will be the union of these two global fronts, West/East and North/South.

Innocents on all sides could be caught in this global crossfire. World affairs, however, is not a zero-sum game where the United States is necessarily at odds with the whole non-globalized world. The stentorian message of the Seattle WTO protests and subsequent anti-globalization demonstrations is that America's most fundamental interests (as distinct from U.S. corporate interests) are fast converging with those of the South. Such syncretism couples the goals of a still to be achieved America with the South's most pressing needs.

Consider the case of tobacco promotion in the developing world. In the 1980s the United States followed Sen. Jesse Helms into this moral crevasse, forcing world markets to accept U.S. tobacco in the name of "free trade." As Japan and its Pacific imitators surged ahead in a wide spectrum of high-tech production, America took refuge in its solid status as the leading exporter of lung cancer.[36] Its grip on the world's 1.1 billion smokers—which is expected to be 1.6 billion in twenty years—went uncontested until May 2003, when the World Health Organization (WHO) concluded a unanimous agreement with 192 countries to wage war on smoking-related disease through advertising restrictions, labeling laws, and higher tobacco taxes.[37]

Like the Lone Ranger and Tanto, the United States and the Dominican Republic rushed to the aid of the downtrodden Marlboro Man. Together they resisted the kind of labeling laws and advertising restrictions that America itself enforced domestically. Indeed, in June 2003 the U.S. surgeon general spoke out for a total ban on tobacco products. This glaring double standard strips away the moral cloak that America uses to shroud its economic unilateralism.

Apart from a few unreformed neoliberals, does anyone seriously believe that what is good for Altria (Philip Morris) is good for the world? Against the charge that U.S. trade tactics tax the developing world in terms of health costs, the tobacco industry fired back with hard "evidence" that the reverse was true. Philip Morris boasted, for example, that it had saved the Czech Republic $30 million a year in pensions, housing, and health costs for the elderly by *reducing Czech life expectancy*.[38]

Resistance to this genocidal mentality, in the form of WHO-sponsored advertising reforms, has been treated by the United States as an assault on Joe Camel's rights of free speech. But at least WHO gets a response. Public resistance to global corporatism gets ignored. This programmatic indifference is getting harder to maintain, however. The string of anti-globalization demonstrations that began in Seattle metamorphosed into the global anti-war movement of early 2003. Such civil anti-globalism may be the best available weapon against the uncivil variety.[39] To ignore it is to send the message that only terroristic resistance gets results.

Present U.S. unilateralism—realism with a neoconservative twist—also fans the flames of terrorism through its tunnel vision regarding the nature of U.S. "interests." Realism per se is not the problem. Nor is a full retreat from "national interests" the solution. What is urgently needed is a moral-realist redefinition of those interests. Any genuine realism must come to terms with soft power,[40] thereby bridging the chasm that divided twentieth-century realism and idealism. That dichotomy prevents the Left and Right alike from realistically confronting the insecurities that hit home on 9/11.

While neoconservatives divorce the demands of security from those of human rights and social justice (even while wrapping security goals in the language of democracy promotion),[41] Seattle-style anti-globalists typically bifurcate security and trade issues. Moral realism closes both gaps, joining Michael Walzer in his call for a "decent Left" that links geopolitical realism with practical reform.[42] Darrell Moellendorf agrees that the Left no longer has the luxury of an uncompromising anti-war posture, as if all wars and geopolitics are inherently unjust.[43] There are times when nonintervention can be every bit as immoral as overt imperialism. Sins of omission, such as Rwanda and the current Sudan crisis, are no more forgivable than sins of commission, such as Vietnam and today's Iraq.

In the post–Cold War era, more than ever, the United States carries global responsibilities that reach beyond immediate "national interest." Action to stop the civil wars in Liberia and the Democratic Republic of the Congo could easily qualify as moral imperatives. Yet, as Dennis Jett points out, the president who promised to bring "moral clarity" to America's foreign policy has left these matters to the French, whom he famously vilified for their moral intransigence concerning Iraq. Reform in these areas could provide a "realist" payback insofar as peace and rudimentary justice are more than ever in the interest of *all* nations. That global convergence is the bedrock of moral realism.

Usually this transnational end can be advanced by peaceful means. On its "realist" side, moral realism recognizes the risk of imperial overstretch, as Paul Kennedy dubs it,[44] while on its moral side it honors ethical constraints that mean nothing to a traditional realist such as Kissinger or a neocon trainee such as Bush II. Those constraints can be overridden only by the categorical imperative that Walzer terms moral minimalism: the kind of issue that cuts so "close to the bone" that nonintervention ceases to be an option.[45]

Even in such cases, moral realism favors diplomatic and multilateral procedures wherever possible. Unilateralism carries too high a price in an interconnected world where not only foreign governments but foreign public opinion must be weighed on the geopolitical scales of "soft power." 9/11 put the United States at a soft-power crossroads, as pro-American sentiments crested around the world. Unfortunately Washington lost little time in squandering the good will of Europe and most of the world.[46] The Iraq invasion, opposed by a majority in every country except the United States and Israel, clinched this reversal. As world opinion reached a full boil, civil societies were bonded across East/West and South/North lines, even more than at Seattle.

Public outrage was especially strident in France and Germany, but even in Spain, which officially backed Washington, a mere 14 percent of public opinion endorsed the Bush assault on Iraq. Similar results were common throughout Asia and Latin America.[47] True to form, the Bush administration kept score, and soon launched a reward-and-punishment program whereby trade advantages were granted to authoritarian Singapore for overruling public opposition to the invasion, while similar benefits were denied to Chile for upholding the democratic will of its people. Similarly, Deputy Defense Secretary Paul Wolfowitz expressed consternation toward the Turkish military for not playing "a strong leadership role" in undermining the democratic will of Turkish citizens. The really bad news, in terms of soft power, is that the world now looks upon the United States as the archetype of this same invidious "leadership role" on a global scale.

The irony is that the Cold War had forced the United States to exercise some minimal restraint in its dealings with the global South, which had at least two alternatives: affiliation with the Soviets or with the nonaligned movement. The debt crises of the 1980s and the fall of the Soviet Union not only killed those alternatives, but expelled any realist concern for human rights and human development. These issues became the exclusive domain of idealism, which never had deep pockets or much geopolitical clout.

By the mid-1990s, however, rumors began to circulate in high places that realism might still apply in such matters. "The coming anarchy" at "the ends of earth" (to borrow two influential titles from Robert Kaplan) was starting to metastasize. And after 9/11 there could be no doubt that the socioeconomic meltdown of the Third World has profound security implications for places like New York and Washington. The question was what to do about it: "reengage" the Third World, so as to halt the meltdown, or get a bigger stick with which to keep the miscreants in line? Defensive action of one kind or another was mandated. It came down to a question of preventive assistance or preemptive war—moral realism or neoglobalism. By choosing the big stick, America not only failed to preclude the alternative world it feared, but also lost much of the leadership role that in the twenty-first century, more than ever, can be secured only through soft power.

Resistance of Last Resort

The anti-war upsurge of 2003 confirmed two facts: that the world did not buy the Bush war dance, and Bush did not much care. Civil resistance was therefore futile. The Muslim world had suspected that all along. And being more on the receiving end, its revulsion ran deeper. Even before the Iraq invasion, Saudis registered a 97 percent disapproval of U.S. policies.[48] Islamic antipathy toward the United States was most pronounced, in fact, in areas that have shown a real fondness for McValues. In Egypt, for example, there was a sense of betrayal among the 57 percent of the population that is under 25. The fact that these youth are mesmerized by American culture only makes U.S. aggression a more personal blow to them. Many try to resolve the contradiction by distinguishing the U.S. government from the American people;[49] but eventually the fact will sink in that Americans are quite comfortable with the new imperialism so long as it keeps gas prices low and does not trigger tax hikes.

A Pew survey of twenty countries released in June 2003 revealed that most Muslims admire American democracy and related values. Yet they so deplore U.S. foreign policy that many trust Yassar Arafat or even Osama bin Laden over Bush to "do the right thing." Neither the White House nor the American public seems to care. Such complacence invites the retrieval of an especially heinous power politics. This is hardly a feature of the Empire celebrated by Hardt and Negri as an innocuous "network power" that keeps cultural space open and "has nothing to do with imperialism."[50] The Bush Doctrine, as applied to Iraq, vindicates Chalmers Johnson's far more statist conception of Empire,[51] except that the centrality he assigns to Washington obscures what Hardt and Negri get right: their prescient focus on Empire's "virtual center."

Virtuality, however, can cut both ways. After the passage of NAFTA in 1994, Mexico's Zapitistas (rebel peasant farmers from Chiapas) not only took up arms, but also went online, launching what Castells considers the "first informational guerrilla movement." Virtual Empire had given rise to virtual resistance. Conceivably this challenges the power that the transnational capitalist class, as Leslie Sklair terms it, has reaped by virtue of its highly mobile and utterly noncommittal capital assets. For now, however, the contest remains a mismatch. Far from effecting a liberatory diffusion of power, the exile of "place" from Empire concentrates power in the TCC. This nomadic power elite, being unburdened by any sense of local responsibility, always keeps its bags packed. This erodes the ground for bargaining on the part of whole nations as well as labor unions or other resistant groups. No *civil* resistance has been able to strike such a moving target.

That radical dis/placement removes all imperial constraints, for if no "place" is special for Empire, it is equally the case that no place is off limits. The "openness" that Hardt and Negri applaud offers a license to invade any space and subvert any culture or politics. Such utter boundlessness sets the stage for the full collision of "McWorld and jihad" that Benjamin Barber warned of in the early 1990s.[52] After 9/11 we know too well that Barber's dialectic is even more lethal than he could have imagined at that time. The fact that its locus is no longer globalization as McWorld, but rather as Empire, raises the stakes immeasurably. What was mere cultural aversion becomes a *resistance of last resort.*

That exigency brings out the worst on both sides of the East/West civilizational divide. It also reveals the disutility of prevailing theory on this cultural front. Consider the case of the last stand of the French in Algeria. The late French general Jacques Massu finally admitted the shocking extent of French atrocities in that mother of all cultural conflicts. A standard "postcolonial" reading of Massu's confession would miss the key point by putting the full onus on the West, whereas the real tragedy lies in the dialectical escalation of violence and inhumanity on both sides.

This is the colonial malady that Conrad and Orwell exposed with regard to the Congo and Burma, respectively. Postcolonial regimes have recycled that horror, and neoconservative analysts such as Robert Kaplan are quick to declare this outcome inevitable in places like the Sudan and Algeria, where democracy was in his opinion launched prematurely. By contrast he praises the nondemocratic peace and stability of Tunisia.[53] His studies of Third World disaster zones provide a useful antidote to naïve idealism, but this realist pendulum too easily swings to the opposite pole.

A case in point is Morocco, where a quasi-enlightened monarch rules in the presumed interest of future (but forever postponed) democracy. After 9/11, and especially after the local terrorist assaults of May 2003, Morocco followed the U.S. example of trading much of its liberty for security. This was supposed to guard against fundamentalist extremism, but its main victim is likely to be civil Islam, which along with the country's numerous NGOs has been laying a foundation for actual political choice. Democracy, argues Aboubakr Jamai, is the best weapon against terrorism.[54]

In short, Kaplan makes for a better travel guide than political analyst. The reactionary cast of his realism is dated insofar as power politics now depends as much on the communication of social hope as on mere stability. Realism, therefore, is no longer the exclusive property of the Right, just as moral argument (hence Walzer's "decent Left") is no longer the exclusive preserve of the anti-realist Left.[55] Left realism, as I treat it in *Fire on the Rim*, must stake its claim to twenty-first-century geopolitics or face a world divided between the twin terrorisms of Empire and Jihad. This moral realism has its counterpart in Eastern modes of reform such as civil Islam, premised on the kind of alternative Asian values that suffuse, for example, Pramoedya Ananta Toer's vision of a postmilitarist Indonesia. By escaping both colonial and postcolonial patterns of oppression, Pramoedya's hope speaks for the entire developing world.

That real but fragile hope could easily be snuffed out by the current war on terrorism. Up against Empire, resistance can no longer settle for the communicative strategies of simple protest. The alternatives vary widely, ranging from paramilitary resistance (e.g., the sometimes violent but non-terroristic tactics of the Zapatistas or the Guadalcanal Liberation Front) to the "in your

face" but nonviolent tactics of Greenpeace or the more politic agenda of
Brazil's Acre Popular Front, lead by Chico Mendes's former associate, Jorge
Viana. Unfortunately there is also the terrorist alternative, as surfaced at Bali,
not to mention 9/11. So long as resistance worked within the confines of civil
counterdiscourse, the basic humanity of one's adversary was assumed. Terrorism, however, communicates nothing so much as the incommunicability that
spawns it. Certainly the same can be said for such "conventional" weapons of
incommunicability as napalm, daisy cutters, and cluster bombs, the staple in-
struments of state and now *Empire state* terrorism. Each side dehumanizes the
other, reducing it to the status of a contaminant to be expunged by any means.

True to President Bush's us/them riposte to 9/11—which forced, in effect, a
global referendum on U.S. primacy[56]—resistance springs from a stubborn determination *not to be us.* Countless millions of non-Muslims share that sentiment,
though only Islamic extremists possess the necessary organization and jihadic
virulence to transform cultural reflex into militant action on a global scale. In
that respect al Qaeda serves as a proxy for all those who cannot fight back.

The pressing question is not how such hostility could arise, but how globalists could have expected any other response. How did they fail to anticipate
that some people would choose armed resistance and even suicide tactics over
cultural annexation? Academically popular euphemisms such as "hybridiza-
tion" and "glocalization" have smoke screened what globalization does to
"nonconnected" peoples and cultures. Despite the clarion efforts of some fine
bridge builders—most notably the late Edward Said—admonitions from the
Arab world still fall on deaf ears. Is it any surprise that when moderate protest
goes unnoticed, resort is taken to a means of communication that cannot be
ignored?

Enemy of Our Enemy

The best way to prevent this tragic escalation of means is to nurture civil
voices of all kinds, even when they seem anathema to "U.S. interests" in the
short run. Unfortunately, like the Soviets before, the United States has habitually worked to silence all forms and factions of Islamism that cannot be put
to immediate strategic advantage. Thus Algeria's democratic Islamism was
proscribed,[57] and Indonesia's is suffering the same fate. Such policies almost
invariably come back to haunt—hence the CIA term "blowback." The ultimate case in point is 9/11, a tragedy made possible by the suppression of civil
Islam.

No degree of external surveillance can eradicate the threat of terrorism, but
fortunately this job can be done internally. When Osama bin Laden issued a

call for global jihad against the United States after 9/11, the vast majority of Muslim clerics throughout the world urged restraint. Though they chaff at the material and military excesses of Western culture, they no less deplore the un-Koranic brutality of al Qaeda. These clerics are our natural allies, though after Iraq many are issuing their own fatwas against America.

Our cities will not be safe from terrorist attack until this pan-Islamic reaction is allayed. The best defense against future 9/11s rests less in the geopolitics of Empire or added layers of "homeland security" than in soft-power strategies for prevention. Our best ally toward that end is the foremost *enemy of our enemy:* civil Islam. The tragedy of 9/11 is compounded by the damage it has done to this crucial ally, and to true jihad.

Nothing could be more beneficial to al Qaeda than a war on terror that collapses the distinction between civil and uncivil Islam—unless it is America's unilateral contempt for other anti-terrorist allies. What is needed is neither a new imperialism nor a new isolationism, but a different kind of engagement. Instead of frontal military campaigns, which will inflame the whole Islamic world, we should assist civil Islamists in their principal jihadic struggle: their search for an effective rapprochement with modernity. Otherwise, cultural exclusivity will fill the jihadic void. Our task must be to avoid the kind of civilizational clash that would inspire thousands of budding Islamists to enter the killing fields of anti-Western jihad. Instead, the neoglobalist fusion of neoliberalism and neoconservatism after 9/11 burned our intercultural bridges. By 2003, with the Iraq invasion, globalization had thrown off its pacifist camouflage to emerge as veritable Empire.

Conclusion: Survival Skill

The intellectual ground for Empire had been prepared on the Right as early as the 1970s as a counter to the "appeasement" policies of Nixon/Kissinger realism. It came of age institutionally under Reagan's unprecedented peacetime militarization, and found its true perch—but also its greatest challenge—in the unipolar world of the 1990s. The imperialist opportunity of the post-Cold War was threatened by the absence of a manifest geopolitical adversary. 9/11 solved that problem, reminding even the most doctrinaire globalists that the world, like it or not, was still mired in "history." Hence America was still the "indispensable nation," as Madeleine Albright was pleased to point out.

By no means was this militant recourse entirely new, or entirely Republican. Anthony Lake, Clinton's National Security Adviser, was equally at odds with post–Cold War pacifism in the early 1990s.[58] The globalization he favored would keep power politics very much in the game. From there it would be but a short step to the "for or against" line in the sand that President Bush drew after 9/11. Globalists presaged that "moral clarity" by casting themselves as a civilizational vanguard, for whom democracy promotion and self-promotion all but merged. What most distinguished them, however, was their newfound sense of security, which put them on the offensive globally. Soon, as Prem Shankar Jha charges, globalism began to resemble "the totalitarian creeds that it vanquished."[59]

In fact, the seeds of Empire were embedded in globalism from the start. What all globalisms share is a dearth of civilizational dialogue. Huntington's advice, that we rush back into our Atlanticist shell, is but the flip side of Fukuyama's determination to Atlanticize the entire world. Both treat the cultural Other with disdain, yet neither takes this philistinism so far as does the Bush Doctrine, which combines the cultural closure of neoliberalism with the unprecedented geopolitical hubris of neoconservatism.

The resulting will-to-Empire, premised on the delusion that the United States can go it alone, is a non-sustainable blunder. This fallacy collides with Empire's major claim to legitimacy: its much advertised support for global democracy—hence President's Bush's freedom theme in his second inaugural address. To the extent that democratic values are actually being globalized,[60] unilateralism is going to be a tough sell outside the United States. Sooner or later, having given no quarter to disparate cultural voices, America will reap what it sows. Before 9/11 the democratic art of listening was promoted, if at all, as a moral imperative. Now we come to realize it is also a survival skill.

Notes

1. This trend has been reversed in the cabinet of Bush II. See "A Weakened Treasury," *International Herald Tribune* (May 22, 2003), <www.iht.com/cgi-bin/generic.cgi?template=articleprint.tmplh&ArticleId=97039>.

2. Recognizing that globalization is not univocal saves us from Tom Nairn's mistake of construing America's post-9/11 foreign policy as anti-globalist rather than neoglobalist, as this study argues. See Nairn's "America: Enemy of Globalisation," *openDemocracy* (January 9, 2003), <www.opendemocracy.net/articles/ViewPopUpArticle.Jsp?id=3&articleId=879>.

3. Robert Kagan, "Power and Weakness," *Policy Review* (June/July 2002), <www.policyreview.org/JUN02/kagan_print.html>.

4. It is against this backdrop that David Halberstam's title, *War in a Time of Peace*, carries a contrarian punch. His subtext is that power politics was a silent partner of globalist policy throughout the halcyon 1990s.

5. "The Solidarité Summit," *The Economist* (May 30, 2003), <economist.com/agenda/PrinterFriendly.cfm. Story_ID=1811612>. At the WTO's Doha Round of November 2001 there was at least a rhetorical nod toward broader developmental con-

cerns, and President Chirac of France attempted to introduce such issues at the Evian G-8 meeting of June 2003. But the United States adroitly played its Iraq card to table this agenda, exploiting France's fervent desire to mend fences with Washington by giving exclusive priority to security issues. See Eric Pfanner, "U.S. Agenda Dominates G-8 Talks," *International Herald Tribune* (June 4, 2003), <www.iht.com/cgi-bin/generic.cgi?template=articleprint.tmplh&ArticleID=98426>.

6. Manuel Castells, *End of Millennium* (Oxford, U.K.: Blackwell, 1998), 174–75. Concern over this threat was piqued in June 2003 when Thai authorities arrested a man trying to sell radioactive material smuggled out of Russia. Terrorism experts consider it is only a matter of time before a terrorist group such as al Qaeda secures such materials and tries to put them to use. Ironically al Qaeda's known contacts with nuclear scientists have not been in so-called "Axis of Evil" countries, but rather in U.S.-supported Pakistan. See Yonan Alexander and Milton Hoenig, "WMD Terrorism: The Next Phase?" *The Christian Science Monitor* (June 18, 2003), <www.csmonitor.com/2003/ 0618/p09s01-coop.htm>.

7. The privatization of water is actively contested in many countries, such as Bolivia, Ecuador, and Argentina, but it is in South Africa that the issue has reached a critical mass. When the country's first democratic government came to power in 1994, it guaranteed the right of "sufficient food and water" in the new constitution. But at the same time it instituted "cost recovery" policies that would shift the financial burden of basic services to an impoverished population, one-third of which lived on less than $2 per day. Water utilities were converted into profit-making institutions, which are now being farmed out to multinational corporations. In the view of Robert Mukolo, head of the Crisis Water Committee, "privatization is a new kind of apartheid." See Ginger Thompson, "Water Tap Often Shut to South Africa's Poor," *New York Times* (May 29, 2003), <www.nytimes.com/2003/05/29/international/africa/29WATE.html>.

8. Joseph Kahn, "Making Trinkets in China, and a Deadly Dust," *New York Times* (June 18, 2003), <www.nytimes.com/2003/06/18/international/asia/18GEMS.html>.

9. Iris Young, "From Guilt to Solidarity: Sweatshops and Political Responsibility," *Dissent* (spring 2003), <www.dissentmagazine.org/menutest/articles/sp03/young.htm>.

10. Europe prides itself on having a more responsible attitude toward the developing world than America has. But when the European Union unveiled its draft for a new constitution in June 2003, it conspicuously omitted any reform of the infamous agricultural subsidies that eat up half the EU's budget at the expense of both European consumers and small farmers throughout the non-European world. See "Europe Snubs World's Poor," *New York Times* (June 23, 2003), <www.nytimes.com/2003/06/23/opinion/23MON1.html>.

11. Only recently, under pressure from the European Commission, have global banking institutions indirectly acknowledged their contribution to global ecocide and related ethnocide. In effect they are admitting that massive environmental destruction does not come cheap. It comes in large part from First World funding practices. Ten of the world's leading banks have signed the Equator Principles code, belatedly sponsored by the World Bank, which pledges at least some environmental caution. A more mandatory code, complete with heavy penalties for violations, would be much better, but this is at least a start. See David Kalmowitz, "Banks Come

to the Rescue of Threatened Forests," *International Herald Tribune* (June 10, 2003), <www.iht.com/cgi-bin/generic.cgi?template=articleprint.tmplh&ArticleId=98987>.

12. Coral Bell, "Normative Shift," *The National Interest*, No. 70 (winter 2002/2003), <www.nationalinterest.org/issues/70/Bell.html>.

13. Bryan S. Turner, *Orientalism, Postmodernism and Globalism* (New York: Routledge, 1994), 12.

14. Arundhati Roy and Amy Goodman, "Arundhati Roy on Empire and the Corporate Media," *Democracy Now* transcript of May 31, 2003 on *Znet*, <zmag.org/content/print_article.cfm?itemID=3704&sectionID=13>.

15. Thomas Frank, *One Market under God: Extreme Capitalism, Market Populism, and the End of Economic Democracy* (New York: Doubleday, 2000), 358.

16. Manuel Castells, *The Power of Identity* (Oxford, U.K.: Blackwell, 1997), 69.

17. Bruce R. Scott, "The Great Divide in the Global Village," *Foreign Affairs* 80, no. 1 (January/February 2001): 176 (160–77).

18. Terrorism is an inexcusable atrocity no matter what conditions provoke it. Yet to ignore its causal conditions is to abort the project of prevention. It is in this vain that Gore Vidal must be defended against his many acerbic critics for trying to understand the perverse logic behind Timothy McVeigh's bombing of the Oklahoma City federal building on April 19, 1995. Like Osama bin Laden, McVeigh was outraged by Washington's often brutal treatment of other societies, and of vulnerable segments of American society. He was especially incensed by the federal "shredding of the Bill of Rights" at Waco, Texas—a warning bell that America failed to heed. See Gore Vidal, *Perpetual War for Perpetual Peace: How We Got to Be So Hated* (New York: Thunder's Mouth Press/Nation Books, 2002), 46 and 59–60.

19. It certainly was not good for Burmese villagers, who were compelled by the Myanmar government to work under harsh conditions and without remuneration on the construction of Unocal's $1.2 billion pipeline in the 1990s. Villagers from the Tenasserim region of southeastern Myanmar have since filed a lawsuit against Unocal in the United States under the Alien Tort Claims Act of 1789. See Alex Markels, "Showdown for a Tool in Human Rights Lawsuits," *New York Times* (June 15, 2003), <www.nytimes.com/2003/06/15/business/yourmoney/15TORT.html>.

20. See Harold Meyerson, "Past Tense," *Prospect* (June 5, 2003), <www.prospect.org/webfeatures/2003/ 06/meyerson-h-06-05.html>.

21. This munificent support for Musharraf has been rationalized in terms of his presumed anti-terrorist vigilance, even as al Qaeda operates with near impunity along the Afghan border, using Pakistan as a safe haven. When U.S. military officials complained about being barred from pursuing these insurgents across the border, the ban was justified on the ironic ground that it was necessary to stabilize Musharraf's rule. So his regime must be supported in order to fight terrorism, and terrorists must be tolerated in order to preserve his regime. On the military's complaint see Steven R. Weisman, "The Mideast Thicket Continues to Test Bush's Leadership," *New York Times* (May 27, 2003), <www.nytimes.com/2003/05/27/international/worldspecial/27DIPL.html>.

22. Paula J. Dobriansky and Thomas Carothers, "Democracy Promotion," *Foreign Affairs* (May/June 2003), <www.foreignaffairs.org/20030501faresponse11226/paula-j-dobriansky-thomas-carot>.

23. Dobriansky and Carothers, "Democracy Promotion"; and Thomas Carothers, "Promoting Democracy and Fighting Terror," *Foreign Affairs* 82, no. 1 (January/February 2003): 94 (84–97).

24. Regarding this concept see Thomas P. M. Barnett, "The Pentagon's New Map," *Esquire* (March 2003), <www.nwc.navy.mil/newrulesets/ThePentagonsNewMap.htm>.

25. See Francis Fukuyama, "Has History Started Again?" *Policy* (winter 2002), <www.cis.org.au/Policy/ winter02/polwin02-1.htm>; and Francis Fukuyama, "The West Has Won," *The Guardian* (October 11, 2001), <www.guardian.co.uk/Print/ 0,3858,4274753,00.html>.

26. Francis Fukuyama, "The West May Be Cracking," *International Herald Tribune* (August 9, 2002), reprinted by the Global Policy Forum, <www.globalpolicy.org/ wtc/analysis/2002/0809cracking.htm>.

27. Abdel Bari Atwan, "Americans Are Masters of Destruction," *Observer* (March 10, 2002), www.observer.co.uk/Print/0,3558,4371587,00.html. In June 2003 the Justice Department's own inspector general issued a caustic, 200-page report criticizing the government's manner of detaining and often abusing noncitizen suspects, many of whom were held a month or more without formal charges. Many innocent detainees were held for weeks or months in harsh conditions while the FBI made little attempt to clear them. See "The Post–Sept. 11 Prisoners," *International Herald Tribune* (June 4, 2003), <www.iht.com/cgi-bin/generic.cgi?template=articleprint.tmplh&ArticleId= 98406>. Adding insult to injury, U.S. Attorney General John Ashcroft responded to the inspector general's report by asking the House Judiciary Committee for still greater power to hold suspects indefinitely. See "Ashcroft's America," *St. Petersburg Times* (June 8, 2003), <www.sptimes.com/2003/06/08/news_pf/Perspective/Ashcroft_s_America.shtml>.

28. This trade-off worked so well for President Gloria Arroyo that her popularity rebounded, allowing her to reverse her announcement of December 2002 that she would not be a candidate for the May 2004 presidential election. See Philip Bowring, "Arroyo, on a Role, May Decide to Run Again after All," *International Herald Tribune* (June 3, 2003), <www.iht.com/cgi-bin/generic.cgi?template=articleprint. tmplh& ArticleId=98277>.

29. The quotation marks are necessary in a country where even moderate civil resistance is defined as a criminal or terrorist activity, and democratic activists are commonly locked away as "political maniacs." See Xu Wenli, "What It Will Take to Transform China," *Washington Post* (May 19, 2003): A19; and Jonathan Mirsky, "China's Psychiatric Terror," *New York Review of Books* 50, no. 3 (February 27, 2003): 38 (38–42).

30. He broke this de facto contract, however, in his speech of June 19, 2003, at the annual meeting of his party. Clearly addressing the entire Muslim world, in anticipation of his departure from office in October, he warned of the renewed threat of Western capitalist domination in the post-9/11 world. See Wayne Arnold, "Mahathir Blasts U.S. and Britain," *International Herald Tribune* (June 19, 2003), <www.iht.com/ cgi-bin/ generic.cgi?template=articleprint.tmplh&ArticleId=100094>.

31. Thus the "war on terrorism" tacitly doubles as a war on both Islamic reformism and grassroots leftism. On the former see Peter Maass, "Dirty War: How America's Friends Really Fight Terrorism," *The New Republic* (November 11, 2002), <www.the newrepublic.com/doc.mhtml?i=20021111&s=maass 111102>.

32. Joan Didion, "Fixed Opinions, or The Hinge of History," *New York Review of Books* 50, no. 1 (January 16, 2003): 56 (54–59).

33. Both quotations are from Todd Gitlin, "Anti-Anti-Americanism," *Dissent* (winter 2003), <www.dissentmagazine.org/menutest/articles/wi03/gitlin.htm>.

34. Quoted in Mitchell Cohen's reply to Donald Johnson, in "Michael Hardt and others respond to Mitchell Cohen's 'An Empire of Cant,'" *Dissent* archive, <www.dissentmagazine.org/archive/fa02/letters.shtml>.

35. See William H. Thornton, "Back to Basics: Human Rights and Power Politics in the New Moral Realism," *International Journal of Politics, Culture and Society* 14, no. 2 (winter 2000): 315–32. I further develop this argument in chapter 8 of *Fire on the Rim: The Cultural Dynamics of East/West Power Politics* (Lanham, MD: Rowman & Littlefield, 2002).

36. The United States did hold its own, however, as the world's leading exporter of high-tech weapons, selling almost indiscriminately to some of the world's worst human rights violators, including Iraq during its war with Iran. See Carl Boggs, *End of Politics: Corporate Power and the Decline of the Public Sphere* (New York: Guilford Press, 2000), 57. As for tobacco exports, U.S. companies have had a hidden weapon in the form of the incredibly high levels of nitrosamine in their leading brands. The level in Marlboro is at least twice as high, and sometimes as much as twenty-two times higher than the typical local product. Insidiously, Philip Morris often mimics the composition of local brands, including nitrosamine levels, when it invades a new market. It raises these levels as soon as it gains command of the market. See Marc Kaufman, "Marlboro's High in One Carcinogen, Study Says," *Washington Post* (May 30, 2003): A04.

37. Ron Scherer, "World Cracks Down on Big Tobacco," *Christian Science Monitor* (May 22, 2003), <www.csmonitor.com/2003/0522/p01s04-wogi.htm>.

38. Ellen Goodman, "Smoking: America's Gift to the World," *Washington Post* (May 3, 2003): A23.

39. See my argument to this effect in William H. Thornton, "Civil Antiglobalism and the Question of Class," *Social Analysis: The International Journal of Cultural and Social Practice* 46, no. 2 (summer 2002): 123–30.

40. Soft power, as Joseph Nye describes it, works through such indirect means as the admiration that other countries have for American values. See Joseph S. Nye Jr., *The Paradox of American Power: Why the World's Only Superpower Can't Go It Alone* (Oxford: Oxford University Press, 2002), 8–9.

41. Thomas Carothers, "Promoting Democracy and Fighting Terror," *Foreign Affairs* (January/February 2003): 94 (84–97).

42. Michael Walzer, "Can There Be a Decent Left?" *Dissent* (spring 2002), <www2.kenyon.edu/depts/ religion/fac/adler/Politics/Waltzer.htm>.

43. See Darrell Moellendorf, "Is the War in Afghanistan Just?" *Imprints: A Journal of Analytical Socialism* 6, no. 2 (2002), <info.bris.ac.uk/~plcdib/imprints/moellendorf.html>.

44. Paul Kennedy, *The Rise and Fall of the Great Powers: Economic Change and Military Conflict from 1500 to 2000* (London: Fontana, 1989), 666.

45. Michael Walzer, *Thick and Thin: Moral Argument at Home and Abroad* (Notre Dame: University of Notre Dame, 1994), 6.

46. The resulting Atlantic schism, which Robert Kagan casts in a positive light in his notorious *Policy Review* article of summer 2002, is more soberly diagnosed by Philip H. Gordon. See Gordon's "Bridging the Atlantic Divide," *Foreign Affairs* (January/February 2003): 70–83.

47. "Bagdad vit dans l'attente des premières offensives américaines," *Le Monde* (March 19, 2003), <www.lemonde.fr/imprimer_article_ref/0,5987,3462—313424,00 .html>; and Robert J. Samuelson, "The Gulf of World Opinion," *Washington Post* (March 27, 2003): A21.

48. "A Country of Fear," *The Atlantic Online* (April 2, 2003), <www.theatlantic.com/ unbound/polipro/pp2003-04-02.htm>.

49. Emily Wax, "In Egypt, Anger at U.S. Displaces Admiration," *Washington Post* (March 24, 2003): A25.

50. Michael Hardt and Antonio Negri, *Empire* (Cambridge, MA: Harvard University Press, 2000), 166–67.

51. Chalmers Johnson, *Blowback: The Costs and Consequences of American Empire* (New York: Henry Holt and Co., 2000), 7. Manuel Castells provides a balanced assessment of the role of the nation state in the new global (dis)order. In that sense he mediates Johnson's too statist approach and Hardt and Negri's inordinate virtuality. See all three volumes of Castells's *The Information Age*, e.g., Vol. I, *The Rise of the Network Society* (Oxford, U.K.: Blackwell, 1996), 98.

52. Barber's seminal article, "Jihad vs. McWorld," appeared in the March 1992 issue of *Atlantic Monthly* (available online at www.theatlantic.com/politics/foreign/barberf.htm), and culminated in his *Jihad vs. McWorld* (New York: Ballantine Books, 1995).

53. Robert D. Kaplan, "Was Democracy Just a Moment?" *The Atlantic Online* (December 1997), <www.theatlantic.com/issues/97dec/democ.htm>.

54. Aboubakr Jamai, "Morocco's Choice: Openness or Terror," *New York Times* (May 31, 2003), <www.nytimes.com/2003/05/31/opinion/31JAMA.html>.

55. My term "moral realism" is closely akin to Michael Walzer's "decent Left," except that it recognizes the need for strange bedfellows alliances with enlightened non-leftists who subscribe to moral realism on the instrumental ground of "soft-power" advantage.

56. See Andrew J. Bacevich, "New Rome, New Jerusalem," *The Wilson Quarterly* (summer 2002), <wwics.si.edu/index.cfm?fuseaction=wq.print&essay_id=17318& stoplayout=true>.

57. Algeria's pro-democratic but anti-American FIS (Islamic Salvation Front) was overthrown by the army after winning the country's first multiparty election in 1992. It is hardly surprising that Huntington considers this overthrow favorable to America's interests. See Michael Steinberger's interview with Huntington, "So, Are Civilizations at War?" *Observer* (October 21, 2001), <www.observer.co.uk/Print/ 0,3858,4281700,00.html>.

58. Prem Shankar Jha, "Democracy, Globalisation and War: New Myths to Save the West from the Rest," *World Affairs* 5, no. 2 (April/June 2001): 33 (26–47).

59. Jha, "Democracy, Globalisation and War," 33.

60. One of the best cases for an ongoing "third wave" of democratization is made by Larry Diamond, "Universal Democracy?" *Policy Review*, No. 119 (June 2003),

<www.policyreview.org/jun03/diamond_print.html>. What Diamond neglects is the undertow effect whereby democratic processes are co-opted by multinationals and other institutions of global corporatism. This is not to deny the raw democratic potential of Seattle-style grassroots mobilization, or what I have termed "global anti-globalism" (see *Fire*, 193–97), but its limitations in terms of geopolitical effectivity were graphically demonstrated early in 2003 in the case of the worldwide protest movement against the Iraq invasion. When up to 10 million protesters took to the streets worldwide on a single day, the Bush administration simply ignored them, with no apparent harm to his popularity ratings in the United States. See Bernard Weiner, "America Two Years after 9/11: 25 Things We Now Know," *The Crisis Papers* (August 18, 2003), <www.crisispapers.org/Editorials/25-things-we-know.htm>.

2

Marching as to War: 9/11 and the Making of Neoglobalism

A New Power Politics

THE TERRORISM THAT VISITED AMERICA ON 9/11 was a new kind of geopoliti-cal force. More lethal for being unstructured, it lacked any moral or polit-ical compunction concerning mass carnage. The relative restraint of tradi-tional Left resistance, rooted in Marx and Engels and surviving even in the tactics of 1970s anarcho-communists,[1] was jettisoned. 9/11 put global war in a new key, both in terms of its NGO origins and its cultural motivation. In that sense it was not so much aimed at America the nation as at the cultural nerve center of global capitalism.

The resulting culture war traces to the globalist imperium of the ebbing Cold War era. As late as 1978 Nicos Poulantzas could write that what is "spe-cific to the capitalist state is that it . . . monopolizes . . . networks of domi-nation and power."[2] No longer. As Manuel Castells observes, "State control over space and time is increasingly bypassed by global flows of capital, goods, services, technology, communication, and information."[3] The result is nothing like the liberatory hybridity that postmodernists extol. Rather it comes down to a higher order of dialectical closure. Writing near the end of the Cold War, Jonathan Friedman noted the skewed dualism whereby cul-tural difference is increasingly engulfed by consumer culture.[4] Eduardo Galeano understands this ongoing capitalist incursion in terms of power politics: "During the Cold War, each half of the world could find in the other an alibi for its crimes and a justification for its horrors. Each claimed to be better because the other was worse. Orphaned of its enemy, capitalism can celebrate its unhampered hegemony to use and abuse. . . . "[5]

That abuse amounts to terrorism-from-above, and is bound to inspire a radical recoil from below—hence the geopolitical symbiosis that Benjamin Barber alludes to in his polemic title, *Jihad vs. McWorld* (1995). Assenting to either side of this dialectic, in Barber's view, "commits us to a dark world of *jihad* and counter*jihad* (what President Bush initially called his crusade), in which issues of democracy, civil comity and social justice—let alone nuance, complexity and interdependence—simply vanish."[6] Even as these antithetical terrorisms blast at one another, they jointly undermine the remnants of civil society and any semblance of social solidarity other than the bare necessities of risk management.[7]

For Barber the term "Jihad" is not restricted to a uniquely Islamic reaction, but rather denotes any "rabid response to colonization or imperialism and their economic children, capitalism and modernity; it is diversity run amok, multiculturalism turned cancerous. . . ."[8] Jihad has deep cultural roots but has gained critical mass only after the Cold War, striking not just at Western capitalism but at social and political modernity as such—something that even the Red Brigades could not have contemplated. Such terrorism defies definition except in terms of its cultural or "Huntingtonesque" recidivism.

This cultural turn, at once premodern and postmodern, added to the confusion of the September 11 attack, whose very scope marks it as an act of war. Modern war has so long been associated with the interests and devices of nation-states that it is hard to conceive of a culturally rhizomic geopolitics. Realist thought remains locked in its modernist fixation on the balancing acts of nations or national coalitions. Although American "unipolarity" is a major factor here, it is America's role as the essential globalist police state that makes it the lightning rod for postnational balancing acts such as 9/11.

In a much maligned essay written for *The New Yorker* a week after the attack, Susan Sontag pondered how a robotic president and the usual chorus of commentators were peddling psychotherapy in lieu of geopolitical analysis: "Where is the acknowledgment that this was not a 'cowardly' attack on 'civilization' or 'liberty' or 'humanity' or 'the free world' but an attack on the world's self-proclaimed superpower, undertaken as a consequence of specific American alliances and actions?"[9] In terms of neorealist theory, the twin genres of geopolitical terror (globalist and anti-globalist) can fairly be labeled *geoterrorist*. Together they set in motion a vicious cycle in which the only real winner is terrorism itself.

This dialectic goes beyond the simple recognition that poverty breeds resentment and resentment has consequences. It has been a stock assumption of the Left that terrorism is the product of poverty and marginalization, and that these in turn are products of globalization. Doug Henwood points out, however, that East Asia and Latin America—the areas most directly impacted by the flood of global capital over the last two decades—have produced little in the way of international terrorism. Rather, one of the major fonts of recent terrorism has been oil-rich Saudi Arabia. The scent of jihadic geopolitics, rather than poverty or culture clash alone, is too strong here to ignore.

This geopolitical dialectic helps to explain why the prime beneficiaries of 9/11 were the targeted institutions themselves: national defense and transnational capitalism.[10] United as never before, they serve an increasingly militarized New World Order. Many on the Left call it Empire,[11] and some on the Right have begun to embrace this stigmatic word in the name of a newly assertive "realism." Against the retreat from nation building and military adventurism that President Bush endorsed before 9/11, a radical new "conservatism" is emerging. William Kristol's "Project for the New American Century" (PNAC) promotes a new manifest destiny based on cultural rather than territorial hegemony. More to the point, it also calls for a return to Cold War levels of military spending as a percentage of GDP: 10 percent as opposed to the 3.5 percent of the Clinton years.

This is much the same cultural agenda that Victor Hanson (*Carnage and Culture*, 2001) celebrates under the rubric "civic militarism." If cultural imperialism were its only goal, why would the PNAC want to nearly triple military spending relative to GDP? It is curious, also, that this policy has been pushed in the name of conservatism, a tradition that (give it this much) has been skeptical toward the wholesale export of any given set of national values. Such cultural imperialism has more commonly been sold under the label of liberal progressivism.

9/11 helped to sideline more authentic conservatisms such as John Gray's "postliberalism," which might have held militant globalism in check. So too it retired any residual liberal resistance to full-fledged (i.e., militarized) neoliberalism. The geopolitical brunt of Empire is now so effectively legitimated under the flag of anti-terrorism that its own brand of terror escapes notice, at least in the United States. Elsewhere this vanishing act fails miserably. In the developing world it is common knowledge that what the West took for the triumphal end of the Cold War was in fact the start of an equally truculent Cold Peace—a less overt but no less odious power politics. Thinking itself invincible, the only remaining superpower turned its military and economic guns on a seemingly defenseless world outside the New World Order.

In this respect the Peace was the exclusive product of 1990s America. In *War in a Time of Peace* (2001), David Halberstam critiques the curious blend of global intervention and sheer indifference that developed as American "infotainment" won out over serious journalism and especially over issues of foreign policy.[12] The voting public was too busy watching the Dow to notice how this policy was viewed on the "outside." Even as transnational corporations were amassing geopolitical power to match their economic clout, public idolization of corporatism reached new heights. With 10,000 new websites opening per day by the late 1990s, it is hardly surprising that many would look on the Silicon Valley (where success meant being a billionaire, not just a millionaire) as a refurbished capitalist model.[13] By the end of the decade, however, the old corporatism was staging a definitive comeback against any radical wiring of democratic values, such as the vaunted informational "pull" of the Net.[14]

The Empire struck back via media giants like Time Warner (now AOL/Time Warner) and Disney/ABC,[15] whose literal incorporation of public discourse met little serious resistance. Not even a recession and a major stock plunge could dent the new corporate image. Indeed, the only seriously considered solution to this economic slippage was *more* corporatism. By linking his special authority to combat terrorism to his "fast track" trade promotion authority (TPA), President Bush got his "free-trade" agenda through the House on December 6, 2001, by a down-to-the-wire vote of 215 to 214. In previous months that bill seemed doomed, with thirty Republican congressmen firmly opposed and many "new Democrats" turned off by the president's divisive rhetoric concerning labor and the environment. In a chillingly accurate prognosis, the editors of *The Economist* stated on June 21, 2001, that nothing short of a "forcing event" could keep TPA afloat. That "forcing event" was soon provided from an unexpected quarter. Nothing since the fall of the Soviet Union has done as much as 9/11 to buttress global corporatism.

The Myth of Reform Globalism

This was just what the neoliberal establishment needed to deflect attention from its elephant in the bedroom, as Merrill Goozner describes the growing inequality of income and wealth. By 1998 the top fifth of America's families raked in nearly half the national income and held 83.4 percent of the national wealth.[16] It is all the more remarkable, given this mammoth social divide, that the general public would vicariously embrace the corporate tenets of "market populism," as Thomas Frank terms it. The same "irrational exuberance" that Allen Greenspan warned of on Wall Street bathed the New Economy in a Heavenly light. It took a considerable act of faith to accept Rupert Murdoch as a man of the people,[17] or the absurdly bloated stock market as a functional extension of democracy.[18] Meanwhile the most pressing domestic issues—those falling under the regulatory purview of the Labor or Interior Departments as opposed to Commerce, Treasury, or the Fed—were either downsized or dropped entirely.

What the New Economy was to national news, globalization was to international. Again the dark underside of the story went untold. When it came up at all, it was usually set in the context of globalist "*TINA*" (There Is No Alternative), which has become the theme song of reform globalism (cosmopolitanism, Third Wayism, etc.) in its attempt to banish welfare liberalism and social democracy, not to mention the actual Left. Many on the real Left are edging in this same direction. Michael Hardt and Antonio Negri hold that liberation from the emerging capitalist Empire requires the forfeiture of all moralism, resentment, or nostalgia. Indeed, they jettison all activist resistance. Having posed the question of how the "multitude" can become political, they can offer no means toward this end other than the utopian ideals of unlimited worker mobility and "global citizenship." They grant that unfettered labor flows, like unregulated capital flows, are at the top of any TNC wish list, but this is unimportant since to them globalization is driven by and for the multitude.

This fantasy puts them surprisingly close to the neoliberal prattle of Thomas Friedman, who sees globalization as powered from below.[19] The difference is that for Friedman there is no need for an exit door (who would want to leave this Crystal Palace?), whereas Hardt and Negri's TINAism of the Left embraces the new imperial order so as to push through Empire to exit from the other side. Sadly they have posted their exit sign over a globalist broom closet. For them, as for globalists in general, there is no exit from extant globalization. Much as pro-globalists have naturalized globalization, anti-globalists tend to fatalize it. Both come to the same thing where resistance is concerned. The present challenge is to locate a real and proximate exit door. It is time to move not only beyond modernist universalism but also past the dislocated "difference" of nominal postmodernism.

What the liberation of cultural difference requires is not more identity politics, but the reform impetus of common histories and common dreams.[20] In their frenzied effort to extirpate every static norm known to mankind, "postmodernism" (e.g., multiculturalism, postcolonialism, and most of what passes for cultural studies) has fenced off the cultural commons that could be the last line of defense against Empire as well as jihad. Such cultural resistance is not only at odds with the normalizing straightjacket of globalism, but the *ab*normalizing vertigo of poststructuralism.[21] Bryan Turner sees this vertiginous strain of postmodernism as offering no "political vision of the modern world apart from an implicit injunction to enjoy diversity. This lack of politico-moral direction exists in a context of increasing alienation of intellectuals from McUniversity. . . ."[22]

Since McUniversity is McWorld in microcosm, these words pack an anti-globalist punch. Turner is in effect a *grounded* cosmopolitan. More ethereal cosmopolitans or Third Wayers may superficially concur with him, but their idea of revisionist globalism is usually more of a tune-up than an overhaul. Anthony Giddens goes so far as to proffer globalization as the essential medium of civil society and democracy in our time.[23] He takes due note of the paradox that democracy is spreading around the world even as citizens in older democracies are becoming politically disillusioned; yet, by an arcane logic understood only by Third Way illuminati, he concludes that the erosion of democratic culture in established democracies can be rectified by only *more globalization*,[24] as if globalization itself were not a major contributor to the erosion of democratic values. Such reform globalism is to real reform what Nazi national socialism was to actual socialism.

To cast himself as a "radical," Giddens must completely redefine the term, with globalization processes understood from the top down. Seen from the bottom, or from the South, the post–Cold War era is one of gross contradictions: growing economic distress in a time of unprecedented "development," and political powerlessness in the wake of "third wave" democratization. The Cold War, by comparison, had some redeeming qualities. It encouraged a measure of distributive justice in the form of economic aid to developing countries (never mind the motive). And since its strategy of mutually assured destruction targeted precisely those nations most responsible for the arms race, an effective balance was achieved.

The Cold War's demise put an end to that balance without curtailing the terror it stockpiled. Triumphalism trumped other possibilities. Though the fall of the Second World had opened opportunities for a substantive "peace dividend" and a morally engaged foreign policy,[25] the United States simply shifted the focus of its militancy by enlisting a growing arsenal of nonmilitary tactics. Their force can be measured in terms of capital flows and commercial leverage rather than megatons. These devices dispense with Cold War "justice" insofar as they primarily target the developing (or undeveloping) world. They exercise, moreover, little of the restraint that even colonial and Cold War policies found necessary—the former because it had to keep up a missionary façade, and the latter because it had to compete for the moral high ground with a formidable Second World adversary.

As the Cold War waned, the United States withdrew from that moral competition. The amorality of Cold War realism found a new home in globalization, and a geopolitics to match—hence the neoglobalism of my title. It is common knowledge outside the Washington Consensus that today's unipolar asymmetry inspires a new breed of resistance. As long as there is McTerror, there will be Jihad. That is why realist tactics of Cold War vintage can never win the "war against terrorism." The lesson of 9/11 is that force alone can win battles but not wars. Purely militarist solutions produce more "blowback" than stability. But neither can idealism alone achieve lasting peace. Only a new moral realism can get us off the geopolitical treadmill of Empire vs. jihad.

The antithesis of such moral realism is not so much the old amoral realism as the quasi-moral imperialism that was unleashed after 9/11 in the form of the Bush Doctrine. Unabashed imperialists such as Robert Kagan and Robert Kaplan support this call for preemptive defense, where the idea is to do unto others before they do unto you. Throwing out the liberal rule book on winning friends and influencing world affairs, Kaplan concentrates on the ancient art of defeating enemies and dictating world affairs, with or without friends. For this he adopts a nuts and bolts paganism patterned on second-century Rome.[26] This shocking choice of role models is tempered, to be sure, by the very un-Roman objective of global democratization. It is obvious, however, that Kaplan is artfully reversing his means and ends. Instead of using his "warrior politics" to secure democracy, democracy becomes a pretext for military adventurism.

That duplicity is almost enough to make one appreciate the raw candor of Max Boot, who openly embraces imperialism on its own merits. But in the grand tradition of "white man's burden," neocons usually wrap their imperialism in multiple layers of moralism. In this sense their foreign policy is reminiscent of the nation's colonial flirtation a century before. Both Theodore Roosevelt and Woodrow Wilson sang this song at one point, but after hard experience they reversed themselves—Roosevelt in practice and Wilson in both practice and creed. The nation as a whole had learned some hard lessons. Less than a decade after the U.S. seizure of Spanish holdings in the Caribbean and the Pacific, America's imperial mission was aborted. Speaking to the Senate in 1920, Wilson asserted that America faced a stark choice between the ideal of democracy and that of imperialism. That admonition is even more pertinent in today's unipolar world. The neocon strategy makes traditional realism look almost appealing in its balance and restraint. The dark secret of the new militancy is the sinister twist it gives to Wilsonian values. By pursuing Empire in the name of democratization, the Bush Doctrine turns idealism on its head.

The Three Faces of Bush

Ironically, one of the prime beneficiaries of the Bush Doctrine has been President Clinton, who by comparison is remembered as a paragon of international goodwill. To remove this halo it is only necessary to recall the familiar sounding charges that were laid on Clinton after he ordered air strikes on Iraq in 1993. The world press accused him of risking the lives of innocent civilians, of flouting the New World Order, and using the conflict to deflect attention from his economic woes at home. Even when he wore his "Third Way" halo, Clinton's foreign policy often recycled some of the least attractive features of Bush I internationalism. Witness the sanctions imposed on Iraq by Resolution 661 of the UN Security Council, which both presidents steadfastly upheld. By conservative estimates 661 cost the lives of hundreds of thousands of Iraqi children, and one Unicef report put the figure at 500,000.

All that pales, however, before the designs of Bush II and his neoconservative mentors, who considered 661 too soft on Iraq. For an international prototype they have looked to Reagan or sometimes Nixon rather than the relatively pliant Bush I.[27] By inclination Bush II was the most domestic-minded president since Johnson (prior to his Vietnam entrapment). Like most nominal conservatives Bush reviled liberal internationalist entanglement in places like Iraq and Yugoslavia.[28] But like Johnson he would soon be up to his neck in the kind of foreign affairs he was least prepared for. Dogged by recession and corporate scandals at home, he was driven increasingly into the camp of neoconservative internationalism. For a broad strata of American voters, especially after 9/11, that "me first" approach to international relations passes for world leadership.

The "neoconization" of Bush II would require, however, a great deal of pruning. His campaign platform still contained remnants of his father's rhetorical influence, such as the pledge that under him America would act as a "humble" nation, seeking global "partners, not satellites." That pre-neocon disposition was reflected in his selection of Colin Powell as secretary of state. Neocon resentment of that choice would simmer until 2003, when Rumsfeld's crony Newt Gingrich—former speaker of the House and present member of the Defense Policy Board—authored an obviously orchestrated diatribe titled "Rogue State Department," in *Foreign Policy.* Gingrich accused Powell's team of abdicating "American values" in favor of accommodation and passivity[29] (i.e., in favor of an un-American preference for diplomacy over war). At that point the neocons were stridently at odds not only with liberalism but with all rival modes of conservatism.

Except for the State Department, 9/11 had put neoconservatism in the administrative driver's seat. The last vestiges of an older conservative restraint had vanished by 9/20, when the accidental president drew his infamous line in the sand: "Either you are with us, or you are with the terrorists." Enter Bush III. No longer the simple retreatist who peevishly rejected the Kyoto Accords, Bush emerged as a new breed of "wag the dog" interventionist. His battle plan was outlined in his January 2002 State of the Union Speech, which focused so obsessively on war that it spotlighted the question of what was behind the smoke screen. Needless to say there was no mention of Enron, and the recession got little more than passing reference.

Even within his war-on-terror theme, Bush applied obvious diversion tactics, shifting emphasis from the signal danger of al Qaeda to the largely speculative threat of two out of the three rogue nations on his "Axis of Evil" list: Iraq and Iran. The third, North Korea, constituted a real and present nuclear danger, and for that very reason it was under little threat of U.S. invasion. Thus the war on terror was fused with the issue of nuclear proliferation, which would be the gateway for Bush's long-awaited invasion of Iraq.

Four months later, at West Point, Bush broached his strategy for military preponderance, effectively claiming a U.S. monopoly on the use of coercive force worldwide.[30] By alluding to the tradition of Eisenhower, MacArthur, Patton, and Bradley—"commanders who saved a civilization"—he placed himself in that hallowed line. Then came the clincher: the war on terror "will not be won on the defensive." A new direction is required to "confront the worst threats before they emerge."[31] This not only meant expelling Cold War containment strategies but also reviving the essence of Cold War bipolarity: a Reaganite sense of the enemy as a totalistic "evil empire." Both militarily and morally, a total solution was sought.

Such "moral clarity," Bush averred, was essential to America's Cold War victory. Thus the United States must lead the world in a frankly "undiplomatic" struggle between "good and evil." Such a strategy could easily rekindle that other feature of the Cold War: the arms race. To eliminate that possibility Bush prescribed more of the same medicine: such overwhelming force that an arms race would be rendered "pointless." This was hardly a realist strategy, for it put the balance-of-power principle in mothballs. Russia and China were to be assuaged by their cut of the new globalist pie, along with a mutually useful partnership in the war on terrorism.

For pundits on the New Right, such as Rich Lowry of the *National Review*, the West Point speech raised hopes that Bush was ready to expand the war on terrorism by linking it to the long simmering war on WMD (weapons of mass destruction) development by rogue nations. Lowry hailed this merger as a realistic acceptance of hard facts, for "once your enemy has a well-formed WMD capability it may be too late to do anything about it."[32] The president likewise rooted his strategy in the unprecedented nature of the new security challenge. It all came down to a simple choice: "attack now or forever hold your peace."

At the opposite critical pole, Bill Vann and David North look past these proximate sources to the Cold War roots of preemption. We are reminded that even in the early postwar period there was a Spartan faction that rejected containment in favor of "rollback." Although this was a dispute over tactics, not basic principles, it nonetheless produced a militant undercurrent on the

Right. The economic crisis of the 1970s gave new life to the "rollback" school, and laid the foundation for Reagan's military buildup of the next decade.[33] The end of the Cold War caught Bush I off guard, but the Gulf War brought out the hawk in him. Iraq's invasion of Kuwait looked to him (so the story goes) like the fascist aggression he fought in World War II. Even under Clinton the American war machine was being geared for its new *globalist* mission.

The notion of a post–Cold War peace dividend had long since disappeared from serious consideration. By the mid-1990s the salient policy issue was which kind of militarism was best suited for dealing with the New World *Disorder*. After 9/11 the closest thing to a "dove" stance in this debate was the cautious militarism of neo–containment strategists like Powell, who by then were under siege from neoconservatives hawks like Rumsfeld.[34] The West Point speech—Bush's first major address since his European tour met a stone wall of suspicion as to his motives—removed all doubt as to the president's complete conversion to the neocon camp. It appeared that Lowry's hopes for an expanded war would soon to be realized. There was little doubt that this agenda pointed straight at Iraq. The only question was who would be marching with the United States on the road to Baghdad.

Finally, in September 2002, the Bush Doctrine was officially set forth in a comprehensive *National Security Strategy of the United States*. As in the West Point speech, erstwhile geopolitical rivals such as China and Russia were recast as allies in the cause of anti-terrorism. This would help to buy their silence on preemption, the most radical departure of the Bush Doctrine. As Todd Gitlin sees it, *Strategy* was more preventive than preemptive, since the dangers it targeted could be extremely remote or even imaginary. It thus amounted to a geopolitical blank check, and a substitute for international law.

Strategy's pledge that Americans do not exercise their power "to press for unilateral advantage" may ring hollow abroad, but plays well domestically. As if clarification were needed, it is spelled out that there is but "a single sustainable model for national success" in the world, and this happens to be America's combination of "freedom, democracy and free enterprise." Never mind, as Gitlin points out, that China is an ostensible success with none of these qualities, while Argentina is a failure despite having all three.[35]

Strategy's doctrine of preemption effectively voids a basic principle of the UN Charter: the denial of any signatory's right to use force against other nations except in self-defense or with the authorization of the UN Security Council. Under *Strategy*'s terms of engagement, it was just a matter of choosing the right rogue nation to preempt (one that was close to collapse anyway). With Osama bin Laden proving too elusive, and Kim Jong Il too dangerous, Saddam Hussein ended up on ground zero. An outraged James Baker, Bush I's secretary of state, broke Republican ranks to defend his old boss's multilateralism. But nothing could halt the neoconservative charge at that point, least of all the absence of hard evidence in support of Saddam's putative threat to world peace.[36] Neocon foreign policy was an a priori affair, unburdened by such liberal constraints. America, accordingly, would soon be searching ex post facto, as in Vietnam, for the reason it had gone to war.[37]

9/11 and the Making of Neoglobalism

The message of the Bush Doctrine to the non-globalized world was no longer the standard globalist exhortation to "join us and profit," but rather the neoglobalist "join us *or else*." This ultimatum, however, was only new in its openness. Caspar Henderson detects its presence, for example, in Madeleine Albright's famous "walk tall" speech, which cast the United States as "the indispensable nation." She was more than hinting that the wishes of the rest of the world were quite dispensable.[38]

After 9/11 there was little incentive for even that degree of subtlety. The Bush, Jr. political team astutely recognized that it was time for a remake of *High Noon*, with Jr. cast as the forsaken lawman. "Old Europe" inadvertently played its part by refusing to stand with the sheriff. It would have spoiled everything if France and Germany had decided to join the attack on Iraq. Having Blair there was troublesome enough, as he kept pressing for compromises that no self-respecting neocon could abide, but at least his presence validated the president's globalist credentials. With the wolf coming out of its sheep's clothing, globalism now had teeth.

Except for Blair, who would pay dearly on the home front for his neoglobalist adventure, mainstream globalists were sent packing by what is sometimes referred to as the "Rumsfeld strategy." Here, in the words of the master, "the mission determines the coalition, and not the other way round."[39] The rudiments of this strategy had been applied before—e.g., in Bush I's Gulf War and Clinton's NATO-based Kosovo alliance—but such cases had been looked upon as exceptions to the globalist rule. The Bush Doctrine removed those exceptions by normalizing the new globalist militancy.

It remains to be seen which way this ball will bounce. On the one hand, Suzanne Nossel contends that the global outcry against the invasion of Iraq marks a turn toward the democratization of geopolitics. As such it constitutes "one of the most multipolar moments in history."[40] On the other hand, the United States seemed almost to court this reaction, as if to prove how little it mattered. Was this the advent of full and unmitigated unipolarity, or of a new grassroots multilateralism? Either way, the prevailing globalist power structure has been fully exposed by the Bush Doctrine. It is no longer possible to pretend that globalization—as a practice rather than an ideal—does not operate under distinctly American auspices. After 9/11 that means pursuing a highly non-idealist agenda—but also, as discussed above, a non-realist agenda. To survive, globalism has radically changed its stripes, fusing neoliberalism and neoconservatism.

In fact these two globalisms were never so far apart as myth has it. Both had seen the world in largely "us/them" terms. Granted, neocons had been more inclined to enforce those terms on the level of raw coercion, while neoliberals usually preferred economic duress. 9/11 seemed to tip the scales in favor of the neocons, but it would be more accurate to describe the new breed of conservatism as neoliberalism with a big stick. Thus empowered, neoliberalism's borderless agenda spelled the end of time-tested policy limits such as the national sovereignty guarantees of the UN Charter. The door was opened not only for preemptive war, but for unabashed CIA assassinations and judicial proceedings that can only be described as summary injustice.

9/11, then, marked the end of any real ideological contest between America's rival globalisms. Bush came out of the fray with what Reagan never had: not only a Reaganite congressional majority, but also a like-minded Supreme Court.[41] The neocons in turn came out with a president unburdened by prior knowledge of foreign affairs. This made him a perfect match for neoconservatism's ample stock of easy answers. Especially he swallowed the neocon interpretation of the Gulf War as a lost opportunity. From there it was but a short hop to the neoglobalist vision of U.S. hegemony over Iraq and the Middle East. As the story goes, Bush I's internationalism tied his hands, preventing him from finishing what he started in Kuwait. "Bush III" would set that straight. After 9/11 his unilateralism took on (even in name, at first) the nature of a crusade. Americans noticed the change and called it "presidential." He got his mandate, the neocons got their man, and through his high ratings they both tapped the popular base they would need to radically revise the globalist agenda for the twenty-first century.

It would be a mistake, however, to see the neocons as anti-globalists. They were simply correcting a fatal flaw of 1990s globalism, which failed to recognize that actually existing globalization had more in common with the worldview of Hobbes than of Francis Fukuyama. While triumphal globalism took center stage, a chorus of dissenting voices gained prominence on the American Right. These contrarians faced up to two very Hobbesian facts: (a) that the post–Cold War world was even less secure than the bipolar world had been, and (b) that the new global hazards could no more be shored off through EU-style multilateralism than by conservative isolationism. Impending dangers would have to be confronted assertively, and unilaterally if necessary. It is little wonder that neoconservatives, who seem to turn globalism on its head, have often been viewed as anti-globalists. In fact they are supra-globalists—the only group that stands ready to enforce globalization as a nonnegotiable imperative rather than a polite invitation.

But that frankly imperialist project would have to wait. Before dealing with the world, neoconservatives would have to win America over, starting with its president. The first two post–Cold War presidents proved uneducable, having come to office with the wrong kind of ideological baggage. Bush I was too much a product of Cold War internationalism to learn new tricks, while Clinton was too immersed in neoliberal economism to recognize the new power politics as a globalist force in its own right. Bush II, by contrast, was the perfect blank slate. His need for easy answers made him ripe for neoconservative tutelege. The first task was to drive a wedge between this prospective unilateralist and his relatively multilateral father. The second, using the Oval Office as a base camp, was to de-Clintonize the Washington Consensus. The idea was not to bury neoliberalism, but to "neoconize" it.

Arch-conservative Roger Scruton attests that 9/11 opened a window of opportunity for the Right by thrusting ordinary Americans back into the fold of a common culture. Those who had never read Russell Kirk, Hilton Kramer, or Irving Kristol suddenly got a cram course on the charms of cultural retrenchment. Middle America was invited to partake in the defining (and confining) act of conservatism: its division of humanity into neat categories of "us" and "them." After 9/11 this global bifurcation was no longer wedded to isolationism. It was no longer feasible to remove ourselves from "them" in the old conservative manner. Instead, the "other" must be subdued, as in Iraq.

This was the neoconservative road to globalization, as mapped by Paul Wolfowitz, the Bush administration's chief Straussian. In the name of "moral clarity," the president confronted a world in need of radical reformation. Like the pot calling the kettle black, neocon fundamentalists all but replicated the binary lines of the Cold War by depicting Islamic fundamentalists as "religious Stalinists." Like his true believing opposite, Osama bin Laden, Bush divided the whole panoply of human experience into impermeable categories of good (us) versus evil (them), never noticing that the real enemy is the one in the mirror.[42] Neoconservative aggression is likely to produce, by way of blowback, the opposite of its intended effect. Like Trotskyist millenarianism (which actually influenced some early strains of neoconservatism) neocons believe their mission is to destroy the forces of unrighteousness.

Such global pugnacity is of course a scandalous perversion of the traditional conservative conviction, reaching back to Burke and Herder, that cultural reality is far too complex to comprehend, much less restructure. In the view of Clyde Prestowitz, a small-government conservative and Reagan administration veteran, "neoconservatism is not conservatism at all but radicalism, egoism, and adventurism. . . ."[43] Francis Fukuyama adds that what Americans call "conservativism" Europeans call "liberalism," because it is all about "free market" individualism, not the collective rights that, on the American side, are stridently upheld by anti-globalist activists.[44]

Conservatism, then, is already a fractured ideology, and to survive politically it will have to open itself up to centrist voters. This conservative populism is the Right's only ticket in a democratic context. Bush must attract what one White House insider describes as "base plus," retaining the loyalty of Republican stalwarts while reaching out to the political mainstream. The former task could prove as hard as the latter. By the summer of 2003 the president's combination of monumental tax cuts (enough to risk a foreign run on the Treasury's solvency) with record military budgets was giving fiscal conservatives fits of anxiety. With estimates for the next year's budget deficit exceeding $450 billion, complaints were mounting on Capitol Hill from within the GOP itself.[45] The trick was to get that pedestrian "plus" to identify with foundational conservative issues.

That is where 9/11 was decisive. For the moment, a common cause united the conservative "base" with the country's political center. The question was how long this center would hold. Could the "war on terrorism" keep the 9/11 spirit alive? Just in case it could not, there was no time to waste. Neoconservatism quickly pressed its real agenda, including upper-income tax cuts at home and corporate militancy abroad. Luckily for the neocons, the cultural prerequisites for a general "Right turn" were already in place. On the domestic side, the 1990s had seen a steady drift toward the social acceptance of gross inequality. Even the word "dynasty" had lost so much of its taint that neither the Democrats nor Republicans hesitated to endorse dynastic candidates in the 2000 presidential race.

On the foreign side, the "Bush Doctrine" had less need of an egalitarian or democratic front, given the short attention span of the American public on foreign affairs apart from full-scale war. Public indifference and factual license are two sides of the same neocon coin. Suffice it to say that the us/them boundaries of the current war on terrorism are geopolitically adjustable. America has long applied the term "terror state" to countries that happen to run afoul of the United States for almost any reason.[46] States with no proven terrorist record find themselves listed, while many known supporters of terrorism are showered with U.S. aid.

A telling case in point is the Bush administration's decision to renew the flow of aid to Indonesia's military. Such funding had been suspended since September 1999, when Indonesian troops and hired thugs committed massive atrocities in East Timor. The issue was compounded when two Americans were murdered in Papua Province in August 2002. The FBI was sent in after police in the area concluded that Indonesian soldiers were probably responsible. Without waiting for the FBI's findings, the Bush administration—pressed by former Indonesian ambassador and present Deputy Defense Secretary Paul Wolfowitz—expedited the release of a $400,000 first installment in training funds.[47]

An even more egregious case of geocronyism is the lavish funding of Pakistan under its self-appointed president, General Pervez Musharraf. A $3 billion aid package was recently extended to Pakistan, despite the fact that it has been and remains the prime conduit for terrorist backing in Kashmir and Afghanistan. Bush even threw in words of praise for the general's success in constructing a "tolerant and prosperous Pakistan."[48] The Afghan government exercised more "moral clarity" when, in the summer of 2003, it temporarily shut down Pakistan's embassy in retaliation for Musharraf's ongoing support of Taliban insurgency. India's view of the matter—symbolized by its 1,800-mile border fence project[49]—speaks for itself.

Conclusion: Neoglobalist Solidarity

These were minor concerns, however, for a president who considered himself chosen by God. Divine selection trumped the fact that Bush had not been chosen by a majority of American voters. So too constitutional and human rights could be sacrificed on the altar of anti-terrorism. The Justice Department drew on this certitude in framing anti-terrorist policies, such as its claim of the right to hold American citizens in prison indefinitely and without access to legal counsel if they are deemed "enemy combatants." Many alleged terrorists were secretly detained and given closed hearings without access to attorneys. Yielding to the president's war powers, the courts looked the other way, while Attorney General John Ashcroft ignored members of Congress who questioned such policies.

By no accident, the president's constant recourse to God's will bears ominous resemblance to nineteenth-century America's recourse to Manifest Destiny. Scott Appleby, a religious historian, ties the whole thrust of today's unilateralism to the religious Right's theologically driven teleology.[50] Westward-looking Americans knew how to deal with Native Americans who got in their way. As Horace Greeley approvingly summed it up in 1859, "These people must die out."[51] This is the providential tradition that Bush III regenerated after 9/11, substituting Muslims for Native Americans.

Putting aside the question of how Bush reconciled his us/them Manichaeanism with his much professed Christianity, there was a practical problem with this politics of divide and hate: it virtually guaranteed that the world would hate "us" back. In an age of global communication, the message that got through to Middle America also got through to the Middle East. Indeed, Muslims who admired the principles of American democracy were especially prone to resent the perversion of those principles in the interest of Empire. Already the Bush administration had forfeited most of the global sympathy that America reaped after 9/11. Abu Ghraib added insult to injury. As the editors of one paper put it, "there is something seriously wrong when a foreign policy intended to build a universal front against terrorism . . . ends up turning so many against the United States."[52] The war on Iraq not only increased the popular base for terrorist recruitment, but set in motion what many would have thought impossible a few years before: a budding courtship between secular Arab nationalists and radical Islamists. This anti-American common cause is the Islamic equivalent of Bush's monolithic "us." The loser on both sides has been moderation.[53]

The Bush Doctrine, however, is not so novel as its critics suggest. In many respects it represents the full expression rather than negation of pre-9/11 globalism. This of course is vehemently denied by neoliberals with close ties to the Democratic Party. Former Clinton staffers Ronald Asmus and Kenneth Pollack insist that neocon power strategies, and preemptive strikes in particular, should never have been raised to the status of "normal tools" of intervention. They duly note that the real challenge in Afghanistan and Iraq was not so much victory in war as in peace.[54] The Bush administration was so averse to that task that as of August 2003 it had spent only about $300 million of the $3.3 billion assistance package appropriated by Congress in the fall of 2001 for Afghanistan.

Notice, however, that Asmus and Pollack do not reject the neocon goal of reshaping the world along Washington Consensus lines. Their invective is more directed toward the means than the ends of the Bush Doctrine. As the editors of *The New Republic* point out, few neocons would insist upon a preemptive strike as a *first* option. And many, such as Wolfowitz, have been advocates of tendentious nation building. These right-wing idealists had to restrain themselves, however, for they had to coexist with a wide spectrum of Republican "realists,"[55] including a phalanx of "Nixonian" neocons such as Cheney and Rumsfeld.

After 9/11 there was a great deal more solidarity within neoconservative ranks, and likewise there was much less distance between neoliberalism and neoconservatism than Asmus and Pollack suggest. 9/11 exposed and nurtured the fealty both camps gave to Washington-based globalization. This deep structural bond, and the prior triumph of neoliberalism within Democratic ranks, gave rise to neoglobalism as the core of a frightfully broad Washington Consensus. This congruence was underscored by Senator Kerry's re-luctance to challenge one of the weakest links in the Bush war on terrorism: his diversion of security resources to the war in Iraq. The thrust of post-9/11 securitization was more than endorsed by Kerry. He only criticized Bush for not pushing this militarist agenda even farther. Meanwhile, as Martha Nuss-baum complained, no major party laid stress on the urgent needs of human-ity in general.[56]

Where neoliberals and neoconservatives have most diverged is not in their globalist objectives but in their way of handling *resistance* to globalization.[57] The similarity of their objectives was camouflaged by the ostensibly softer co-ercion of neoliberalism. 9/11, however, brought their means and ends together under neoglobalism, which embarked on a crusade to crush the worst anti-globalist offenders by whatever means were necessary. By no means were ter-rorists the only targets of the new anti-terrorism.

Among its victims were some of the cardinal rights of law-abiding dissi-dents, including American citizens. The Bush Doctrine and its domestic ana-logue, the Patriot Act, enjoyed bipartisan congressional support. No serious challenge was raised to this vastly expanded executive license, including the right to launch preemptive strikes and to set aside normal juridical safeguards in the handling of terrorist suspects. Though wrapped in democratic idealism, neoglobalism nurtures an "us/them" worldview that sweeps both civil dissent at home and civil Islam abroad into the "them" camp.

9/11 turned that worldview into a foreign policy. The end of the Cold War had invited glossy visions of an uncontested New World Order, but darker vi-sions soon materialized. The resulting double vision was not a simple rift be-tween a capitalistic Right that endorsed global corporatism versus a Left that rejected it. Many who claimed liberal Left credentials had long since meta-morphosed into neoliberals or Third Way quasi-reformists, while many on the Right—notably Samuel Huntington, Robert Kaplan, and John Gray—looked past globalist hubris to a mounting New World Disorder. If 9/11 won the case for Huntington et. al, the subsequent "war on terrorism" increases an already massive imbalance of power on the globalist side. Terrorist "blowback" is sure to follow as a balancing agent of last resort.

Notes

1. On the attitudes of Marx and Engels toward the Fenian terrorism of their days, see Walter Laquer, *The Age of Terrorism* (Boston: Little, Brown, 1987), 61; and on the relative restraint of Left terrorism of the 1970s see Richard E. Rubenstein, *Alchemists of Revolution: Terrorism in the Modern World* (New York: Basic Books, 1987), 91–92.

2. Quoted in Manuel Castells, *The Power of Identity* (Oxford, U.K.: Blackwell, 1997), 243, trans. by Castells.

3. Castells, *The Power of Identity*, 243.

4. Jonathan Friedman, "Being in the World: Globalization and Localization," in Mike Featherstone, ed., *Global Culture: Nationalism, Globalization and Modernity* (London: Sage, 1990), 311 (311–28).

5. Eduarto Galeano, *Upside Down: A Primer for the Looking-Glass World*, trans. by Mark Fried (New York: Metropolitan Books, 1998 [trans. 2000]), 309.

6. Benjamin R. Barber, "Beyond Jihad vs. McWorld," *The Nation* (January 11, 2002), <www.thenation.com/docPrint.mhtml?I=20020121&s=barber>.

7. Benjamin R. Barber, *Jihad vs. McWorld* (New York: Ballantine Books, 1995), 5–6; and on risk-inspired solidarity see Ulrich Beck, *Risk Society* (London: Sage, 1992).

8. Barber, *Jihad vs. McWorld*, 11.

9. Susan Sontag, in "The Talk of the Town," *The New Yorker* (issue of September 24, 2001), <www.newyorker.com/PRINTABLE/?talk/010924ta_talk_wtc>.

10. Concerning al Qaeda's contribution to American capitalism and geopolitics, see "Bin Laden—Promoter of Globalization?" *The Globalist* (November 28, 2001), <www.theglobalist.com/nor/richter/2001/11-28-01.shtml>.

11. E.g., Michael Hardt and Antonio Negri, *Empire* (Cambridge, MA: Harvard University Press, 2000); and Chalmers Johnson, *Blowback: The Costs and Consequences of American Empire* (New York: Henry Holt, 2000). Hardt and Negri, however, treat "Empire" as a virtual structure apart from the American imperialism that occupies Johnson.

12. David Halberstam, *War in a Time of Peace: Bush, Clinton, and the Generals* (New York: Scribner, 2001), 496.

13. Haynes Johnson, *The Best of Times: America in the Clinton Years* (New York: Harcourt, 2001), 25.

14. Songok Han Thornton, "Let Them Eat IT: The Myth of the Global Village as an Interactive Utopia," *Ctheory* (January 17, 2002): A103.

15. Carl Boggs, *The End of Politics: Corporate Power and the Decline of the Public Sphere* (New York: The Guilford Press, 2000), 70.

16. Merrill Goozner, "Blinded by the Boom: What's Missing in the Coverage of the New Economy?" *Columbia Journalism Review* (November/December 2000), <www.cjr.org/year/00/4/goozner.asp>.

17. Thomas Frank, *One Market under God: Extreme Capitalism, Market Populism, and the End of Economic Democracy* (New York: Doubleday, 2000), 31.

18. Thornton, "Let Them Eat IT."

19. Gopal Balakrishnan, "Hardt and Negri's Empire," *New Left Review* 5 (September/October 2000), <www.newleftreview.net/NLR23909.shtml>.

20. See Todd Gitlin, *The Twilight of Common Dreams* (New York: Metropolitan Books, 1995).

21. Michael Buraway, "Introduction: Reaching for the Global," in Michael Buraway, Joseph A. Blum, et al., eds., *Global Ethnography: Forces, Connections, and Imaginations in a Postmodern World* (Berkeley: University of California Press, 2000), 28 (1–40).

22. Bryan S. Turner, *Classical Sociology* (London: Sage, 1999), 283.

23. Anthony Giddens, *The Third Way: The Renewal of Social Democracy* (Cambridge, U.K.: Polity Press, 1998), 137–38.

24. Anthony Giddens, *Runaway World: How Globalization Is Reshaping Our Lives* (New York: Routledge, 2000), 89–93.

25. An excellent case for what I call moral realism is made by Barber (see Barber, "Beyond").

26. See Anatol Lieven, "The Hard Edge of American Values," an *Atlantic* interview with Kaplan in the June 18, 2003, issue of *The Atlantic Online*, <www.theatlantic.com/cgi-bin/send.cgi?page=http%3A//www.theatlantic.com/unboun…>.

27. Former Nixon speech writer William Safire has noted the Nixon parallel, which Reihan Salem relates to what he considers the nationalist faction of the Bush II camp—that of the Nixon/Ford veterans Cheney and Rumsfeld. Salem sees this as the source of the "America first" argument that Bush applied to his rejection of Kyoto and the International Criminal Court. He regards Wolfowitz, by contrast, as carrying the flame of Reagan's right-wing idealism. Whatever the merit of Salem's thesis in the early days of the Bush II administration, the two factions all but merged after 9/11. See Reihan Salam, "Domestic Disturbance," *The New Republic* (July 28, 2003), <www.tnr.com/doc.mhtml?i=express&s=salem07803>.

28. William Saletan, "Humanitarian Hawks," *Mother Jones* (July/August 1999), <www.motherjones.com/mother-jones/JA99/saletan.html>.

29. Newt Ginrich, "Rogue State Department," *Foreign Policy* (July/August, 2003), <www.foreign.com/story.php?storyID=13742>.

30. "Present at the Dissolution," *The Nation* (August 18, 2003), <www.thenation.com/docprint.mhtml?i=20030818&s=editors>.

31. "Complete Text of Bush's West Point Address," *NewsMax.com* (June 3, 2002), <www.newsmax.com/cgi-bin/printer_friendly.pl?page=http://www.newsmax.com/arc…>.

32. Rich Lowry, "A Fighting Doctrine," *National Review* (June 4, 2002), <www.nationalreview.com/lowry/lowry/060402.asp>.

33. Bill Vann and David North, "Bush Speaks at West Point: From Containment to 'Rollback,'" *World Socialist Web Site* (June 4, 2002), <www.wsws.org/articles/2002/jun2002/bush-j04.shtml>.

34. That debate was presaged in the early 1990s by Powell's contest with Bosnian hawk Merrill McPeak, the air force chief of staff who was ready to jettison post-Vietnam caution in favor of a robust global interventionism. See Halberstam, *War in a Time of Peace*, 39.

35. Todd Gitlin, "America's Age of Empire: The Bush Doctrine," *Mother Jones* (January/February 2003), <www.mojones.com/commentary/columns/2003/02/ma_205_01.html>.

36. That evidence was not only critical in terms of world opinion, but in terms of UN resolutions that presumably have the force of international law. Resolution 687, issued after the Gulf War cease-fire of April 1991, specified that Iraq's violation of the terms of the cease-fire, which included a strict prohibition of weapons of mass destruction, would nullify the cease-fire. In short, proof of WMD stockpiling would render the Iraq War a continuation of the Gulf War rather than a unilateral action. See

Robert Lane Greene, "Law and Order," *The New Republic* (July 29, 2003), <www.tnr.com/doc.mhtml?i=foreign&s=green072903>.

37. See Maureen Dowd, "Bomb and Switch," *New York Times* (June 4, 2003), <www.nytimes.com/2003/06/04/opinion/04/DOWD.html>. Dowd's concern over this retroactive search is well justified, but she is wrong to suggest that this was an American first.

38. Caspar Henderson, "Bi-polar Disorder," o*penDemocracy* (July 29, 2003), <www.opendemocracy.net/articles/ViewPopUpArticle.jsp?id=6&articleId=1392>.

39. Rumsfeld qtd. in Joseph Joffe, "Gulliver Unbound: Can America Rule the World," *CIS Occasional Paper* 85, from the 20th Annual John Bonython Lecture, Sydney (August 5, 2003), <www.cis.org.au/Events/JBL/JBL03.htm>.

40. Suzanne Nossel, "Democracy Confronts the Superpower: The New Globalist Politics," *Dissent* (summer 2003), <www.dissentmagazine.org/menutest/articles/su03/nossel.htm>.

41. See William Greider, "Rolling Back the 20th Century," *The Nation* (May 12, 2003), <www.thenation.com/docprint.mhtml?I=20030512&s=greider>.

42. This metaphor is drawn from Roxanne L. Euben, *Enemy in the Mirror: Islamic Fundamentalism and the Limits of Modern Rationalism—A Work of Comparative Political Theory* (Princeton, NJ: Princeton University Press, 1999). On the fundamentalist commonality between Bush and Osama see David Aikman, "The Great Revival: Understanding Religious 'Fundamentalism,'" *Foreign Affairs* 82, no. 4 (July/August, 2003): 188–93.

43. Qtd. in John Rossant, "Has America Become a Bullyboy," *BusinessWeek* (June 16, 2003), <www.businessweek.com/print/magazine/content/03_24/b3837024_mz005.htm?db>.

44. Francis Fukuyama, "Beyond Our Shores: Today's 'Conservative' Foreign Policy Has an Idealist Agenda," *The Wall Street Journal* (December 24, 2002), <www.opinionjournal.com/forms/printThis.html?id=110002814>.

45. Steven E. Schier, "President Bush: A Radical with a Plan," *The Hill* (July 30, 2003), <www.thehill.com/op_ed/073003/.aspx>.

46. Frank Füredi, *The New Ideology of Imperialism* (London: Pluto Press, 1994), 34.

47. Congress, by contrast, voted in July 2003 to withhold further funding for fiscal year 2004 unless Indonesia prosecutes the guilty parties. See Dan Murphy, "U.S. Rewards Indonesian Military as Probe Continues," *The Christian Science Monitor* (July 22, 2003), <www.csmonitor.com/2003/0722/ p07s01-woap.htm>.

48. David E. Sanger, "Bush Offers Pakistan Aid, but No F-16s," *New York Times* (June 25, 2003), <www.nytimes.com/2003/06/25/international/asia/25PREX.html>.

49. Rami Lakshmi, "India's Border Fence Extended to Kashmir: Country Aims to Stop Pakistani Infiltration," *Washington Post* (July 30, 2003): A16.

50. "Divine Intervention" *Foreign Policy* (July/August 2003), <www.foreignpolicy.com/story/printer.php?storyID=137141>.

51. Qtd. in Jackson Lears, "How a War Became a Crusade," *New York Times* (March 11, 2003), <www.nytimes.com/2003/03/11/opinion/11LEAR.html>.

52. "American Power," *International Herald Tribune* (June 4, 2003), <www.int.com/cgi-bin/generic.cgi?template=articleprint.tmplh&ArticleId=98232>.

53. See Husain Haqqani, "Islam's Weakened Moderates," *Foreign Policy* (July/August 2003), <www.foreignpolicy.com/story/story.php?storyID=13761>.

54. Ronald D. Asmus and Kenneth M. Pollack, "The Neoliberal Take on the Middle East," *Washington Post* (July 22, 2003): A17.

55. "The Neo Con," *The New Republic* (July 22, 2003), <www.tnr.com/etc.mhtml>.

56. Martha Nussbaum, "Rules for the World Stage," *Newsday* (April 20, 2003), archived <www.law.uchicago.edu/news/nussbaum-grotius.html>.

57. Even that tactical difference has been exaggerated. Gore Vidal discerns, for example, the germ of the Guantanamo Bay mentality in the Anti-Terrorism Act of 1996. See Gore Vidal, *Perpetual War for Perpetual Peace: How We Got to Be So Hated* (New York: Thunder's Mouth Press/Nation Books, 2002), 19.

3

Second Front: Anti-Terrorism and the Plight of Post-Crash Reform on the Rim

The New Security Paradigm

ONE OF THE DEFINING FEATURES OF COLD WAR REALISM, as filtered through Henry Kissinger and Jeane Kirkpatrick, was its view of human rights as an impediment to good statecraft. Nor did that attitude evaporate at the end of the Cold War. Not until October 1997, when President Clinton signed the Leahy Amendment into law, did security and human rights begin to converge in what can be called moral realism. Though it was first restricted to counternarcotics efforts, Leahy's range was soon extended to all military aid. Repressive regimes were served notice that state terrorism could cost them their military aid and Pentagon ties. The only losers in this policy shift, in the words of Stephen Rickard of Amnesty International, were "the world's thugs and torturers—and their apologists."

There is a catch, however. The secretary of defense retains the right to waive Leahy if he thinks it appropriate due to "extraordinary circumstances." Granted, he must explain such a waiver to relevant congressional committees within fifteen days, but there are no clear guidelines on what constitutes an "extraordinary circumstance." No doubt the current "war on terrorism" more than qualifies. Thus the reform movement that Leahy signals is a dying cause.

Much as developing countries were once subjected to CIA-sponsored subversion if they failed to join America's war on communism—a policy which ironically pushed many Southeast Asian nationalists into the communist camp[1]—they were now informed by President Bush that they have but two choices regarding the "war on terrorism": join us or fight us. In his speech to corporate leaders at the APEC (Asia Pacific Economic Cooperation) forum in Shanghai, President Bush admonished that "Every nation now must oppose this enemy, or be, in turn, its target." The illogic of terrorists making a target of those who do *not* oppose them leaves little doubt as to what the president really means: that his own "war on terrorism" will target those who do not join it.[2]

To slam the gate on interest-free idealism, a moratorium on moral interventionism was tossed into the bargain—except of course in oil-saturated Iraq. After Kosovo the world waited to see if transnational interventionism, which had been so conspicuously absent in Rwanda, would become a central feature of North/South relations. Or was the liberal face of neoliberal policy a mere mask for vital (i.e., Northern) interests. Whether or not America's action in Kosovo was imperialistic,[3] the fact that this breach of national sovereignty was made in the name of moral intervention was enough to set the police states of the world on edge. To the consternation of China and many Asian regimes, human rights were starting to take on geopolitical weight, as moral realism became a frontline issue of North/South relations for the new century.

The question was whether the New World Order would furnish anything more than an apparatus for global security. Would it offer a "Third Way" for the Third World? Or, as Chalmers Johnson contends, would it cloak a new American "Empire"?[4] Events in East Timor brought these questions front and center in Asian security relations. Powerful voices in the United States, including the *New York Times*, were calling for a suspension of international loans—Indonesia's foreign debt having already reached $130 billion—unless Jakarta acted to curb the violence in East Timor. Suharto's successor, President Habibie, came under UN pressure to allay tensions by granting East Timor a referendum on the question of its independence. At first he opposed the idea, but in April 1999 he granted a vote under the supervision of UNAMET (the UN Mission in East Timor).

This move only intensified the fighting between government-backed paramilitary forces and Timorese separatists. When voters overwhelmingly endorsed independence, the militias went on a vengeful rampage, even as 15,000 Indonesian troops looked on or even participated. Neither Habibie nor the nearly autonomous General Wiranto showed any interest in stemming the violence. Nor, for that matter, did the UN exhibit much concern. Having officially sponsored the referendum, it simply stepped aside, as did Indonesia's civil administration, including its police and utilities officials. This left the militias free to do as they wished. Only after the fledgling country was in ruins was an Australian-led peacekeeping force sent to restore order (and, more to the point, to prevent hordes of refugees from migrating to Australia).

Finally, in accord with Leahy, the U.S. Congress rose above Clinton's corporate-inspired inertia to suspend military assistance to Indonesia.[5] This put U.S.-based multinationals in a no-win situation. If Jakarta defied Leahy, they stood to lose part of their geopolitical support system. But they could lose even more if the regime took the reform path, spelling the end of corporate cronyism. What they needed in the wake of Kosovo and East Timor was a politic way to ditch the reform dynamic that Leahy epitomized.

Enter Osama bin Laden. Notwithstanding his war on global capitalism, he came gift wrapped as the enemy of an even more perilous foe. He arrived just in time to save corporate globalism from what can be called the "fourth wave" of democratization: the challenge of substantive reform within the pro forma democracies that rode in on the "third wave." The prospect of real political development was especially noxious to Asian power elites who lost their purchase on public docility after the Crash. The security paradigm that set in after 9/11 was their salvation. Even the State Department's own annual report on human rights confirms that many of the Bush administration's allies in the "war on terrorism" are paragons of state terrorism. Clearly securitization is a dual-purpose sword.

Securitization in America has been marked by a similar duality. After 9/11 it capitalized on the prospect of protracted "war" to secure record-breaking approval ratings for President Bush, even in the midst of a flagging and "Enronized" economy. Seeing the advantage of security as a global solvent, the administration quickly muzzled the president's initial "crusader" rhetoric. In Washington, at least, the "blame Islam" syndrome was contained by the need to enlist Muslim nations in a global anti-terrorist coalition. Lower Rim countries such as Indonesia, Malaysia, and Brunei, which sit on top of their own Islamic powder kegs, have become pivotal. Failure to secure their backing would preclude the support Washington seeks from ASEAN (the Association of South-East Asian Nations).[6] All things considered, the United States was lucky to get the attenuated anti-terrorist resolution that was patched together at the November 5, 2001, ASEAN meeting in Brunei.[7]

In the absence of a well-defined enemy, securitization easily metamorphoses into a war on political difference. Jonathan Glover notes that while U.S.-backed insurrection is called *resistance*, other insurgents are labeled *terrorists*.[8] The present "war," moreover, removes the banana republic association of much pre-9/11 counterinsurgency. Anti-terrorism offers a new globalist ticket for post-Crash regimes (one they certainly prefer to that other ticket, economic restructurization, though they may end up with both). Meanwhile U.S. strategists are liberated from the moral impostures of the 1990s, returning us to the unabashed realism of Cold War alliances.

Green Light at APEC

The Bush administration's retreat from Leahy conforms to those same priorities. The magnitude of this policy reversal is suggested by a comparison of the president's stance at the October 2001 APEC Ministerial Meeting in Shanghai with his November 1999 campaign speech at the Reagan Library. There he portrayed China as a strategic competitor as opposed to a Clintonesque "strategic partner." In line with what he described as realism "in the service of American ideals," Bush called for a "fellowship of free Pacific nations as strong and united as our Atlantic partnership." In short he was suggesting a NATO-like Pacific alliance,[9] with China assigned the role of the former Soviet Union. This was to be the Asian branch of a "distinctly American internationalism." Its linchpin was an unambiguous security pledge to Taiwan, along with moral support for oppositional voices within China.[10]

China's predictable response was vented during the Hainan Incident of April 2001, a defining moment in a newly commercialized geopolitics. The diplomatic furor that followed the collision of a U.S. surveillance plane and a Chinese fighter jet was allayed by the backroom intercession of China's new-found corporate partners. The president's inevitable "about face" started that very month and was completed at the APEC meeting in October. China would meet no protest from the United States or other APEC members when it rejected Taiwan's delegates. Nor was there any criticism of China's extension of the word "terrorism" to include virtually all dissidents in Xinjiang Province (occupied East Turkestan, as some prefer to call it) and elsewhere.[11]

Such reticence has consequences. China tested the potency of its "anti-terrorist" diplomacy by summarily executing eleven Xinjiang "separatists" just prior to the March 2000 meeting of the United Nations Human Rights Commission (UNHRC). UNHRC kept its silence. In June China secured monumental trade deals with the EU and the U.S., clearing the way for its acceptance into the WTO. Within a few days it celebrated this triumph by executing five more "Islamic terrorists," while sentencing others to long prison terms, including two life sentences. The Western press took little interest,[12] and the academic world took even less.

This same "anti-terrorist" pretext allowed Bush and Malaysia's Mahathir Mohamad to reconcile in Shanghai. Prior to 9/11 Mahathir had desperately sought a meeting with Bush as a show of tacit support for his mounting repression after the arrest and show trial of his former Deputy Prime Minister Anwar Ibrahim. This was not to be. It was 9/11 that got Mahathir a warm invitation to the White House.[13] This green light allowed the dictator to enjoy the full privileges of his Internal Security Act (ISA), which authorizes such draconian measures as unlimited detention without trial. Most of the "terrorists" thus jailed just happened to be members of the main opposition party, PAS (the Islamic Party of Malaysia), which the government was pleased to compare to the Taliban.[14] This ploy worked beautifully. Many of the non-Muslims who voted for PAS in the general elections of 1999—raising hopes for a genuine two-party system—abandoned the opposition.[15] Pro-Anwar demonstrations also lost steam, and even sympathizers who stubbornly kept the issue alive tended to focus more on the need for a new prime minister than for legal reform.

There is some question as to what Bush thought he was getting in return for this green light. Only Britain and Australia had at that time committed troops to the Afghan War. In effect Bush and Mahathir were buying each other's silence. On October 12, 2001, in response to burgeoning protests against what many saw as a war on Islam, Mahathir called for a halt to U.S. air strikes, and later he pushed unsuccessfully for an ASEAN resolution to that effect. Having cast himself as the squeaky wheel of Southeast Asia, he was now well positioned to bargain at once for a less strident regionalism and a touch of anti-terrorist oil.

This rights-for-security trade-off profoundly impacted North/South relations. In Afghanistan, for example, known terrorists were hired to fight terrorists. The most egregious case in point was the Uzbek "General" Abdul Rashid Dostum, who had hired himself out to the Soviets during their war here, and stood out even by Afghan standards for his campaigns of rape, torture, and assorted atrocities. After 1992 he led factions of the Mujahedeen in their postwar pillage of Kabul, thus inviting the Taliban's rise to power. By any objective standard the Northern Alliance, America's hired gun, was itself a terrorist organization. If the "war on terrorism" is to pass for anything more than another geopolitical machination—a globalist replay of Cold War realism—U.S. policy must restore a balance between rights and security.

This reform imperative must reach beyond democratic proceduralism—the presumed gateway to "third wave" democratic consolidation.[16] Most democratization of the 1980s and early 1990s served to reinforce elitist power structures by lending them a populist veneer. This enabled Reagan, Bush I, and Clinton to paste a cover over American foreign policy. The National Endowment for Democracy functioned as a late Cold War and early post–Cold War mopping-up operation, its real task being to neoliberalize Third World opposition politics. Set in this context, Bush II's push for global democratization is simply business as usual. "Democracy" on these terms is part of a global/local bargain between international capital and local oligarchs who are simply rotated in office.

Washington looks favorably upon these rotations as an alternative to less manageable autocracies such as the Marcos or Suharto family networks. Technocrats such as Habibie or Arroyo can better serve the United States as a fifth column for neoliberal restructurization. An overt U.S. military presence was unnecessary after the Cold War, and ran against the 1990s grain of "economized" geopolitics. Already in the 1980s ASEAN had shed its security orientation in favor of raw economism. Thereby it was positioned to meet the challenge of NAFTA and the EU—especially in the form of AFTA (the ASEAN Free Trade Agreement). Such economism has by no means been displaced by post-9/11 securitization; rather the two power systems, military and economic, are entering a mutually supportive phase on both sides of the Pacific. Much as neoliberal globalization used the Asian Crash as a pretext for renewed economic incursions, it now uses the "war on terror" as a gateway for geopolitical reentry.

APEC is emerging as the power broker to watch within this new geopolitics. The regional closure of AFTA[17]—not to mention Mahathir's vision of a still more insular EAEC (East Asian Economic Caucus)—is giving way to APEC's "open regionalism."[18] This is in fact a euphemism for regional acceptance of U.S.-administered globalization. Washington urges lower Rim regimes to adopt a bloated definition of terrorism, and they need little encouragement. This not only includes secessionism, as in Aceh, but almost any activism on behalf of human rights, social justice, or opposition politics. Thus the "second front" of the "war on terrorism" is looking very much like a war on post-Crash reformism.

Surrogate Miracle

Current Washington convention holds that Southeast Asia is under siege from the same terrorist forces that struck the United States on 9/11. Islamic insurgency on the Rim, however, has more to do with local unrest than with al Qaeda and its affiliates. Nor is this radical surge specific to Islamic communities. It is more pronounced among Muslims because they have been the most oppressed of the oppressed. The economic malaise that set in after the Asian Crash of 1997 exacerbated their already deplorable condition.

The most enduring effect of the Crash is political,[19] but its prime mover was economic: the stampede exit of $100 billion from the Rim in 1997. Absolute poverty soared to levels commonly associated with full-scale war, while output losses came to $2 trillion from 1998 to 2000, sparking images of a long economic malaise such as Latin America's "lost decade" of the 1980s. Strangely, the response of Western institutions seemed designed to ensure that very outcome. Key figures at the World Bank rightly feared that austerity measures imposed by the IMF would deepen the recession and foster political unrest.[20] The Bank's former chief economist, Joseph Stiglitz, cogently argues that the burden of IMF restructuring fell squarely on the poor.

What Stiglitz declines to mention is that the malady behind the Crash owed as much to World Bank machinations as to the IMF. Both had promoted an export regimen so dependent on foreign capital as to put sustainability at risk, and so dependent on cheap labor as to stunt domestic purchasing power. Ravi Kanbur's version of the Bank's *World Development Report* bucked the system by pushing for economic redistribution. Not surprisingly, Kanbur felt compelled to resign in June 2000 when his draft was revised in favor of orthodox neoliberalism.[21] Stiglitz had left in January under similar pressure. Even such moderate critics as these had no place in the emerging "Washington Consensus."

Unemployment tripled in those countries that surrendered to IMF auspices after the Crash: Indonesia, Thailand, South Korea, and the Philippines. This brought a long simmering crisis to a boil. Given the mounting insecurities of globalization, including chronic overcapacity and deflation, the question is how the Crash took so long in coming. Falling prices could be compensated only so long as unit sales were rising, while wage arbitrage had no remedy other than still lower wages, more layoffs, and more heinous labor conditions.[22] Warning should have been taken from hard economic experience, such as the deflationary spiral of the 1930s. The real Asian miracle, from this vantage, is that the region's growing income gap was successfully depoliticized for so long. Radicalism had been devitalized by the myth that all boats rise on a rising tide, with little thought given to what lay in store when the tide finally turned.

Granted, most radical resistance perished along with Left networks after the Cold War. This left no organizational grid for coherent radical action. Japan's long slide of the 1990s seemed to testify that more is required than economic stagnation to forge effective opposition, much less radical resistance. Even South Korea's more potent oppositional tradition could not be activated after the Crash. It is telling that the veteran dissident-turned-president Kim Dae Jung—in a reversal every bit as striking as that of Brazil's Cardoso—would be the one to assiduously implement IMF "reform." Kim used his vaunted "sunshine policy" with North Korea to deflect attention from this colossal Trojan horse, for which subterfuge he got a Nobel prize in 2000.[23]

In Southeast Asia, however, post-Crash politics took a very different turn. Having accomplished little in the way of political development, the southern "tigers" depended all the more on economic prowess for their legitimacy. It follows that any economic disruption would all the more destabilize the southern Rim. It was here that the prerequisites for full-fledged radicalism came together after the Crash. These included (a) a dearth of substantive democracy, (b) dire poverty in the midst of grossly exposed affluence, and most uniquely, (c) a pervasive organizational matrix in the form of political (albeit mostly civil) Islamism. The area's post-Crash leaders understood that Islam could serve as a medium for serious resistance, much as Latin American Catholicism had given sanctuary to liberation theology and radical movements such as Brazil's Pastoral Commission on Land (CPT).[24] While some Southeast Asian administrations resorted to rigid security measures, others took the safer route of issue avoidance. Both were running from the specter of Islamism.

Globalists tend to view this growing security crisis as an exogenous product of al Qaeda, but regional leaders are fully aware that the Crash released its own energies of resistance. They play along with the global "war on terror" because anti-terrorism affords a surrogate "Asian miracle," and indeed two miracles in one: broad support at home and geopolitical backing from abroad. Securitization promises these regimes the stability they require for economic revival and hence their own political survival.

That is why the anti-terrorist cause found a home in APEC and even in the officially apolitical ASEAN. The prototypic case is Singapore, which not incidentally has been rated the "most global" nation in the world.[25] Its definition of terrorism is therefore more expansive than most, covering not only movements that are anti-regime, but also anti–World Order. Securitization offers Singapore a badly needed source of post-Crash legitimacy. Having already offered itself as a logistics base for the U.S. Navy, the city-state was fast to join America's latest war dance.

This was enough to provoke the Jemaah Islamiyah, a local terrorist cell with al Qaeda links, to plan a bomb attack on U.S. ships and Western embassies. When the plot was exposed, the public stood solidly behind one of the most invasive security systems in the world, confirming that terrorism tends to reinforce existing power structures. Despite long-standing Muslim discontent among the Malay underclass, the four opposition parties of the Singapore Democratic Alliance (SDAL) have signaled their support for the Internal Security Act.[26]

A similar politics of securitization was taking shape on a regional scale by the time of the APEC meeting of October 22, 2002, at Cabo San Lucas. In return for compliance with American geopolitical goals, the United States has quietly endorsed the region's most egregious "security" priorities. This reciprocity reinstates the old realist accord that was suspended when Congress passed the "Leahy Law" in 1997, cutting military aid to highly repressive regimes.

A new era of foreign policy seemed to have dawned when Leahy was applied to Indonesia after the East Timor tragedy; but this ethical turn proved fleeting. Congress appropriated a token but highly symbolic $400,000 for military-related civilian instruction in 2002 (an ominous specification in view of

Jakarta's habit of using "civilian" militias for genocidal operations), with another $400,000 approved for 2003; and in August 2002 Secretary of State Colin Powell promised Indonesia a $50 million anti-terrorism package. Though $47 million of this was tagged for police support, $3 million was to go for military training. Powell insisted that human rights still had a place in this security agenda, but emerging Washington policy told a different story. Like anti-communism before, anti-terrorism put U.S. policy in step with unreformed power elites. Indeed, in countries where all real opposition is considered subversive, Washington is pressing lower Rim governments to fully militarize their response to political Islamism.

The Islamization of Anti-Islamism in Indonesia

Under Suharto, Pancasila ideology—which imposed a distinctly Javanese (*abangan*) political secularism on all organizations—served to depoliticize Indonesian society. Even in the mid-1990s the state's means of political repression bore striking resemblance to that of colonial times.[27] Meanwhile Western development gurus sang in tune with the World Bank on the wonders of Suharto's restructured economy.[28] As late as 1996, Hal Hill mocked those critics who talked of storm clouds on the horizon.[29] The question of rights hardly registered in the region's developmental discourse, since neoliberal teleology assumed that rights would flow automatically from growth.

This naivety is nothing new. Although *The Economist* insisted during the 1980s that Suharto was "at heart benign"[30] (as proven, apparently, by his kindness to international corporations), even passive reformism could be lethal under the shadow of Suharto's 465,000-man armed forces (the Armed Forces of Indonesia, or ABRI). Unlike Malaysia, where a stable power elite kept political unrest at bay, it was precisely the democratic proclivity of Indonesian political culture that necessitated the military's role as an agent of control.[31] As the largest political organization in the country, and the ultimate defender of Pancasila, ABRI dedicated itself to the defeat of its real nemesis: liberal democracy.

Though Jakarta was clearly a weak link in the Bush administration's "war on terrorism," it drafted a securitization law along the lines of Singapore and Malaysia. No doubt this helped the U.S. State Department make its case for $16 million in securitization aid to Indonesia, just for starters. That will further empower a military that already spurns civilian control. The question is whether full U.S. military cooperation will be part of this security package. Leahy stipulates that justice must first be obtained for the military's horrific human rights abuses in East Timor and elsewhere. But Megawati Sukarnopu-tri's regime—which like Gloria Arroyo's in the Philippines was heavily backed by the military—circumvented this requirement by means of mock trials. Meanwhile senior officers who commanded in East Timor were promoted. This should not come as a complete surprise, for neither Megawati nor her PDI (Indonesian Democracy Party) took an active role in the pro-democracy movement prior to Suharto's fall.[32] Too late we learned what was behind Megawati's famous silences.

The United States urged her to revive Indonesia's martial habits where ter-rorism is concerned.[33] The October 2002 bombing in Bali and the August 2003 Marriott Hotel bombing in Jakarta pushed her to comply, if only for commercial reasons: the exit of foreign investors, not to mention tourists, cast doubt on Indonesia's post-Crash recovery. Thus Megawati had to confront the delicate question of Islamism. Her dependence on the military (TNI—for-merly ABRI) prevented her from reaping the moderate Muslim support that was available to her from organizations such as the National Awakening Party (PKB). Her husband, Taufik Kiemas, tried to bridge this gap by way of an al-liance between the ruling PDI-P (Indonesian Democratic Party of Struggle), the PKB, and Golkar, the former ruling party.

That such an UMNO-style coalition (modeled on Malaysia's dominant po-litical machine, which long ago co-opted Muslim support) would be seriously contemplated suggests the vitality of the new Muslim politics in Indonesia, both as a progressive and reactionary force. The danger was that a Muslim presidential rival such as Amien Rais could easily tie Islamic sectarianism to economic interests commonly associated with the Left. This radical fusion could unleash a Latin-style reaction against policies that promise general re-form while actually serving the interest of foreign investors and nonnative Indonesians. This is what recommends the PKB as a useful ally for PDI and Golkar alike. It could deliver up to 60 percent of the national vote from Mus-lim "moderates," while pushing reform Islamists into the same radical fringe they occupied in the 1999 general election.[34]

This strategy is straight out of Suharto's playbook. After trying for years to deactivate Islamism under the flag of Pancasila, Suharto seemed to reverse himself in December 1990 by approving the formation of the Association of Indonesian Muslim Intellectuals (ICMI) under the direction of a presumably apolitical technocrat, B. J. Habibie. As startling as this departure was to West-ern observers, it was understood domestically as a shrewd political maneuver to offset Suharto's flagging military support.[35] Suharto, however, played his Is-lamic card too little and too late.[36] Muslims could see that even as he courted Islamic support, he waged war on real Islamic opposition. In 1984 he ordered the infamous massacre of Muslim protesters in Jakarta's Priok Port area,[37] and in the 1990s many thousands more (estimates range from 5,000 to 35,000) would be killed in Aceh.[38]

The popular cleric Abdurrahman Wahid, then the head of the powerful Nahdlatul Ulama (NU) party, rightly charged that ICMI was launched as a "preemptive strike" to contain rather than advance Islamism; but when Wahid himself became president, he took up where Suharto had left off, claiming that what he was containing was a radicalism imported from the Middle East. That was poor camouflage for the continuing atrocities being committed in Aceh, where Islamic resistance was assuredly not imported. Once again Aceh's Merdeka (freedom-fighting) rebels were defined as religious fanatics, much as they had been under the Dutch.[39]

This Islamicization of anti-Islamism had been honed at ICMI by Habibie, who took over the presidency from Suharto on May 21, 1998. He had been chosen as vice president specifically because—lacking both personal dynamism and an independent power base, such as Wahid's NU[40]—he was so obviously incapable of filling Suharto's shoes. As pressures mounted for his resignation, Suharto could point to his would-be successor as a threat; and in the seventeen months of his rule Habibie did little to upgrade that image. He himself granted that his foremost accomplishment was to become the nation's first democratic casualty by letting himself be voted out of office. Had it been otherwise there could have been civil war.

Far from promoting democracy, as he claimed, Habibie sought Muslim support against the rising democracy movement. He enjoyed the fervent support of Komaruddin Rachmat, chairman of FURKON, an umbrella organization for twenty-four Muslim groups. Late in 1998, when Habibie came under pressure from massive student pro-democracy demonstrations, Komaruddin hired a small army of Muslim "security volunteers" with bamboo sticks to beat back the unarmed students. When forced to choose between democratization and pro-government Islamism, the traditionally secular military chose the latter. Habibie reciprocated by keeping the back door open for army politics, thereby adding fuel to the flames of popular dissent. Though active middle-class resistance had subsided, the urban poor took their place in street protests beside pro-democratic students.

Reform pressure rendered the government increasingly dependent on reactionary Muslims. Habibie bequeathed to Wahid the idea of dividing good and bad (i.e., resistant) Islamism. While the former got new mosques and roads, the latter got state terrorism. Along similar lines, two Islamic political camps emerged: Wahid's secular nationalism (the good) versus Rais's more subversive sectarianism, which also tended to be anti-Western and anti-Chinese.[41] Though the post-Crash Rais was no less a liberal democrat than Wahid (for the foreign influences he contested were usually anti-democratic in practice),[42] Wahid's relative secularism was far more acceptable from a globalist perspective. That helped him win the presidency at a time when international favor could make or break the Indonesian economy. His Islamic credentials, meanwhile, could be useful for national cohesion. Although Megawati's party won the majority vote in the 1999 general elections, Wahid was declared the victor through the usual political devices. Megawati became his deputy, thereby bonding nationalism with "good" Islamism.

The very qualities that made Wahid an international favorite, however, raised military suspicions. With the clear intention of destabilizing his administration, TNI began supporting reactionary Muslim operations such as Jafar Umar Thalib's Laskar Jihad ("Holy Warriors"). Suharto stalwarts made sure the military did nothing to impede Laskar's mounting role in the Muslim/Christian clash in the Maluku Islands—a charge made by the governor of the Malukus. Worse still, by casting doubt on Wahid's Islamism, Jafar sabotaged the post-Suharto cohesion that Wahid promised the country.[43]

Feeling the heat, Wahid began looking for ways to placate the military, circumventing the principle of civilian rule he had sworn to uphold. Toward that end he slipped retired general and future president Susilo Bambang Yudhoyono into his cabinet. Under mounting pressure to do something to avert further national disintegration, Wahid gave Yudhoyono, now his security minister, the unofficial role of prime minister, even as he formally ceded much of the country's daily management to Megawati.

Wahid's hopes for a rapprochement with TNI collapsed when a government human rights commission charged the most powerful military man, General Wiranto, with responsibility for much of the carnage in East Timor. When Wiranto was pressed to resign in order to stand trial, he flatly refused, even though Wahid promised him a pardon if convicted. Soon the president found himself at odds with the whole military structure, which had never adjusted to its political decommissioning.

Early in 2001, with inflation rising and the economy floundering, Wahid came under threat of impeachment on corruption charges. In the weeks to come his supporters poured into Jakarta, holding mass rallies and forming armed "suicide squads," with Wahid's obvious approval. This unofficial palace guard went on a rampage that May, burning churches and threatening government operations. No doubt Wahid would have liked to declare martial law, so as to dismiss an antagonistic parliament, but he balked after learning that neither the military nor even his own cabinet was behind him.

On July 23 he was sacked, as the military looked with increasing favor upon Megawati's nationalism and willingness to take a harder line against separatists. Equally attractive, no doubt, was the power void this left for TNI to fill. With her in office, civilian and military elites wielded power they could hardly have dreamed of under Suharto. It soon became clear, as she put together a technocratic and market-friendly economic team, that globalists would also be winners in this post-Suharto system. She was grandly rewarded at a World Bank donor's conference where Indonesia took home a $2.7 billion loan.

The problem would be taking home the 2004 election, for Megawati could no longer credibly present herself as the people's candidate. At best she could be credited with fulfilling *half* her promise to foster democracy and remove corruption: by spreading the spoils, she democratized corruption itself. Struggling to satisfy both her globalist creditors and her military sponsors, she avoided conflict with both poles of the Muslim polity, the modernist/reformist and the traditional/reactionary.[44] These were delicate balancing acts for a president whose main input at policy meetings was often a comment or two on the snacks and refreshments.[45] But in all fairness it should be added that unlike Suharto or her father, Sukarno, Megawati was more an accidental than a willful authoritarian. As Robert Hefner puts it, "the most serious obstacle to Indonesia's democratization is less the person of the president than . . . military dominance of the political system as a whole."[46]

A typical case in point was the "Binjai incident" of September 2002, in which soldiers from an army airborne unit attacked and torched two police stations using submachine guns and grenade launchers. They then took over an electrical relay station, blacking out the entire city of Binjai, near Medan. Seven police and three civilians were killed in what turned out to be a reprisal against the police for refusing to release an arrested drug dealer. The dealer, as is common practice, had purchased military protection, or *beking* (backing). Previously the military brass could simply have ordered his release, but since late 1998, as part of the country's post-Crash reform, the police have been removed from the military chain of command.[47] Such incidents are now common, often being sparked by nothing more than a traffic ticket.

The international dimension of military *beking* was exposed by an attack of August 2002 on a group of teachers working for the Freeport Mining Company. Two Americans and one Indonesian were murdered by automatic weapons fire on an isolated road in Irian Jaya (Papua). Although Freeport had received numerous threats from a local military unit for reducing the perks it doles out for military "protection" from a slush fund,[48] the company joined the military in a spiteful fabrication: blaming the murders on the Free Papua Movement. Many Papuans do loathe Freeport for its environmental despoliation and its failure to share profits with local communities, but the rebels have wisely adopted a policy of not attacking outsiders. Moreover, a police report made it clear that the bullets fired in the assault, and the quantity used, pointed straight at the military.

The inquiry came to a dead end, as the police are prohibited from investigating military conduct. Having already said too much, the police chief was silenced and reassigned, while Freeport refused all comment. It was the Australian government that delivered the smoking gun in the form of an intercepted conversation between TNI commanders that removed all doubt as to the military's full involvement. The attack turned out to be the work of Kopassus, the Indonesian Special Forces. According to a report in the *Sydney Morning Herald*, the army was trying to force Freeport to pay $10 million in "protection" money.

Countless human rights reports leave no doubt that the country's major terrorist organization is none other than the military itself. For the Bush administration to fund TNI in the name of anti-terrorism is rather like hiring "anti-terrorist" services from al Qaeda, or from Pakistan's pro-Taliban ISI, which the United States does effectively employ. The only question is what organization can stand up to the military. Like it or not, the only dependable friend of Merdeka in Indonesia is the very Islamism that Washington is determined to suppress. Here and elsewhere in Southeast Asia the progressive wing of Islamism reinforces post-Crash reformism. But now, thanks to the "war on terrorism," the tide which turned toward reform after the Crash is turning once more.

Indonesia's democratic prospect will stand or fall on the will of Muslim reformists to swim against this tide without falling prey to jihadic sentiments. Until Suharto's last months in power, the New Order had successfully muzzled all would-be opposition on campuses and in labor organizations, business associations, etc. So too it marginalized the two leading opposition parties, the PDI (Indonesian Democratic Party) and the PPP (United Development Party). This left only Muslim social organizations as a forum for critical discourse.[49]

Civil Islam, then, took on a resistance role by default. While that function seemed to lose some of its urgency with Suharto's fall, the IMF-sponsored demand for full economic restructuring in the wake of the 1997 Crash gave moderate Islamism a new oppositional mission.[50] After 9/11 that role was rendered all the more pressing as the incursions of neoliberal globalism were joined by those of neoconservative imperialism. Muslims worldwide felt compelled to fight fire with fire, at the expense of more moderate channels of reaction. Even in Indonesia, where reform Islam is deeply rooted, moderates found themselves caught in the no-man's-land of a two-front war between jihad and neoglobalism.

As terrorist activities mounted in Indonesia and throughout the region, the question was how the public would react. It was good news for civil Islam when, five days after the Marriott bombing, Majelis Mujahedeen (the public wing of the militant Islamic group Jemaah Islamiyah) met disappointment when it staged a mass rally to show popular support for its cause. The turnout was weak, and no mainstream politicians attended. Although he was listed on the program, Vice President Hamza Haz (long an open supporter of the organization's founder, Abu Bakar Bashir) was conspicuously absent. This public rebuff underscored the organization's inability to achieve legitimacy. Moderate Muslims won that round, but still faced the daunting task of having to mount resistance on two global fronts: versus an anti-democratic and globally funded ruling elite and an equally anti-democratic pan-Islamism. Civil Islam can fulfill this task only by keeping its local moorings, and by recovering the original meaning of *Merdeka*—freedom from all forms of oppression.

The geopolitical tide is turning against indigenous and exogenous reformism—both Merdeka and Leahy respectively. After 9/11 Washington has been only too willing to accept Jakarta's equation of secessionism with terrorism.[51] Military and paramilitary brutality—the kind of state terrorism that inspired separatist sentiments in the first place—is on the rise throughout the archipelago, and U.S. fingerprints are all over the crime scene. Even the neoliberal commentator Thomas Friedman reports the concern of his Indonesian contacts that authoritarian regimes such as Malaysia and Pakistan have become the darlings of post-9/11 American policy, while Indonesia—"a messy, but real, democracy"—is encouraged to remilitarize. Noting that Indonesian democracy could offer a valuable counter to Arab Islamism, Friedman sensibly concludes that fostering "that example is a lot more in America's long-term interest than arresting a few stray al Qaeda fighters in the jungles of Borneo."[52]

He is wrong, however, to credit the United States with having been the major pro-democracy force in countries like Indonesia after the Cold War. In 1991, at the dawn of post–Cold War globalization, Congress authorized the establishment of the Joint Combined Exchange Training (JCET) program, which by 1998 had missions in 110 countries. In this way, as Chalmers Johnson puts it, "Congress inadvertently gave the military's special forces a green light to penetrate virtually every country on earth."[53] Special ties have been formed with Indonesia's Kopassus "red berets," who specialize in rape, torture, and permanent "disappearances."

Under the direction of Suharto's son-in-law, Lt. General Prabowo Soemitro Subianto, countless Islamic secessionists were executed by Kopassus between 1995 and Suharto's fall. Applying the skills he acquired through military training at Fort Benning and Fort Bragg, Prabowo increased Kopassus ranks from 3,500 to 6,000, and personally supervised ten years of state terrorism in East Timor. The U.S. position on all this was amply conveyed when Secretary of Defense Cohen paid Prabowo the honor of a three-hour visit at Kopassus Headquarters during Cohen's visit to Jakarta in January 1998.[54] 9/11, then, did not inaugurate Washington's promotion of state terrorism in Indonesia. It simply brought it out of the closet.

The root problem is America's tendency to demonize Islamic politics in general. Far from being an anti-democratic monolith, the Islamic cultures of Indonesia can better be described as a polarity which promotes proto-democratic pluralism on the one side and reactionary modernism or anti-modernism on the other. The modernizing wing culminated in B. J. Habibie's ICMI.[55] By the mid-1990s Suharto was actively courting these tractable techno-modernists. The flip side of this "ICMIzation" was Suharto's suspicion of intractable Muslim modernists such as Amien Rais, who gravitated in the 1990s from radical Islamism toward the political pluralism that Robert Hefner dubs "civil Islam."[56] As Graham Fuller argues, it is precisely the suppression of civil Islam that paves the way for the uncivil variety.[57]

Given the military's long contest with Muslim politics, the resurgence of both civil and uncivil Islam was bound to weaken ABRI's grip on public affairs. Meanwhile the fall of Suharto set two contradictory forces in motion: a simultaneous redemocratization (known as *Reformasi*)[58] and political re-militarization. After taking office in July 2001, President Megawati forged close relations with the military, which also put her in good stead with the United States, especially after 9/11. Strategic rather than fiscal concerns prompted the IMF to resume the lending it suspended in 2000.

If Washington goes so far as to waive Leahy, at this of all times, the prime beneficiary will be the military. One big loser will be civil Islam, along with the native pluralism that sustains Merdeka. Only briefly, with Leahy, was U.S. policy even remotely on the side of that native ideal, and this position may not survive the "war on terrorism." Jakarta was angered when Lee Kuan Yew, Singapore's senior minister, charged that Indonesia is a repository of globally connected terrorism. In fact, Lee's words served Jakarta's militarist objectives by helping to shift international concern from rights to security.

In that respect it hardly mattered who won the presidential run-off election of September 20, 2004, for both candidates were firmly in the grip of the military. While Western editorials hailed the election as the crowning achievement of *Reformasi*, the main issue on most voters' minds was the economy. They were choosing between a flaccid military puppet and an assertive general who—with his strong credentials as a martial law administrator in Aceh—could presumably make the trains run on time. The only good news was that an even worst choice, the world-class war criminal General Wiranto, had been edged out in the first-round election of July 5. It says much about America's pro-democracy stance that Washington is gleeful over these results; for the winner, Yudhoyono, is a veritable poster boy for U.S. military training.

Malaysia's UMNO Strikes Back (With a Little Help from PAS)

If Indonesian Islamism has been politically drafted as a last resort, Malaysian Islamism was co-opted from the start. To control this social base is to control Malaysian politics, and for a whole generation that is precisely what Prime Minister Mahathir Mohamad accomplished, cloaking his regime in the vestments of Islamic solidarity. His show of outrage over Muslim repression in faraway places such as Bosnia or Palestine was a brilliant ruse, not matched by any visible concern for Acehnese refugees at his gates. He had thousands of them repatriated at a time when mass executions were in progress in Aceh.[59] It was never so easy for him to deal with Muslim resistance *inside* his gates. A formidable Muslim opposition took shape after the Crash, and especially after the arrest and show trial of Anwar Ibrahim, Mahathir's deputy minister and would-be successor. So it was that UMNO (the United Malays National Organization) came to look upon the new mandate for anti-terrorism as its political salvation. In lieu of a full economic recovery, this could offer UMNO a new legitimacy ticket—a surrogate Asian miracle.

Seeing what happened to Suharto, Mahathir struck hard and fast on behalf of the party, which of course he expected to control behind the scenes after his official retirement in October 2003. He stepped up his campaign to subdue not only Muslim extremism but Islamism in general. While UMNO'S stated target is the al Qaeda–linked Jemaah Islamiyah—at least sixty members of which have been arrested without trial under the infamous Internal Security Act (ISA)—it is no secret that the ultimate target is PAS (the Islamic Party of Malaysia), which now rules two of the country's thirteen states.

UMNO's Islamic façade gained credibility in 1982 when Anwar—then a leading student activist with the Malaysian Muslim Youth Movement (ABIM)—was won over. By the end of the 1980s UMNO had in effect (at least as a public relations ploy) been "ABIMized," which did nothing to blunt its assault on real Islamic politics.[60] Long before Suharto, Mahathir grasped the importance of putting a Muslim face on anti-Islamism. He simply intensified the process after the Crash.

His decision to rid himself of his Islamic point man, Anwar, ran against this grain, but had to be done, since Anwar was starting to give substance to UMNO's reformist claims. The public's tolerance for a crackdown was tested in August 1998 with the conviction of Lim Guan Eng, a leading DAP (Democratic Action Party) member of Parliament, on charges of sedition. Meanwhile Mahathir inserted an old crony, Daim Zainuddin, into his cabinet, slipping him many of Anwar's economic responsibilities.[61] To control public reaction he pulled strings to have several of Anwar's supporters in the media fired. Even the Internet came under scrutiny, arrests being made without trial under the ISA. With the judiciary backing the crackdown, all criticism of the government vanished from the media.[62]

That did not prevent an avalanche of street protest when Anwar was sacked in September 1998. For the next year peaceful demonstrations were beaten back, with hundreds of arrests made, often on charges based on colonial-era sedition laws.[63] In a speech delivered in New York, Mahathir tied these anti-Islamist actions to the government's forty-two-year war on communism. The idea was to conflate the two "terrorisms" as a continuous defense of true (UMNOesque) Islam.[64] This made for good diplomatic spin, but did not work on the home front. PAS scored high in the November 1999 elections, replacing the mainly Chinese DAP as the major opposition party within the Barisan Alternatif (Alternative Front) alliance. In a speech of June 1, 2000, PAS president Fadzil Mohamed affiliated his version of Islam with an unlikely ally: globalization. Confident that PAS would soon be in command, not in opposition, he was already playing to a world audience, while Mahathir often seemed to be playing for the opposing team. His hostile remarks concerning Chinese "extremists" managed to offend nearly all Chinese, thus guaranteeing the critical two-thirds parliamentary majority that the opposition needed to bury him politically.[65]

With its popularity sinking, UMNO prodded Mahathir to soften his stance toward his critics. But even as he made a token move in that direction by seeking a meeting with several opponents, he had ten others arrested under the ISA. The mainstream media tried to ignore the issue, but in the midst of an economic slowdown and rising unemployment, Mahathir's ruling days seemed numbered. What saved him and his party was 9/11. At first there was general skepticism toward UMNO's charge that PAS harbored Taliban sympathies and maintained close connections to the Malaysian Mujahedeen. Then PAS overplayed its Islamist hand. Casting off the constraints of civil Islam, it called for a jihad against the United States and organized demonstrations in front of the U.S. embassy in Kuala Lumpur. The tide abruptly turned not only against PAS but the whole thrust of post-Crash reform. Now army and security forces could suppress even nonviolent opposition with impunity.[66] No less important, the opposition that survived lost much of the progressive punch that had animated it after Anwar's arrest.

Meanwhile Mahathir's actions did much to reinforce the Islamic extremism he claimed to combat. While UMNO was the immediate winner on the counterterrorism front, reactionary Islamism could be the biggest beneficiary over time. The clear losers, in any case, have been civil Islam and post-Crash reform—a fact that makes no dent on "Washington Consensus" strategy. When President Bush met Mahathir at the Shanghai APEC summit of October 2001, he saw no reason even to mention Malaysia's human rights record.[67]

Philippine People Power (III)

That same suspension of judgment is now applied throughout Southeast Asia, hitting hardest where Islam is a minority faith. Anti-Islamism can then be militarized without fear of mass reaction. In the Philippines, for example, Washington furnished more than $90 million in military aid between fall 2001 and January 2003, compared with less than $2 million per year previously. Not since withdrawing from its Clark and Subic Bay bases has America enjoyed such geopolitical leverage here. And not since the glory days of Marcos has the Philippine military enjoyed such munificent support.

The given excuse for U.S. involvement is a dodge, for the Philippine government is quite capable of dealing with indigenous Muslim insurrection on its own, if only it will redress the social grievances that stoke the crisis. The same can be said for the larger democratic conflict, where the government has more to fear from Christians than Muslims, for a signal force behind post-Marcos reform has been the Catholic Church. Jaime Cardinal Sin was especially instrumental in mobilizing the "People Power" movement that tossed Marcos out,[68] along with the American adopt-a-dictator system for regional hegemony. It is almost comic that the United States would then take credit for restoring democracy to the country, just as it would in Korea (1987) and Thailand (1992).[69] The main American contribution was to offer the Marcos family with all its liquid holdings a safe haven on U.S. soil. That favor was not just given for services rendered, but to prevent civil war and a possible victory for the Left.

As the Cold War waned, the United States was looking for more malleable and less expensive allies than Marcos and Suharto, who dug too deeply into corporate coffers. Corazon Aquino played her part well, ushering in what Walden Bello identifies as the second phase of structural adjustment. The first phase, implemented by Marcos out of eleventh hour desperation, had concentrated on trade liberalization. The second focused on the repayment of the country's $26 billion foreign debt, at the expense of economic recovery and natural resource sustainability. What this "model debtor" experiment ended up proving was the direct connection between structural adjustment, stagnation, and environmental destruction. A third phase, set in motion by the Ramos administration as of 1992, lowered restrictions on foreign investment. The result was massive capital speculation, which artificially inflated the country's financial and real estate markets. Meanwhile the floodgates were left wide open for rapid capital exit when the bubble burst in 1997–1998.[70]

Fidel Ramos's political legacy was no better. While preaching free market values, this career army engineer wasted no time in packing top government positions with retired generals whose expertise lay in the containment of all forms of opposition, including "People Power." The best that can be said of Ramos is that he worked hard for the interests he served. When Lee Kuan Yew visited him in Manila, he stressed that the Philippines needed "discipline more than democracy,"[71] which is to say that it needed *to discipline democracy*. To complete that task Ramos and his generals needed a second term, which in turn would take a constitutional amendment. That failed, but Ramos had done enough to put the public in the mood for a distinctly *un*disciplined president next time.

Thus, on the rebound, they got Joseph Estrada, a former B-grade movie star known for his Robin Hood heroics. Unfortunately Estrada was more interested in nightclubs and gambling than governing. Moreover, far from his Robin Hood pose, he turned out to be a fan of the world according to the World Bank, complete with market liberalization, deregulation, and privatization. His decision to amend the constitution in the interest of foreign investors sent 75,000 protesters into the streets of Manila's financial district, including former president Aquino, a host of Roman Catholic leaders, and small-business owners concerned about Estrada's favoritism toward big business. Many People Power veterans such as Cardinal Jaime Sin joined the opposition that would impeach Estrada on November 13, 2000.

People Power II, as the movement came to be called, culminated in a march of tens of thousands of protesters on the Malacanang presidential palace. Estrada knew it was over when he found himself abandoned by the armed forces, the police, and most of his cabinet. Unfortunately his vice president and replacement, Gloria Arroyo, the daughter of a former president (Diosdado Macapagal, who lost the chance for a second term to Marcos), answered to the usual business and military interests. Using her police and military backing, Arroyo cracked down on a counterprotest of around 40,000 which marched on the palace. Most of these Estrada loyalists came from the impoverished countryside, where more than a third subsist on less than $1 a day. Many end up living out of city garbage dumps, and still find that more lucrative than what they left behind. Arroyo's technocratic agenda offers little hope to them or the 40 percent of the workforce locked in agricultural poverty. This opens the door for groups on the Left, such as Bayan, which claimed millions of supporters even before Estrada's fall.

The Left lost out to Aquino in 1986, but is getting a second chance on the crest of People Power II. It can seize that chance, however, only if it finds a way to add substance to its usual hyperbole. Some groups are simply out of touch with reality. Kilusang Mayo Uno, for example, vowed to send "millions" to the barricades against Arroyo's globalism. Others seem to suffer from ideological vertigo, hawking themselves as mercenaries for ex-crony capitalists from the ranks of Marcos and Estrada. In short, the Left's vanguard role in People Power II is anything but secure.

The only sure bet, as things now stand, is that the new Philippine politics will do little for Muslim minorities. If the United States could do anything for these doubly repressed communities—condemned to both poverty and religious discrimination—that would be a sound investment in the region's long-term stability. But to assist in military operations against Muslim resistance is not only unjust, but also improvident, for it invites the very transnational Islamic infiltration that U.S. intervention is supposed to prevent.

A major flash point of that resistance is in the south, where Muslim guerrillas have been active since the 1970s. Civil war erupted in June 1997 when the AFP (Armed Forces of the Philippines) mounted a campaign against the MILF (Moro Islamic Liberation Front). A cease-fire soon followed, but did nothing to allay tensions. When government troops launched a full assault in February 2003, Arroyo stressed that the target was not the MILF itself, but a criminal gang within it. Obviously she was fearful of a general Muslim reaction, either local or international. MILF's international connections are an open question. Ghazali Jaafar, vice chairman of the MILF, admits that the organization has backers in Indonesia, Malaysia, and Brunei; and Ghazali is known to have had private talks with Malaysia's Information Minister Khalil Yaakob.

Perhaps it was because Abu Sayyaf was not so well connected, and was less capable of putting up much military resistance, that Washington's new "realists" targeted it instead of the larger and better organized MILF. Abu Sayyaf was little more than a criminal network, but what it lacked in revolutionary purpose it made up for in brutality. Like Laskar Jihad, it used its Islamic credentials to legitimate activities that were are strictly un-Koranic. These were local thugs, not soldiers, and certainly not soldiers of Islam.

Neither wide public opposition nor a spate of treason charges against Arroyo could keep her from jumping at the chance to draw in U.S. forces against Abu Sayyaf, whose former links to Osama bin Laden (no later than 1995) made it a cash prize for the government. Soon the United States was offering not only on-site "training" by special operations forces in western Mindanao and $100 million worth of equipment—including at least eight UH-1H Huey helicopters and 30,000 machine guns—but also billions in foreign investment and economic aid. Dubbed Operation Balikatan ("shouldering the load together"), it could well have been named Operation Overkill. It hardly seemed to matter that this use of American troops for domestic police work was in patent violation of the 1987 Philippine constitution.

Given the Pentagon's historic use of "advisers," the *New York Times* felt justified in asking for a better explanation than had been provided for Operation Balikatan. An editorial by a resident *Times* globalist granted that the "real aim of the American mission is political: to demonstrate momentum in the war on terror, deploy troops in a country where they are welcome, show the flag in Southeast Asia, and find an enemy that can be quickly beaten."[72] This is not to deny the horrid nature of Abu Sayyaf, which put itself on the terrorist map by dumping the bodies of two decapitated hostages at the Santa Isabella Cathedral, one of whose priests they also tortured and killed. But this cannot justify U.S. support for the equally opprobrious state terrorism that has blighted Mindanao for years, subjecting peasants and tribes people to arbitrary brutality by a militia composed largely of thugs and known criminals.

Both militarily and ethically, then, Abu Sayyaf was an easy and profitable target. The media, unfortunately, hardly distinguished between the criminal terrorism of Abu Sayyaf and legitimate Muslim resistance. It was forgotten that in Mindanao the Islamic community had been under siege since the 1950s, when the CIA's legendary Colonel Lansdale set up an EDCOR (Economic Development Corporation) project to flood Mindanao's "virgin territory" with Christian migrants.[73] The general plight of the rural poor was to be alleviated at the expense of rural Muslims. This was agrarian reform on the cheap, and later even that skewed effort would be abandoned. World Bank policy under Robert McNamara encouraged a turn from redistribution projects, and Marcos needed little encouragement. Land reform ground to a halt in 1975 when it dawned on Marcos that most of his rural support came from landlords.

Aquino promised to remedy the situation, but again with Washington's prodding she turned to more corporate-friendly activities, such as economic restructuration. Social needs were sidelined in favor of debt repayment, which consumed 50 percent of the nation's budget.[74] Nevertheless, by wrapping itself in a cloak of reform, Aquinoism succeeded in marginalizing the Left—notably the National Democratic Front (NDF) and the New People's Army (NPA). Thus, paradoxically, radicalism suffered from the fall of Marcos. Nor did Ramos or Estrada do anything to revive it, despite the latter's egalitarian rhetoric.[75] Their loyalty likewise went to global capitalism, which they knew would not put its eggs in an unstable basket. By default of agrarian reform, a military solution to rural instability becomes obligatory. This too serves the needs of globalization, which talks the language of liberal democracy while funding order at any price.

Arroyo could not duplicate the theatrics whereby Aquino made the public believe her reforms were for them. With her popularity collapsing in the polls, she announced in December 2002 that she would not seek reelection, but would devote her remaining seventeen months in office to implementing a motley "reform" package that has fairly been described as "underwhelming."[76] It is suggestive of the nation's fiscal predicament that Arroyo looked to new gold-mining operations as the solution to the budget deficit. Unfortunately this deus ex machina hit a snag: the mines in question were located in an area controlled by communist guerrillas. That too is indicative of a national dilemma: the regime's biggest security risk, according to Defense Secretary Angelo Reyes, is not Muslim terrorism but resurgent Left resistance.

There are three good reasons, however, why Islamic resistance cannot be taken lightly. First there is its possible linkage with global jihad, and second its relative intractability, given its deep historical roots. Minanao is part of the Moro culture sphere that has been resisting Christian encroachment since the thirteenth century. While northern lands like the Kingdom of Manila were secured by Spanish colonization, the Moro sultanates held out for centuries. The Spanish divide-and-conquer strategy sundered natives into *Moros* (Muslim Malays) and *Indios* (pagan Malays), the former to be killed and the latter converted. Little changed for the Moros when the Indios effectively took command in 1946, or when People Power took over after Marcos.

The third reason is that Muslim and Left resistance might reach a strategic accord; and both in turn could strike an alliance with liberal-Left reformists. The incorporation of Moro resistance into a more inclusive People Power II would produce an unprecedented radical fusion. Call it People Power III. This could never happen, however, until it is recognized that Muslim resistance is not just an ethnic phenomenon, but is the hind end of a socioeconomic malady that pervades Southeast Asia. Only in that sense is Moro resistance a pan-Islamic product. The only group in the region that remotely conforms to the al Qaeda pattern is Jemaah Islamiyah, best known for the October 2002 bombing in Bali, Indonesia, and the plot to blow up several embassies in Singapore. While some members have been arrested—most notably the al Qaeda strategist Hambali, captured in Thailand in August 2003—they command no popular movement anywhere in the region. Thus the so-called "second front" in the war on terrorism is falsely advertised. Its real target is not so much radical Islamism as a radically inclusive Left: a nascent People Power III.

The force of this grassroots resistance was graphically illustrated in February 2003 when the incipient U.S.-Philippine alliance suffered a stunning setback. While the Arroyo regime claimed that U.S. soldiers were operating in the Philippines only in a training capacity, the Pentagon let it be known that Americans would in fact "actively participate" in combat.[77] This clear violation of the Philippine constitution evoked such public outrage that combat operations had to be cancelled. People power had worked, for the moment, and its influence was again felt in July 2003 when 300 Philippine soldiers mutinied, charging that the Arroyo government itself was responsible for the string of terrorist bombings that had recently struck Mindanao. The rising failed, but the point was made. It was common knowledge that the army had long been selling weapons and ammunition to Islamic rebels, so the mutineers' charges were hardly outlandish.

It must be asked, therefore, why American media took so little interest. Part of the answer is that these media have to a large degree become "embedded" in the foreign policy purview of the current administration, with its fixation on al Qaeda and its Islamic affiliates. To redirect attention to local issues would cast American intervention in an imperialistic light, and would expose Arroyo—one of the first ASEAN leaders to publically support the war on terrorism—as a U.S. puppet. Ulterior motives are obvious on both sides. While tangible support from Washington will buttress Arroyo's globalist credentials, military cooperation will mark America's full geopolitical return to the region. The real loser, along with Muslim dissidents, will be the prospect of "fourth wave" democracy.

Sensing the collapse of their higher democratic hopes, despondent Philippine voters seemed ready to support yet another movie star, Fernando Poe Jr., in the 2004 presidential elections. But Arroyo, having reversed her decision not to run, won by about 1 million votes. Partly this was because she too played the celebrity game, choosing a famous tabloid news anchor as her running mate and including two movie stars on her senate slate. More fundamentally, however, the public understood that a vote for her was a way of facing hard facts. People Power was dead. Arroyo was not so much reelected on a vote of confidence as one of grim concession. In the absence of any meaningful reform alternative, her international connections would have to do. Globalization won the election by default.

Conclusion: The Thai Rural Crisis as Test Site

As in the Philippines, a war on Muslim resistance is being waged in the southern Thai provinces of Narathiwat, Pattani, Yala, Songkhla, and Satun. This too is part of a centuries-old conflict, rekindled by blatant economic injustice. The region had maintained its Islamic identity for hundreds of years before it was annexed in 1902 by Buddhist Thailand as a buffer against the imperialist pressure of British Malaya. Thailand's 6 million Muslims have never been politically integrated, as have the Chinese. Muslim separatism erupted in the 1970s and early 1980s, but more conciliatory policies restored peace to the area over the next two decades. This relatively benign treatment ended when former police Lt. Col. Thaksin Shinawatra became prime minister in February 2001.

The blowback from Thaksin's authoritarian style should serve warning on Washington as it forges an anti-terrorist strategy. His notorious drug war left thousands dead under circumstances that mock any mention of the rule of law. When the government began applying the same tactics to the problem of radical Islamism, simmering Muslim discontent exploded into reciprocal violence. This prompted security forces to slaughter 108 lightly armed Muslim insurgents on April 28, 2004. There is no doubt that a contingent of Jemaah Islamiyah has entered Thailand, where its operations chief Hambali was captured in August 2003. But the Islamists butchered in April were mere amateurs motivated by local issues.[78]

The most pressing of these issues trace to Thaksin's rise to power. It was the popular view that his Democrat Party predecessor, Chuan Leekpai, had been too trusting of the IMF in the wake of the Thai Crash of 1997. Thaksin's Thai Rak Thai (Thais Love Thais) Party won a smashing victory in January 2001 by turning the IMF's praise for Chuan into a political kiss of death.[79] Riding this populist wave, Thaksin has restored such venerable traditions as cronyism, vote buying, and overt authoritarianism, which he wraps in a neat package for export to the rest of Southeast Asia. His patent intention is to secure his place as the successor of Lee Kuan Yew's regional leadership.

At any other time his "Thaksinomic" defiance of IMF guidelines might have put him at odds with Washington. Thaksin has pointedly stated that his early repayment of the country's IMF loan was an act of liberation. But 9/11 changed the rules of the game substantially. Not only could he afford to declare fiscal independence, but political as well. He openly asserted that "democracy is only a tool" for other ends—namely *his* ends. Though his means now included death squads, he got the Bush administration's stamp of approval, even as Bush advertised his goal of promoting democracy throughout the region. At this of all times, with Thaksin adding state terrorism to his repertoire, Washington designated Thailand a "major non-NATO ally." Like Singapore before, it was rewarded with an invitation to negotiate a bilateral free trade agreement.

The timing of this rapprochement could not have been worse for the Muslim south. Thai-U.S. cooperation in the "war on terrorism"—which to Muslims was looking more and more like a war on Islam—was consummated by a decision to send Thai troops to Iraq. By way of reaction, Osama bin Laden was becoming a popular hero in the south, with his image emblazoned on everything from T-shirts to taxis. Fear of this reverse effect raised concern elsewhere in Southeast Asia. Thaksin's increasing resort to force prompted even tough-minded Malaysian military leaders to recommend more holistic solutions to the southern problem. As could be expected, resistance groups such as the Pattani United Liberation Organization (PULO) now warn foreigners to avoid the area's tourist resorts.

Atrocities like those of April 28 are bound to internationalize this local crisis, for global jihad is the only big gun the resistance has at its disposal. What distinguishes the Muslim south from the non-Islamic rural sector is that it does have this international recourse. Meanwhile, globalization has made Bangkok synonymous with the nation itself.[80] Apart from a few families that have greatly profited from capital-intensive farming, agricultural income dropped through the 1980s due to falling crop prices. By the 1990s rural families largely depended upon remittances from one or more relatives working in the city, and there too income distributions were dreadfully skewed. Half of all income growth during the Thai boom went to just one-tenth of the population, putting the country in the world's top-five ranking for regressive economic distribution.[81]

Needless to say this trend hits the rural sector harder, and the Muslim rural sector hardest of all. Thai Muslims feel they have no stake in the country's economic "miracle." No less, however, they feel threatened by "development" schemes that deculturize their communities.[82] To ease this tension the government provides some special employment advantages for Muslims, as well as funds for mosque construction and renovation. But many see these benefits as just another divide-and-conquer scheme.

Meanwhile the contest with PULO and other Islamic resistance groups has escalated into full-scale war near the Malaysian border. Though most Islamic leaders renounce violence, the region is undeniably vulnerable to outside Islamic influence, as was suggested by its broad public support for the Afghan Taliban after 9/11. That is all the more reason for the United States to stay out of such conflicts on a military level, so as to avoid internationalizing the problem. Rather, assistance should be directed towards the rural crisis that here, as in the Philippines, will breed terrorism so long as civil reform is lacking.

In December 1997, just after the Crash, King Bhumibol urged a return to agricultural centrality as the lasting source of Thai prosperity as well as civility. This would entail not only land reform but a rejection of Bangkok's Japan-dominated economism. The crisis of rural Islamism is a subset of this larger social schism. As Walden Bello stresses, a "healthy agricultural sector could have served to absorb industrial production for which demand was falling in foreign markets. It could also have been in a better position to absorb the workers expelled from the cities by industrial recession."[83] By further marginalizing the rural sector, the IMF "rescue package" set the stage for violent Muslim resistance. If the United States and Washington-directed international agencies are unwilling to confront the socioeconomic substructure of this crisis, they should at least borrow the ethical injunction of the medical profession: first, *do no harm*.

To say that America should not intervene in this contest of the city and village—here or in South Asia, as treated in the next chapter—is not to suggest that the United States should do nothing concerning Southeast Asian terrorism. Thailand and its neighbors certainly could use technical assistance in areas such as criminal investigation, airport security, and immigration intelligence. But the Bush-administration policy of funding corrupt and murderous military establishments has been unconscionable. To reduce the present security crisis to a simple "war on terrorism," absent a war on political oppression, is to make war on the social agents of reform, such as civil Islam, that are terrorism's worst enemies.[84]

Notes

1. For a good overview of the Eisenhower/Dulles phase of this paradox see Audrey R. Kuhn and George McT. Kahin, *Subversion as Foreign Policy: The Secret Eisenhower and Dulles Debacle in Indonesia* (Seattle: University of Washington Press, 1995), 8–19.

2. See "President Bush Calls War on Terror 'The Urgent Task of Our Time,'" transcript of the president's October 20, 2001, address to business leaders in Shanghai, from the U.S. Department of State, <usinfo.state.gov/regional/ea/apec/shanghai/wwwh-bush1020.html>. A *Far Eastern Economic Review* editorial defends Bush's friend/foe reflex and his "Axis of Evil" polemics as an improvement over Clinton's flaccid ambiguities. Ominously, however, this in-your-face diplomatic style is compared to the IR theory of the Nazi Carl Schmitt. See "Friend or Foe?" *Far Eastern Economic Review* (March 7, 2002), <www.feer.com/articles/2002/0203_07/p006edit.html>.

3. Noam Chomsky makes this case in both *The New Military Humanism: Lessons from Kosovo* (London: Pluto Press, 1999), and *A New Generation Draws the Line: Kosovo, East Timor and the Standards of the West* (London: Verso, 2001).

4. Chalmers Johnson, *Blowback: The Cost and Consequences of American Empire* (New York: Henry Holt, 2000), 8. Hardt and Negri, by contrast, view globalization less as an extension of American national interests than as a seamless and diffuse "Empire" of "network power". See Michael Hardt and Antonio Negri, *Empire* (Cambridge, MA: Harvard University Press, 2000), 180; and Ed Vulliamy, "Empire Hits Back," *The Guardian* (July 15, 2001), <www.guardian.co.uk/Archive/Article/0,4273,4221990,00.html>.

5. A touch of black humor was thrown in when President Wahid's government blamed the United States for the ongoing violence, on the grounds that without military aid it could not afford the cost of peacekeeping. True to form, Clinton moved rapidly to restore military-to-military ties so far as possible, e.g., permitting medical

training and allowing Indonesian officers to observe joint military exercises with Thailand. But an angry Congress held the line against broader cooperation. See "Indonesia Blames U.S. over Militias," Reuters report in *New York Times* (September 18, 2000), <www.nytimes.com/reuters/world/international-indones.html>; and Eliot Hoffman (a UN-accredited observer at the August 30, 1999, vote in East Timor), "Stop Military Ties with Indonesians," letter to the editor, *New York Times* (May 27, 2000), <www.nytimes.com/yr/mo/day/letters/127ind.html>.

6. Yang Razali Kassim in a speech given at Singapore's Institute of Policy Studies forum of October 10, 2001, <www.ips.sg/fo_war_yang.pdf>.

7. See Ma Nguyen Tong, "Annual Summit: ASEAN Stumbles over So-Called War on Terrorism" (August 11, 2001), <www.geocities.com/dong_nam_a/0112/ASEAN-2001.html>.

8. Jonathan Glover, "State Terrorism," in R. G. Frey and Christopher W. Morris, eds., *Violence, Terrorism, and Justice* (Cambridge: Cambridge University Press, 1991), 256 (256–75).

9. Noted by William Kristol and Robert Kagan in "'A Distinctly American Internationalism,'" *The Weekly Standard* (November 29, 1999): 7.

10. George W. Bush, "A Distinctly American Internationalism" (campaign speech of November 19, 1999), <www.apcss.org/College/SEC20012/BUSH%20Speech-A%20Distinctly%20American...>.

11. Barry Wain, "A Questionable Strategy," *Far Eastern Economic Review* (January 31, 2002), <www.feer.com/articles/2002/0201_31/p019region.html>.

12. "Beijing Executes Muslim Activists to Celebrate Diplomatic Triumphs," report for the *Crescent International* (July 1–15, 2000), <www.muslimedia.com/archives/world00/beijing-exec.htm>.

13. "Silencing the Critics," *The Economist* (April 25, 2002), <www.economist.co.uk/world/asia/Printer Friendly.cfm?Story_ID=1104763&CFID=13>.

14. S. Jayasankaran and Lorien Holland, "Profiting from Fear," *Far Eastern Economic Review* (October 11, 2001), <www.feer.com/2001/0110_11/p032region.html>.

15. S. Jayasankaran, "Lost Ground," *Far Eastern Economic Review* (March 21, 2002), <www.feer.com/ articles/2002/0203_21/p019region.html>.

16. Thomas Carothers, "The End of the Transition Paradigm," *Journal of Democracy* 13, no. 1 (January 2002): 7 (5–21).

17. See Ross Garnaut, *Open Regionalism and Trade Liberalization: An Asia-Pacific Contribution to the World Trade System* (Singapore and Sydney: Institute of Southeast Asian Studies and Allen and Unwin, 1996), 17. Although the more radical closure of "ASEAN maximalism" has remained a minority position, it provided a useful bargaining chip for trade negotiations before China's full opening to world trade reduced Southeast Asia's competitive status. Anti-terrorist cooperation now provides a new bargaining chip in lieu of economic clout. On ASEAN maximalism see Dewi Fortuna Anwar, *Indonesia in ASEAN: Foreign Policy and Regionalism* (New York: St. Martin's Press, 1994), 255–56; and on the EAEC see Rajah Rasiah, "Class Ethnicity and Economic Development in Malaysia," in Garry Rodan, Kevin Hewison, and Richard Robinson, eds., *The Political Economy of South-East Asia: An Introduction* (Oxford: Oxford University Press, 1997), 139 (121–47).

18. ASEAN officially minimizes its distance from APEC, claiming that its "AFTA-plus" objectives are virtually identical to APEC's open regionalism. But it is widely understood that this minimalism is more an expression of failed objectives than of real equivalence, which would contravene the very point of ASEAN. On ASEAN's official position vis-à-vis APEC see ASEAN Secretariat, *ASEAN Economic Co-operation—Transition and Transformation* (Singapore: Institute of Southeast Asian Studies, 1997), 197–98.

19. Elsewhere I argue that the Crash inverted the politics of "Asian values," which had long treated "Western" democracy as an alien and unaffordable luxury: "Now that assertion is turned on its head, as 'Asian values' start to look like the luxuries of good times. Without their miracles, political machines ranging from Indonesia's New Order to Japan's LDP find themselves in danger of losing their economic purchase on legitimacy. In the face of sweeping political reform, they look to globalization for salvation." See William H. Thornton, *Fire on the Rim: The Cultural Dynamics of East/West Power Politics* (Lanham, MD: Rowman & Littlefield, 2002), 65.

20. William K. Tabb, *The Amoral Elephant: Globalization and the Struggle for Social Justice in the Twenty-First Century* (New York: Monthly Review Press, 2001).

21. Alex Callinicos, *Against the Third Way* (Cambridge, U.K.: Polity Press, 2001), 105.

22. On this general dilemma see William Greider, *One World, Ready or Not: The Manic Logic of Global Capitalism* (New York: Touchstone, 1997), 57.

23. Strong evidence suggests that the summit between Kim Dae Jung and Kim Jong Il, which motivated the Nobel Committee to grant the prize four months later, was purchased through a secret transaction involving banks in three countries and seventy-one checks—this from a government sworn to financial transparency and "sunshine" diplomacy. See Doug Struck, "Alleged Payoff to North Tarnishes S. Korea's Kim," *Washington Post* (February 10, 2003): A12.

24. Joao Pedro Stedile, "Landless Battalions: The Sem Terra Movement of Brazil," *New Left Review* 15 (May/June 2002): 78 (77–104).

25. "Measuring Globalization" [from the A. T. Kearney/*Foreign Policy* Globalization Index], *Foreign Policy* (January/February 2001): 56–65.

26. "SDA Condemns Terrorism-Linked Acts," *The Straits Times* Interactive (January 12, 2002), <straitstimes.asia1.com.sg/singapore/story/0,1870,96018-1010872740,00.html>. This almost Spartan militancy comes as a surprise in a country better known for commercialism and a sanitation fetish (it was the proud host, for example, of the November 2001 World Toilet Summit). See "Singapore Conference to Lift Lid on Toilet Talk," *Ireland.com/The Irish Times* (January 14, 2002), <www.ireland.com/newspaper/breaking/2001/1119/breaking21.htm>; and "Singapore: Toilets, Not Terrorism," *Provda* (November 25, 2001), <english.pravda.ru/fun/2001/11/25/21907.html>.

27. Afan Gaffer, "Indonesia 1995: Setting the Tone for Transition towards the Post-Soeharto Era?" in Colin Barlow and Joan Hardjono, eds., *Indonesia Assessment 1995: Development in Eastern Indonesia* (Canberra: Research School of Pacific and Asian Studies/Australia National University, 1996), 45 (43–57).

28. On the World Bank's commendation of Indonesia's high-growth formula see John Wong, "ASEAN Economies: Continuing Dynamic Growth in the 1990s," in Chris

Dixon and David Drakakis-Smith, eds., *Economic and Social Development in Pacific Asia* (London: Routledge, 1993), 121 (115–27).

29. Hal Hill, *The Indonesian Economy since 1966: Southeast Asia's Emerging Giant* (Cambridge: Cambridge University Press, 1996), 240.

30. Quoted in Noam Chomsky, *The Culture of Terrorism* (London: Pluto Press, 1988), 181.

31. Syed Farid Alatas, *Democracy and Authoritarianism in Indonesia and Malaysia: The Rise of the Post-Colonial State* (New York: St. Martin's Press, 1997), 149.

32. Angus McIntyre, "Megawati Sukarnoputri: From President's Daughter to Vice President," *Bulletin of Concerned Asian Scholars* 32/1-2 (January–June 2000), <csf.colorado.edu/bcas/sample/megawati.htm>.

33. Tim Shorrock, "US and Indonesia's Military: Bedfellows Again," *Asia Times Online* (December 10, 2002), <www.atimes.com/atimes/Southeast_Asia/DL10A01.html>.

34. Dini Djalal, "Political Risk," *Far Eastern Economic Review* (December 26, 2002–January 2, 2003): 24.

35. Robert W. Hefner, "Islamization and Democratization in Indonesia," in Robert W. Hefner and Patricia Horvatch, eds., *Islam in an Era of Nation-States: Politics and Religious Renewal in Muslim Southeast Asia* (Honolulu: University of Hawaii Press, 1997), 75–76 (75–117). In Aceh Suharto less successfully used the local branch of MUI (the government-controlled Council of Ulama) to co-opt Islamic leaders. See Jacqueline Aquino Siapno, *Gender, Islam, Nationalism and the State in Aceh: The Paradox of Power, Co-operation and Resistance* (London: Routledge, 2002), 165.

36. So, too, ICMI lost its chance to be part of the civil Islamic call for general reform. Not until Habibie left ICMI did the organization venture even a modest criticism of Suharto's government. In May 1998 it released a public statement describing the president's recent reforms as "too vague, too little and too late." But it was also too late for ICMI itself. It had lost all credibility as a medium of Muslim politics. See "Muslim Group Pressures Indonesian President for Political Change," *Asia Pacific Transcripts* (May 7, 1998), <www.abc.net.au/ra/asiapac/archive/1998/may/raap-8may 1998-1.htm>.

37. A study by the National Commission on Human Rights found that at least twenty-four were killed and fifty-four injured when troops opened fire on protesters seeking the release of several individuals detained for opposing Suharto. See Ian Timberlake, "Indonesia Opens Trial over 1984 Tanjung Priok Massacre," *Clari News*, from Agence France-Presse (September 15, 2003), <quickstart.clari.net/qs_se/webnews/ wed/db/ Qindonesia-rights-priok.RTgY_DSF.html>.

38. Siapno, *Gender, Islam, Nationalism and the State in Aceh*, 165.

39. Siapno, *Gender, Islam, Nationalism and the State in Aceh*, 150 and 167.

40. Songok Han Thornton, "The Techno-Politics of the Indonesian Crash," a forthcoming dissertation chapter.

41. Colin Rubenstein, "The Role of Islam in Contemporary South East Asian Politics," *Jerusalem Letter*, no. 436 (August 15, 2000), <www.jcpa.org/jl/j/436.htm>.

42. These attitudes must be understood within the historic context of Indonesian Merdeka and the long struggle for independence from Dutch colonialism. See Anthony Reid, "Merdeka: The Concept of Freedom in Indonesia," in David Kelly and An-

thony Reid, eds., *Asian Freedoms: The Idea of Freedom in East and Southeast Asia* (Cambridge: Cambridge University Press, 1998), 151 (141–60).

43. Jafar's support in high places was underscored by his acquittal in late January 2003 on all charges regarding the violence he openly encouraged in the Malukus. The sordid injustice of this ruling is reflected in the numbers: Laskar's 3,000 fighters battled a mere 200 commanded by the Christian separatist Alex Manuputty, who by contrast got a three-year prison sentence for subversion. See Jane Perlez, "Indonesia Clears Top Islamic Militant in Attacks on Christians," *New York Times* (January 30, 2003), <www.nytimes. com/2003/01/30/international/asia/30CND-INDO.html>.

44. See John L. Esposito, *Islam: The Straight Path*, expanded ed. (Oxford: Oxford University Press, 1991), 211.

45. Perlez, "Indonesia Clears." Elsewhere it was reported that a diplomat waiting in vain for Megawati's response to a pressing foreign policy question was astonished when she simply handed him a plate and insisted he have another cookie.

46. Hefner, "Islamization," 77.

47. John Roosa, "Brawling, Bombing, and 'Backing,' the Security Forces as a Source of Insecurity," *Inside Indonesia* (January–March 2003), <www.insideindonesia.org/edit73/Roosa%20Brawling.htm>.

48. That reduction was prompted by new American corporate responsibility laws that require full disclosure of such payoffs.

49. Robert W. Hefner, "Islam and Nation in the Post-Suharto Era," in Adam Schwarz and Jonathan Paris, eds., *The Politics of Post-Suharto Indonesia* (New York: Council on Foreign Relations Press, 1999), 43 (40–72).

50. See Robert W. Hefner, *Civil Islam: Muslims and Democratization in Indonesia* (Princeton, NJ: Princeton University Press, 2000), 218.

51. It is worth recalling that in the early postwar years Washington itself supported secessionist rebels in Indonesia. See Kuhn and Kahin, *Subversion as Foreign Policy*, 120–21.

52. Thomas Friedman, "The War on What?" *New York Times* Editorial/Op-Ed (May 8, 2002), <www. nytimes.com/2002/05/08/opinion/08FRIE.html>.

53. Johnson, *Blowback*, 72.

54. Johnson, *Blowback*, 75 and 78.

55. Bilveer Singh, *Succession Politics in Indonesia: The 1998 Presidential Elections and the Fall of Suharto* (New York: St. Martin's Press, 2000), 222.

56. See Hefner's *Civil Islam*; and on Rais's political migration see Adam Schwarz, *A Nation in Waiting: Indonesia's Search for Stability*, 2nd ed. (Boulder, CO: Westview, 2000), 329–30. Suharto's attempt to suppress Rais backfired, however, leading to an ill-timed solidification of opposition ranks just prior to the Crash of 1997. See Hefner, *Civil Islam*, 199.

57. Graham E. Fuller, "The Future of Political Islam," *Foreign Affairs* 81, no. 2 (March/April 2002): 59 (48–60).

58. Lex Rieffel, "Indonesia's Quiet Revolution," *Foreign Affairs* 83, no. 5 (September/October 2004): 98 (98–110).

59. See Siapno, *Gender, Islam, Nationalism and the State in Aceh*, 167.

60. Colin Rubenstein, "The Role of Islam in Contemporary South East Asian Politics," <www.jcpa.org/jl/j/436.htm>.

61. In June 2001 Daim himself would be slipped out of sight in an effort to assuage reformist pressure, and also to convince foreign investor's that something was being done about cronyism. See Arjuna Ranawana, "On His Own," *Asiaweek* (June 15, 2001), <www.asiaweek.com/asi...magazine/business/0,8782,129535, 00.html.

62. "Malaysia's Rough Justice," *The Economist* (August 29, 1998): 27.

63. "Arrests of Activists in Malaysia." *Human Rights Watch World Report* (September 21, 1999), <www.hrw.org/press/1999/sep/malay0922.htm>; and "Human Rights Watch Protests Malaysia Arrests," *Human Rights Watch World Report* (September 2000), <www.hrw.org/press/2000/01/maly0120.htm>.

64. Mahathir Bin Mohamad, "Islam, Terrorism and Malaysia's Response," [speech of February 4, 2000], *Asia Society Speeches*, <www.asiasociety.org/speeches/mahathir .html>.

65. S. Jayasankaran, " Rude Wake-Up for Mahathir," *Far Eastern Economic Review* (December 14, 2000), <www.feer.com/_0012_14/p016region.html>.

66. Joshua Kurlantzick, "Stop Arming Southeast Asia," *The New Republic* (January 20, 2003), <www.thenewrepublic.com/doc.mhtml?i=20030120&s=kurlantzick012003>.

67. "Malaysia's Internal Security Act and Suppression of Political Dissent," a Human Rights Watch Backgrounder (2002), <hrw.org/backgrounder/asia/ malaysia-bck-0513.htm>. This camaraderie would not last long, however. As anger mounted in the Muslim world over the Bush administration's Iraq policy, Mahathir was forced to choose between his newfound Washington partnership and his restive Muslim constituency. In January 2003, at the World Economic Forum at Davos, he once again lambasted U.S. global policies. See Mark Landler, "U.S. Role in the World Dominates Economic Talks as Brazilian Clamors to Be Heard," *New York Times* (January 24, 2003), <www.nytimes.com/2003/01/24/international/ europe/ 24DAVO.html>.

68. Carl H. Landé, "Introduction: Retrospect and Prospect," in Carl H. Landé, ed., *Rebuilding a Nation: Philippine Challenges and American Policy* (Washington, DC: The Washington Institute Press, 1987), 19 (7–44).

69. On America's "third wave" ambivalence see Walden Bello, *The Future in the Balance: Essays on Globalization and Resistance* (Oakland, CA: Food First, 2001), 204.

70. Bello, *Future*, 52–53.

71. Jon Liden, "The Ramos Model for Asian Leadership," *The Asian Wall Street Journal* (October 27, 1998): 10.

72. Nicholas Kristof, "The Wrong War," *New York Times* Opinion (February 19, 2002), <www.nytimes.com/2002/02/19/opinion/19KRIS.html>.

73. Bello, *Future*, 197–98.

74. Bello, *Future*, 53.

75. Bello, *Future*, 198–99.

76. "Lame Duck Plans to Soar," *The Economist* (January 30, 2003), <economist.com/world/asia/Printer Friendly.cfm?Story_ID=1560385>.

77. Naomi Klein, "Mutiny in Manila," *The Nation* (September 1, 2003), <www.thenation.com/docprint.mhtml?i=20030901&s=klein>.

78. John Aglionby, "Facing Up to Reality," *The Guardian* (May 6, 2004), <www.guardian.co.uk/print/0,3858,4917788-105806,00.html>.

79. Peter Symonds, "Thai Billionaire Capitalizes on Anti-IMF Sentiment to Win National Elections," *World Socialist Web Site* (January 11, 2001), <www.wsws.org/articles/2001/jan2001/thai-j11_prn.shtml>.

80. Chris Dixon, *The Thai Economy: Uneven Development and Internationalization* (London: Routledge, 1999), 190.

81. Pasuk Phongpaichit and Chris Baker, *Thailand's Boom and Bust* (Chaing Mai, Thailand: Silkworm Books, 1998), 284–85.

82. Iqbal Ragataf, "Thailand: Hunting Muslims to Death," *IslamOnline.net* (February 13, 2000), <www.islamonline.net/iol-english/dowalia/news-13-2-2000/topnews2.asp>.

83. Walden Bello, Shea Cunningham, and Li Kheng Poh, *A Siamese Tragedy: Development and Disintegration in Modern Thailand* (London: Zed Books, 1998), 133, 160, and 168.

84. Unlike the grassroots reformism of civil Islam, the "democratic" model that the Bush administration envisions for Iraq will have to be imposed from the top down. If there is a single lesson to be drawn from the experience of post–Cold War nation building, in Russia as surely as Afghanistan, it is that democracy must be rooted in the social. This lesson is of course a familiar axiom of conservative thought, as recycled in recent communitarianism, but it was also imparted by Marx in his *Critique of the Gotha Programme*, which warned of the imposture whereby the state dictates to society rather than vice versa.

4

South Asian Meltdown: Hindutva, Jihad, and the Politics of Indo-Globalization

Nehru's Geopolitical Legacy

O N AUGUST 15, 1947, India gained its political independence but lost its civilizational unity. Curiously the Western press focused most of its attention on the less newsworthy of the two events. Independence had been in the works for years, while partition was almost breaking news. No political party had advocated it until 1940, and as late as 1946 the proposal was still much in doubt. It took on certainty only ten weeks before independence, too late for proper planning. The idea had mainly been advanced for bargaining purposes,[1] but Hindu leaders of the congress had not been inclined to bargain. Their concern was to preserve the undiminished central authority of the colonial state, even if it meant wielding that power over a smaller India.[2]

These dismal circumstances cast a long shadow across the political prospects of Asia and the germinal Third World. Writing for *The Nation* in August 1947, Shiva Rao underscored what was at stake as Mountbatten (the last viceroy of India) accelerated the British withdrawal so as to dump an impending famine in the lap of India's first prime minister, Jawaharlal Nehru. With strike fever spreading, and peasants clamoring for immediate land reform, much depended on Nehru. It was imperative that his government deal successfully with this spreading crisis. For all its glaring defects, that government was still the closest thing Asia would have to nondependent democracy (Japan being the very model of dependency) for decades to come. As Rao put it, the flip side of the subcontinent's political wager was Pakistan, "a dictatorship without concealment or apology. If Pakistan under Jinnah can solve its problems more effectively than India under Nehru's leadership, dictatorship will have established a strong claim to the allegiance of India's millions."[3]

The world's leading democracies were content to sit this one out, acting much as they had during the Spanish Civil War, and for much the same reason. The real issue in both cases was not democracy as such, but democracy without world-capitalist dependency. A successful and truly independent India would set a bad precedent. Such an outcome, however, was highly unlikely. There was reason to expect the coming food shortage to dwarf the 2 or 3 million death toll of the 1943 Bengal famine. That would be the end of any substantive Indian independence.

One notable witness to the Bengal tragedy, future Nobel laureate Amartya Sen, explains where skeptics such as Rao went wrong: After "independence and the installation of a multiparty democratic system, there has been no substantial famine, even though severe crop failures . . . have occurred often enough. . . ."[4] Sen's seminal insight is that democracy, however flawed, generates the necessary political incentives and information flows to preclude famine. It follows that basic political rights such as a free press are the prerequisite rather than product of sound and sustainable development.

Sen finds the perfect foil for his "development as freedom" thesis in China during its Great Leap Forward. Duped by its own production propaganda, the Chinese government virtually manufactured the famines of 1958–1961. We now know, thanks to the relative opening of the Deng era, that those unprecedented disasters killed at least 30 million people, or ten times that of India's 1943 famine.[5] For one brief moment in 1962 even Chairman Mao admitted the advantage of democracy when it comes to knowing "what is happening down below. . . ."[6] If further proof of Sen's thesis is needed, China's recent handling of its AIDS and SARS crises should suffice. But the best contemporary case in point, in a class by itself, is North Korea's handling of its chronic food shortages. Two or three million North Koreans have starved to death over the past decade, not so much as a result of the regime's not knowing as its not *caring*. The patent fact is that democratic processes compel politicians to care as well as to know.

This instrumental value of democracy—its ability to serve the underprivileged sectors of society by exposing "what is happening down below"—has its obverse in democracy's dependence on those same social currents for its lifeblood. That Gandhian insight—matched on the Muslim side by the teaching of the great "Frontier Gandhi," Abdul Ghaffar Khan—was suppressed by Nehru and his Congress Party forebears. In Nehru's case this de-Gandhification was a product of misjudgment rather than corruption, but it nonetheless meant that the South Asian choice would henceforth be between degrees of authoritarianism.

In foreign policy, too, Nehru's judgment was accident prone—his misplaced faith in China's goodwill toward India being an accident of Wilsonian proportions. There was one thing he got right, however: the need to keep Indian politics Indian. This was not an easy call, for the Cold War afforded Third World governments a lucrative nondemocratic option: geopolitical prostitution in the service of one of the two superpowers. This was the direction Nehru was determined not to take, but which Pakistan took in stride, prompting the title of Tariq Ali's classic study, *Can Pakistan Survive: The Death of a State* (1983). Ali's working assumptions regarding civil society and the state (the weakness of the former all but requiring the absolutism of the latter) anticipated the work of communitarians such as Robert Putnam, who posit the centrality of "social capital" and "civil society" for genuine political development. Even aid agencies such as USAID now operate within this paradigm.[7]

Especially after Russia's post-Soviet trauma, it is widely recognized that social and cultural capital are as crucial for democratic solvency as are laws and formal institutions. Thus the rootless constitutionalism of Pakistan's founding father, Mohammed Ali Jinnah, was a blueprint for political maldevelopment. Pakistan had even greater need of social cohesion than India did, for British policy had left the region so logged out that soil erosion and flooding were bound to follow. The social stress this caused would be further aggravated by two other British legacies: corruption and programmatic inequality.[8] Having been bled dry for the benefit of the Raj, the region was now cut off from any hope of a reverse resource flow.

Given this insolvent start, Pakistan had little choice but to seek the external support that only a superpower could provide. So it was that Jinnah's nonaligned aspirations would be buried with him in 1948. American aid was pouring in by 1951. Two years later John Foster Dulles would declare Pakistan "a bulwark of freedom in Asia."[9] The freedom he had in mind, clearly, was that of U.S. military and capitalist interests to operate unimpeded wherever they chose. Deepa Ollapally argues that it was India's nationalist protectionism rather than her pro-Soviet proclivity that initially soured Indo-U.S. relations. When the United States sought to discipline India by withholding World Bank funding, Soviet assistance filled the void and opened the gate for expanding Indo-Soviet relations.[10]

By pointing out that this outcome was a result of America's own astringent policies, Ollapally offers a corrective for the standard realist reading of U.S. discord. This counterreading fails to explain, however, America's close relations with a number of equally nationalist and economically illiberal states. South Korea, for example, enjoyed massive U.S. aid and military assistance despite the fact that the Korean economy was as far from market liberalism as India's was.[11] But realists were at least half right: geopolitics is still very much in the game. Though Washington was certainly inclined to look with disfavor on statist economic systems, that inclination was overruled when the country in question happened to lie directly on a geopolitical fault line, or when a forward base was needed for containment purposes, as was the case with Turkey, Pakistan, and South Korea.

This qualified geopolitical priority was nothing new. The Roosevelt administration had nominally supported Indian independence, but refrained from pressing the issue due to its natural alliance with Britain in the face of German and Japanese expansionism.[12] Nor did it help, in the early independence period, that India viewed the communist victory in China with undisguised sympathy. Geopolitics again took center stage in 1954 when the United States officially entered a military alliance with Pakistan.

India fired back in the 1960s with scathing criticism of America's Vietnam policies, and in 1971, under the sway of Nixon-Kissinger realism, Washington returned fire by backing Pakistan on the Bangladesh issue. Thus it was hardly surprising that the Carter administration, in the face of the Iranian Revolution and the Soviet invasion of Afghanistan, would again confound India by extending military assistance to Pakistan as part of an incipient U.S.-Pakistan-China axis.[13]

With the end of the Cold War, however, the geopolitical premises of that axis would start to unravel. At that point only India's recalcitrance kept Pakistan in Washington's good graces, and that incentive came unhinged when Indian Prime Minister Narasimha Rao (1991–96) began promoting economic liberalization in the early 1990s.[14] The situation was looking bleak for Pakistan until Islamic terrorism began to take on global significance as a Cold War surrogate. Quick to capitalize (literally speaking) on this New World Disorder, Pakistan adopted an ingenious dual policy toward terrorism, making a show of combating it while nurturing its fundamentalist roots.

By no means was this new terrorist wave an inevitable product of Islamic theology or even political Islamism. The school of Islam that gave vent to the Taliban originated in Deoband, a northern Indian town in the state of Uttar Pradesh, where even today Muslims and Hindus manage to peacefully coexist. The 135-year-old Darul Uloom seminary, home of Deobandism, has always embraced India's secular constitution and the principle of religious diversity it embodies. India's Deobandis, accordingly, stood by Gandhi in opposing the foundation of a separate Pakistan.[15]

By contrast, the Deobandis of Pakistan and Afghanistan have sought to extend their brand of fundamentalism by way of jihadic holy war. Pakistan's Deobandi madrassas became training grounds for Taliban leaders and terrorists such as Masood Azhar, leader of the Army of Muhammed, while later Deobandis would give sanctuary to Osama bin Laden in Afghanistan. Pakistan's military has funded thousands of these madrassas since the 1980s, funneling assistance from Saudis who wished to encircle Shiite Iran in a Sunni ring of fire. The United States joined the party by backing Islamic militants in the 1980s so as to bedevil the Soviets in Afghanistan.

As Deobandism's dual personality attests, culture can be the deciding factor in religious practice. And behind this cultural conditioning there is often the heavy hand of political machination. Religious strife in India, for example, was in large part a British implant. The final blow, Ali contends, was Britain's refusal to grant India the timely "dominion status" it accorded Canada and Australia. This inspired the rise of Indian nationalism, which in turn prompted the Raj to work even harder at its game of religious divide and control.[16]

If culture could be reduced to religious heritage, pure and simple, then the secessionism of Jinnah and the Muslim League would be vindicated. Religion, however, was not an unbridgeable cultural barrier at the time of partition. It need not have been more divisive than race has been in America. Who would seriously propose that the U.S. race problem should have been solved by partition along racial lines? Over centuries India had forged a workable interfaith accord between Hindus, Muslims, and Sikhs. Much of the religious hatred that raged prior to the British withdrawal was seeded by the congress and the Muslim League. By no means did Muslims uniformly support Jinnah's "two nations" theory. As of 1947 most either opposed the Pakistan concept or failed to grasp its meaning.[17]

Shortly before the split, the British civil servant Malcolm Darling commented on the striking cultural similarity of Muslims and Hindus in the soon-to-be divided regions. Nor were these groups very unified in themselves. The sad fact, as Mushirul Hasan notes, is that the "vivisection of India severed cultural ties, undermined a vibrant, composite intellectual tradition and introduced a discordant note in the civilizational rhythm of Indian society."[18] This weakened the structure of civil society at a time when India could ill afford any more problems. The 1950s and 1960s would witness continuous riots, especially in the south. Some states had to be placed under "President's Rule," but the predicted choice between total authoritarianism and utter breakdown never had to be made.

The key word here is "total"; for, as Narasimha Rao divulges in his tendentious but illuminating book, *The Insider*, the long rule of the Congress Party simply replaced imperial authority with central authority: "Democracy . . . at best consisted of the question: Who should reign?"[19] As Rao sees it, Nehru's paternalistic role set the stage for less benign authoritarianisms to come, including that of his daughter Indira Gandhi, whose appeal to the masses was effectively turned against the party bosses. The centrality that

Rao complains of had reached a point of critical mass. Indian democracy had begun to implode.

Thus empowered, Mrs. Gandhi reacted to a court conviction against election violations by arresting opposition cadres, suspending civil rights, and all but deifying herself under the slogan "Indira is India."[20] Her fifteen months of so-called "emergency" rule were independent India's most authoritarian moment.[21] This was the unwitting domestic side of Nehru's legacy, which put the Congress Party in a camp with Japan's LDP and Mexico's PRI. All that can be said on Nehru's behalf is that the nonaligned strategy he drafted, along with Tito and Nasser, spared the country an even more authoritarian fate. Just as the secularist Nehru saw past India's religious chasm, he bridged the Cold War's ideological rift. Nonalignment was tantamount to ideological secularism, which saved India from Pakistan's camp-follower foreign policy but outraged the high priests of the capitalist world system.

This in effect was a second declaration of independence: freedom from the dictates of superpowers. Had India traded its geopolitical independence for massive American assistance, it almost surely would have gone the route of Korea under Park, Taiwan under Chiang, the Philippines under Marcos, Vietnam under Diem, or Indonesia under Suharto. When Indira Gandhi intervened on behalf of the Bangladesh movement against reactionary West Pakistan, the geopolitical cast of South Asia was fixed for another generation. In the name of "realism" the United States joined China in backing the side of unabashed oppression.

India's Global Nationalism

With the end of the Cold War the rationale for such realism was lost. It should have been possible for U.S. policy at long last to favor democracy and human rights. Instead, favor was bestowed on countries that were well disposed toward neoliberal globalism. India under Rao was more than ready to join this club, but not every Indian state was prepared to tag along. Kerala, India's least capitalistic state, was committed to human development as much as to raw economic growth, and to sustainability as opposed to raw extraction. Under different political circumstances this might have provided an alternative model of development. For that very reason Kerala was vilified and systematically undermined. The myth must be kept alive that there is no alternative to extant globalization. Likewise it would not do for the Indian public to get wind of alternatives to the corrupt and divisive government that holds the nation in thrall.

On both levels, Kerala carries a message that must be snuffed out. Though it is poor even by Indian standards, its inhabitants have an average life expectancy almost as high as Americans, and one of the lowest infant mortality rates in the developing world—half that of China. The key point, Akash Kapur argues, is that the standard modernist and now globalist measure of progress—per capita income—often does not reflect the real quality of life. This recognition, too, is part of Sen's paradigm shift, which lays stress on such indicators of well-being as general health, literacy, and freedom from discrimination. Untouchability has been expunged in Kerala more than anywhere else in India, while women are more politically engaged, and Brahmanist respect for education has been extended to all classes.

All this is now under threat from globalization and its geopolitical twin, global anti-terrorism, which easily devolves into anti-Islamism. Writing in 1992, soon after Rao's fateful turn toward a neoliberal model of development, Arun Ghosh warned that globalization would lead to neocolonialism unless it is coupled with a drive for universal education, full employment, and a minimum income. In a country where villagers commonly subsist on a dollar a day, these elemental reforms would ensure that growth in exports and international services are matched by a broadly expansive domestic market. The idea is to use foreign capital to prime the pump of indigenous capabilities,[22] not to cater to an affluent minority.

A very different kind of internationalism took shape after Atal Bihari Vajpayee came to power in 1998 at the helm of the new ruling party, the BJP (Bharatiya Janata Party, or Indian Peoples' Party). Even as BJP politicians preached the cultural closure of Hindutva (Hinduness, or "Hindian" cultural nationalism), they threw the nation to the winds of international dependency. With many of its financial backers living abroad, the BJP domestic program was largely set by upper-caste needs.

This elitist agenda blocked the prior drift of party politics toward a pluralism that includes agrarian interests;[23] but in itself it was nothing new. Smithu Kothari traces it back to the early days of independence, when colonial administrative structures were adroitly kept in place. This unfortunate continuity guaranteed that the growth politics of the 1950s and 1960s would produce grossly inequitable development. In the 1970s Indira Gandhi launched an anti-poverty campaign, but its top-down structure again served patronage networks that by the early 1980s had begun to surrender the economic side of nonalignment. The full surrender of 1991 led to a tripling of external debt by 1997.[24]

Kothari points out that while globalization was making some Indians fabulously rich, a million people a year were being uprooted from their homes and their only decent means of living. Coupled with the ongoing loss of commons, a shift to cash crops and economic giganticism was especially injurious to those engaged in traditional livelihoods. Again, as under colonialism, India was becoming indentured to external economic forces, while the domestic spoils were divided by the usual triumvirate of business, politics, and bureaucracy.

It is telling that underworld commerce has boomed even as general employment has flagged. Only child labor has shown growth commensurate with GDP gains, such that India now employs half the world's child labor. Growth in elitist consumption rides on the back of Dickensian poverty and malnutrition. Suffice it to say that entrepreneurial and professional classes are reaping the gains of globalization while Dalits (untouchables), tribals, and women workers suffer the consequences.[25] Kothari finds room for optimism in a formative alliance of workers, peasants, and engaged intellectuals, but the bigger story—until the shocking election upset of May 2004 restored the Congress Party to power—was the BJP's success at diverting reform energies into Hindu militancy.

The Far Right factions that spearhead this hate campaign are collectively known as the *Sangh Parivar*. Their political wing is the BJP—the successor of the old Jana Sangh—while their popular base is galvanized by the National Volunteer Force, or RSS (Rashtriya Swayamsevak Sangh), which departs from Hindian purism in its admiring embrace of the principles and methods of Adolf Hitler.[26] Its core doctrine, as defined by the VHP (Vishwa Hindu Parishad, or World Hindu Council), likewise advocates an Indian Final Solution.

After 9/11 the Sangh Parivar found global respectability as an "antiterrorist" association. In return for India's strong support of the Afghan War, and its reticence concerning Iraq, the Bush administration looked the other way as up to 300,000 anti-Muslim and anti-Christian *shakhas* were established under RSS auspices to "educate" the public in the virtues of Hindutva. These training camps mirror the militant function of Islamic madrassas in Pakistan, Afghanistan, and increasingly in Bangladesh,[27] with the two movements fueling each other's xenophobic violence. Ironically, Hindutva spells the death of Hinduism's core principles of tolerance and nonviolence, as personified in Gandhi.

The fuse was lit for the latest religious war when Hindu nationalists decided to build a temple to Lord Ram, a Hindu deity, at the site of the Ayodhya mosque they had destroyed in 1992. On February 27, 2002, a train carrying Hindu activists was torched, killing fifty-eight people. Angry Hindus retaliated by slaughtering hundreds of Muslims between February 28 and March 2, with the police not only failing to protect the victims, but even joining in the attacks. Countless female victims were gang-raped, many being mutilated and burned to death.

While close to 100,000 Muslims were driven from their homes and shops, Prime Minister Vajpayee went about business as usual. It was more than a month before he condescended to visit the scene of these horrors, as if they had issued from some sad but unremarkable natural event, rather than the designs of his own party. He more than hinted in a subsequent speech that the Muslims were themselves to blame, yet he expressed sincere lament that the whole affair would make him lose face in his upcoming trip to Singapore.

Gujarat was distinguished in that here, in what is frequently called India's "laboratory" of Hindu nationalism, the BJP ruled in its own right, without the constraints imposed by coalition politics at the national level. In 1998 Pankaj Mishra could still write (before the lab results were back) that "in states ruled by the BJP there are fewer violent incidents against the Muslims."[28] Many later considered the Gujarat tragedy indicative of what would become of India as a whole if the BJP had had its way.[29] It is debatable how much of the violence was deliberately instigated by Vajpayee's administration, but there is no question that the BJP did little to check the cycle of violence. This did not seem to concern the United States, which kept its silence, while to its credit the European Union compared Gujarat to apartheid and even to Nazi Germany before the war.[30]

It came as no great surprise, after two Bombay car bombings killed 52 and injured another 150 in August 2003, that one of the bombers was a survivor of the Gujarat atrocities. This cycle of violence is now familiar. But behind it all, as an editor of *The Hindu* contends, was the breakdown of the Nehruvian consensus that saw India as a pluralist nation. The prime victims of the Sangh Parivar's war on diversity were civil Hinduism, in the tradition of Gandhi, and the moderate mainstream of Indian Islam, which could have provided a prototype for religious accord throughout the Muslim world.

The BJP came to power on the promise to fight corruption while promoting a true secularism that respects the equality of all races and religions. Such rhetoric won over a credulous Western audience, much as Hitler was believed at Munich. But if there was ever any doubt as to the vile intentions of the BJP and its affiliates, the prime minister removed it on September 9, 2000, in a speech he gave to Hindu supremacists in the United States. Though he has often been described as a moderate in the Sangh Parivar context, he affirmed his unqualified loyalty to the cause of the BJP's "mother" organization, the RSS, which was implicated in Gandhi's assassination and later devoted itself to eradicating all vestiges of Gandhian influence. This purgation would spell the end, likewise, of the developmental goals set forth by Sen. Mishra sees this forfeiture of humanistic development as a key to the BJP's rise to power, for Senian goals are anathema to the kind of globalism that the BJP wedded to Hindu nationalism.

Washington's complacence in the face of mounting paramilitary brutality—including the lynchings of hundreds of Christians after January 1998—was not the fault of Republican policy alone. The Clinton administration led the way with a global "vision statement" jointly issued by Clinton and Vajpayee at the time of Clinton's visit to India in March 2000. Vajpayee put India on the globalist map by promoting market liberalism. But the nation's 40 million beneficiaries must be weighed against more than 500 million who remained locked in dire poverty, and all the more so because of globalization. Opening India to international markets stoked middle-class consumerism while exposing the nation's indigents (40 percent of India's population and a third of the world's poor) to rising food prices.[31]

The frustrations that brought had to be contained or diverted if a stable investment environment was to be secured. Mishra is probably right that India, in its hunger for globalist inclusion, took a lesson from China. The commercial world made it clear after Tiananmen that it did not care about human rights or substantive democracy so long as the profits flowed. Had it been otherwise—if, that is, global commerce had packed its bags and left—the Gujarat horrors might never have transpired, and certainly they would not have been allowed to continue for days, often with police complicity. Globalism is obviously no innocent bystander in these events. The salient fact is that global capitalism supports whatever power structure is in place, so long as it is pro-market.

India is nonetheless a democracy, and that puts a political brake on the BJP's Hindutva aspirations. Consideration must be given to coalition partners that can ill afford to alienate the 12 percent of the population which is Muslim, and which wields a powerful swing vote in Indian elections. The real aim of BJP anti-Islamism, therefore, has not been a Total Solution but a total diversion. By channeling discontent away from pressing issues, religious strife reduces the resistance energy that might otherwise flow into a resurgent, anti-globalist Left.

In the mid-1940s, when villagers formed resistance groups to contest the tyranny of landlords, they lacked the kind of organization and communications that would sustain resistance at a national level. Today's power elite knows that the local can easily become translocal in this global age. The Congress Party and the BJP are committed to the same class privileges, but the latter has a signal advantage in its ability to deflect attention from vital reform issues by inflaming the Hindu masses against Muslims and other minorities.

Nonelite India has long suffered from the development model bequeathed by Nehru. Though he can be credited with keeping India out of the early Cold War, the paradox is that the centrist economism and giganticism he launched has paved the way for the very dependency he dreaded. The Indian ruling class so well learned its lessons from its British counterpart that for all practical purposes there was no postcolonial period, but simply a domestic colonialism under Congress Party auspices. Even that was preferable, however, to the globalist neocolonialism that was brokered by the BJP. Pranab Bardhan points out that India's preglobalist proprietary classes—industrialists, professionals, wealthy farmers, and white-collar bureaucrats—were sufficiently at odds (thanks to weak capitalist development) to allow a muted democratic voice to less privileged segments of society such as unionized workers.[32] The flood tide of 1990s globalization threatened to drown out the heterogeneity that kept democracy afloat under the most adverse Nehruvian circumstances.

Pockets of Gandhian resistance still survive, however, lending hope for an alternative development model, and perhaps even an *alternative India*. This "other India" can be glimpsed in the resistance that has been mounted in the states of Madhya Pradesh, Maharashtra, and Gujarat to the eco-atrocity of two megadams on the Narmada River. The main organ of resistance has been the NBA (Narmada Bachao Andolan, or the Save Narmada Movement), which arose in the 1980s as part of a "small is beautiful" alternative. Drawing heavily on local initiative, the NBA represented a serious challenge to the extractive excesses of economic centrism. Its radical democratism, with implications reaching far beyond South Asia, is part of what Kothari calls "the reversal of the conquest of society by the economy. . ."[33]

If the Gandhian element in this reversal is its moral strength, many would say it is also a political weakness. Barrington Moore spoke for a whole generation of critics with his contention that Gandhi fostered a feckless return to the "idealized" past of the Indian village community, albeit purged of some egregious features such as untouchability.[34] Today's civil resistance can rise above this criticism because it is focused as much on the global village as on the Indian village. It does not betray the latter in the name of some higher good, as did Nehruvian centrism. Rather it links the two villages in a global/local dynamic that I have elsewhere termed "global anti-globalism."[35] So too it gets us past the apotheosis of violent resistance that dominated protest studies of the Cold War era. By that yardstick most Indian resistance, being relatively nonconfrontational, hardly registered in the West. Only now, in the full glare of Jihad and Hindutva, can we fully appreciate what Gandhi was trying to avoid. Some of the qualities that once made Indian civil protest invisible, and seemingly irrelevant, now make it the crucial prerequisite for alternative development.

This alternative traces to the new social movements of the late 1980s, where the focus was on the truly oppressed: peasants, tribals, women, and victims of caste discrimination. If Nehruvian modernization marginalized these sections of the population, current globalization consigns them to social and economic oblivion. The potential for class friction is made greater by the fact that a small but highly celebrated segment of the public is thriving on the same globalization that is choking the silent majority. The RSS and BJP made it their business to fan the flames of religious strife so as to smoke screen this class polarization.

Conversely, it should be the business of the Left to keep the real source of repression in full view. Gail Omvelt sees that task as requiring nothing less than a reinvention of revolution. She finds her prototype for grassroots resistance in the Chipko movement, which arose in the Himalayan foothills of Uttar Pradesh and united three causes in one: that of peasants, women, and the environment.[36] This new civil resistance would do well to heed, also, Gandhi's legacy of civil religious inclusivity and Kerala's long experiment with sustainable development.

While grassroots mobilization is a crucial element of that resistance, this double-edge sword rarely gets its due. Sonia Gandhi's Congress Party appropriated this egalitarian power base in its surprise victory of May 2004. Then came the second shock: even as it tossed out the BJP, Congress implanted Manmohan Singh, the "father of Indian globalization," as the new prime minister. Once again popular resistance was being usurped by power elites. Whereas the BJP drew upon the dark, Hindutva side of populism in its de facto war on minorities, the Congress Party co-opted grassroots progressivism for equally fraudulent purposes. The common voter had challenged both Hindutva and globalization, but the Congress Party ignored the latter half of the message. This subterfuge got hardly a comment from Western media, which almost unanimously sang the praises of India's democratic example for the developing world.

Pakistan's Balancing Act

At first the BJP seemed better equipped than the Congress Party to have it both ways: to unite the grassroots voter appeal of Hindutva with the financial engine of gobalization. Outside Gujarat, however, this rearguard amalgam soon collided with India's democratic mechanics. Constrained by its coalition partners, the BJP had to modify its larger ambition of desecularization and depluralization. Just as Indira Gandhi could not reduce India to herself, the BJP could not reshape the nation the way it did Gujarat, and finally it was thrown out entirely.

Such democratic obstacles are lacking in Pakistan. General Pervez Musharraf—who by self-proclamation became President Musharraf in June

2001—is the fourth military dictator in a country where the army and the omnipresent ISI (Inter-Services Intelligence, i.e., secret police) have not allowed a single elected government to finish its term in office. Salman Rushdie reminds us that Musharraf was the general responsible for training Islamic terrorists for operations in Kashmir. No doubt many of his students were sent by the ISI to al Qaeda camps in Afghanistan. When the previous president, Nawaz Sharif, yielded to American pressure and reined in Musharraf's terrorists, the general was incensed. He overthrew Sharif a few months later.[37] Ahmed Rashid observes that what distinguishes Musharraf from his predecessors is his boldness in not even trying to court civilian allies. Hence he is at odds with every sector of civil society.[38] Even radical fundamentalists, for whom he has done so much, begrudge his deals with the United States.

This unpopularity explains both his dependence on the United States and his resort to dictatorial rule, as seen in his constitutional "reform" of August 2002. By personal fiat he promulgated twenty-nine "amendments" that gave the army, which is to say himself, formal authority over every aspect of the elected government. This was the context in which he allowed a general election in October 2002, so as to give his junta a civilian varnish. Unfortunately his domestic failure has been matched by inordinate diplomatic success. Rashid reminds us that when Musharraf overthrew a democratically elected government to seize power in 1999, Pakistan was widely viewed as a pariah nation. Even its relationship with the United States, its consistent Cold War patron, was fast deteriorating as commercial globalization stole the show from power politics.

9/11 changed all that. Geopolitics was suddenly back in vogue, while the war in Afghanistan dealt Pakistan another winning geopolitical hand. Musharraf's assistance was desperately needed to contain the jihadic monster it had done so much to create. For its promise to wage war on terrorism, and to permit U.S. military operations from its soil, Islamabad got rescheduled foreign debts, an end to nuclear sanctions, a huge aid package, and, last but not least, an invaluable lobbyist in the person of Defense Secretary Donald Rumsfeld. Soon it also gained the approbation of a formerly aloof Washington Consensus, whose neoliberal stripes were starting to look hawkishly neoconservative. Musharraf went through the motions of upholding his end of the bargain. He even fired his ISI chief for disloyalty to Pakistan's renewed pro-U.S. policy. Nevertheless it was impossible to be sure which side of the fence Musharraf was on. The army itself and especially the ISI continued to supply Taliban forces before their fall, and indeed after their fall.

That did not prevent Bush, in June 2003, from pledging $3 billion to this dubious ally over a three-year period. There was more than a trace of déjà vu here. As in the Cold War, U.S. policymakers seem to prefer dealing with one-man dictatorships. Pakistan would be less trusted if it were more democratic, but there is little danger of that. Under Musharraf it has pulled off an unparalleled diplomatic coup, managing to hold its place as both the archetypal terrorist state and the undisputed financial winner of the war on terrorism.[39]

Needless to say, these developments have complicated India's bid for close relations with the United States. At first this post–Cold War hope was raised still higher by 9/11, since India stood ready to support U.S. anti-terrorist strategies. Such expectations were dashed, however, when Pakistan was welcomed back into Washington's fold. Pakistan took quick advantage of this upgrade by striking at India with renewed vigor. On December 13, 2001, the Indian parliament building was attacked by gunmen with almost certain Pakistani connections. To the Indians this was the emotional equivalent of 9/11. They saw no reason why America's stance on Afghanistan—viz., that a nation harboring terrorists was a legitimate target—did not apply toward Pakistan. Indeed, Indian leaders hold that their case for war against Pakistan is better than Washington's case against Afghanistan and especially Iraq.[40]

With U.S. troops staging Afghan operations from four bases in Pakistan, such logic was lost on Washington. True to form, Musharraf grabbed the chance to play the peacemaker, promising a "crackdown" on the militant groups that he and his army had fostered. His personal intercession would not have been necessary in a democratic Pakistan. Opinion polls suggest that only a small percentage of the population considers Kashmir worth so much effort, cost, and risk.[41] But in today's Pakistan public opinion hardly matters unless it is backed by jihadic force. Voices of civil Islamic moderation will remain tangential so long as democracy is thwarted by military or theocratic rule. Without a daily newspaper blitz on the subject, the Kashmir issue would have faded away long ago.

To be sure, India's duplicitous practices have compounded the problem, as rigged elections and festering poverty have stripped Kashmir's Muslims of any stake they might feel in the political status quo. Election fraud and general repression sparked violent resistance in the late 1980s, and by 1992 full rebellion was fomented by the influx of large numbers of Afghan War veterans. This transformed the conflict from one of secular rights into a volatile mix of Pakistani nationalism and international jihad. Today nearly half the militants in the region are thought to be nonindigenous, with most of their funding bearing the stamp of Pakistan. The silver lining is that Pakistan in turn depends on the United States for its solvency. Thus Washington holds cards that could be played on behalf of peace in Kashmir, if only it cared to do so.

Two commonly cited motives for Pakistani terrorist intrusions are the political destabilization of India and revenge for 1971 (when India's support of East Pakistani separatism helped establish Bangladesh). Pakistan's main goal is to evoke hostile reactions on India's part. The army's grip on the nation requires a highly visible enemy, much as Sharonism in Israel needs the visible threat of Hamas. A democratic Pakistan would be less bellicose, and that in turn would do much to defuse Gujarat's Hindutva extremism.[42] The key to pacification on both sides is held by Washington, which by funding Pakistan puts itself, however unwittingly, at the top of the terroristic food chain.

The United States has also played an unwitting part in the region's nuclear proliferation. *Charlie Wilson's War* (2003), by *60 Minutes* producer George Crile, offers a shocking glimpse into America's South Asian machinations during the Reagan era. The point man in this sordid enterprise was former congressman Charlie Wilson, while his nemesis was Stephen Solarz, chairman of the House Foreign Affairs Committee on Asia and the Pacific. Wilson was as determined to boost aid to Pakistan as Solarz was to cut it. Many anti-Soviet realists, such as Zbigniew Brzezinski, sided with Wilson in their effort to look past Pakistan's domestic ravages. What they wanted was a solid (utterly dependent) ally against the Soviets in Afghanistan. Toward that end the United States found it expedient not to notice Pakistan's budding nuclear program.

It was very hard not to notice the clumsily camouflaged cordiality between Pakistan and North Korea. Abdul Qadeer Khan, the former head of Pakistan's nuclear program at the Khan Research Laboratories (KRL), has taken at least thirteen "vacations" in North Korea. He was convicted in absentia by the Netherlands for stealing nuclear secrets before absconding to Pakistan. As a Muslim extremist with close ties to both the ISI and the al Qaeda affiliate Jamaat-ud Dawa (the core jihadic organization in Kashmir), Khan and his KRL colleagues constitute a natural bridgehead for nuclear terrorism.

That of course is the very threat the Bush administration posited as its reason for attacking Iraq. The American media have failed to ask how that danger could be a legitimate ground for war in one case but not the other. The United States embraces the only Muslim state which unquestionably possesses effective weapons of mass destruction (WMD). It is known that Pakistan continued to acquire missiles from North Korea at least until fall 2002, and there can be little doubt that part of the cost of those transactions was met by transfers of nuclear technology from Pakistan. For this the Bush administration tried to punish the KRL lab, not Pakistan. Recently Musharraf gave disturbing assurance that Pakistan was not, *to his knowledge*, passing nuclear technology to North Korea *at this time*. His not very subtle point was that the best protection against nuclear proliferation would be to buttress his dictatorial powers.

This is a country that throughout the 1990s trained and advised the Taliban and other jihadic groups such as Harakat al-Mujahedin, and which has been under military rule for over half of its history. Already the military controlled its banking, transportation, and communications industries, and after Musharraf's constitutional alterations it gained legal authority over nearly all civilian governmental functions. This did not deter the United States from pumping billions of dollars in military and economic aid into Pakistan after 9/11, simply on Musharraf's word that he would assist in the war on terrorism. It can hardly come as a surprise that neither the military nor the ISI has made more than token efforts to apprehend Osama bin Laden, who is thought to be hiding in Pakistan's tribal lands. There are even credible sources which contend bin Laden is getting ISI protection.

This fits a pattern. It is common knowledge in Washington that a group of Pakistani officers sent to Afghanistan prior to the U.S. invasion did not pursue their official mission of encouraging the Taliban to step down. Rather they instructed them on how to survive and protect their weapons in the forthcoming blitz. It is also no great secret that the military and ISI, partly in response to India's close relations to the Karzai government in Afghanistan, are presently supporting Taliban fighters in border areas, even as Islamic militants are once more operating openly in Pakistan. Musharraf's promise to close them down is in league with General Zia's promise not to develop nuclear weaponry in the 1980s. Musharraf's uncanny diplomatic success rests on the widely held belief that his secular dictatorship is preferable to theocratic dictatorship. Better the Shah than Khomeini. Thus we have Tony Blair saluting the "courage and leadership" of Musharraf, a dictator who pours vast sums into nuclear weaponry while leaving the majority of his people ill fed and illiterate.[43]

The Pakistan that Western media have managed to ignore is explored in Bernard-Henri Lévy's *Who Killed Daniel Pearl?* Pearl was *The Wall Street Journal* reporter who was kidnapped and savagely murdered by Islamic militants following his investigation of extremist organizations in Pakistan.[44] Lévy removes all doubt that Pearl's kidnapper, Omar Sheikh, was connected with the ISI as well as the jihadic organizations Pearl was trailing. It is Lévy's contention that Pearl had his throat cut (the video being available for sale outside many Pakistani mosques) not so much because he was American or Jewish, but because he had discovered too much about al Qaeda's developing access to nuclear vendors such as Pakistan and North Korea. The implications this holds for the *next 9/11* go without saying.

Whether or not Lévy is right about the murder motive,[45] he is frightfully convincing as to the threat of WMD terrorism, and the very real possibility that a nuclear version of 9/11 could at this moment be gestating in Pakistan. The question is how to avert this nightmare. Washington is betting on Musharraf, but as we have seen, he is an accomplished trapeze artist, balancing radical extremism against his much advertised secularism. He needs radical Islamists to cement his regime domestically, just as they need him as a conduit for favorable foreign relations. This symbiosis all but guarantees that a large proportion of any aid given to Musharraf will end up in extremist hands. Ironically, Musharraf's dependence on radical Islam serves him well diplomatically. The weaker he seems to be, and the less effective he is in fulfilling his promises, the more saleable he is in Washington. The tragedy of it is that every dollar he gets is an investment in the militarist establishment that stunts political development in Pakistan and, by way of reaction, hampers Indian democracy as well.

Conclusion

Nonetheless there is no doubt as to which of the two putative democracies holds the most promise. The question posed by Shiva Rao in 1947 as to the contest of two developmental systems in South Asia has long since been decided in India's favor. Pakistan lost the contest when it savaged the principle of Koranic tolerance that was adumbrated by Abdul Ghaffar Khan, Gandhi's Islamic counterpart. Khan spent three decades in prison, and is hardly remembered even in Pakistan except as a troublesome Pashtun nationalist.[46] By forgetting him and all he stood for, Pakistan missed its best civil Islamic opportunity. Today its international standing rests on two mixed blessings: the country's possession of nuclear arms and its strategic place in the war on terrorism.

No doubt the specter of radical Islamism worries Musharraf, because it defies state control. Yet he knows his regime owes everything to jihad. Likewise any intelligent Islamist knows that the president must project a "moderate" image for international relations purposes. A reversion to theocracy would invite the pariah status that Iran has suffered since its revolution of 1979. Unlike Pakistan, however, Iran still harbors a vibrant civil society that awaits its political unfolding.

Accordingly, India's current developmental contest is no longer with Pakistan, but with China. Under Deng, China's growth strategy hinged almost entirely on foreign direct investment (FDI). The Chinese Communist Party (CCP) has proved more adept at promoting global capitalism than any democracy could have been. Rao's global opening of 1991 lacked that dictatorial advantage. Nor could the Congress Party match the BJP's ability to divert popular resistance into the emotive politics of Hindutva. India is doing remarkably well considering that it has half the national savings rate of China and 90 percent less FDI. These weaknesses could be more than compensated in the long run by the democratic advantage that Sen adduces.[47]

Unfortunately that factor is being compromised by the politics of Indo-globalization. The BJP's resort to state terrorism produced a Muslim time bomb across India that could have made the Kashmir crisis look tame. Although Indian Muslims were not inclined toward anti-India insurgency, the polarization of Indian society under the BJP pushed the nation to the brink of civil war. If the BJP had not been ousted, groups such as the Gujarat Muslim Revenge Force—which was implicated in the August 2003 explosions in Bombay—would have had no trouble with recruitment in the future.

This disturbing trend had the effect of repelling the FDI that India badly needed to compete globally. BJP apologists argued that the Sangh Parivar offered the best hope for political stability and economic development.[48] In fact, the BJP's short-term victories were tearing India in half. In addition to the clash of Hindus and Muslims there was the perilous dichotomy of haves and have-nots. This is part of the global schism that Raff Carmen sees as creating "two of every society—the two Indias, the two Chiles, the two USAs, the two worlds. . . ."[49] This fault line was clearly drawn by the epoch battle between the World Bank–funded Narmada Valley Development Project (NVDP) and the NBA resistance movement. The NBA won battles at the tactical level, and even forced the World Bank to withdraw. Yet it lost the whole Narmada war in 2000 due to the BJP's Indo-globalist subversion of the Supreme Court.

That defeat, in Chittaroopa Palit's opinion, is a chapter in the strategic failure of the National Alliance of People's Movements (NAPM). What the NAPM could not supply was the kind of holistic solidarity that could counter the Sangh Parivar's fascist communalism.[50] Two decades of grassroots Hindutva have done more to corrode Indian democracy than all the terrorist insurgency of Pakistan combined, though of course the two barbarisms are highly complementary.

The kind of civil holism that Palit prescribes will require the recovery of pluralist integrity in India and Pakistan alike. It is time to salvage the legacies of Gandhi and Khan, respectively. This will be a tall order in an age that marries tribal animosities with commercially mediated narcissism, or what Benjamin Barber terms "Jihad" and "McWorld": "a bloody politics of identity" and a "bloodless economics of profit"[51] (for Barber "Jihad" denotes any anti-globalist militancy, not just the Islamic variety). What is sorely needed is a moral equivalent to Jihad. Accordingly, the world needs more from India than cheaper goods and services. It needs the global equivalent of Gandhi.

Neo-Gandhianism, like Sen's dictum of "freedom as development," hinges on the instrumental as well as intrinsic value of social justice and pluralist tolerance. Pakistan offers a negative case in point. Imran Khan notes how its power elite appropriated the British colonial system, never even trying to evolve a homegrown substitute.[52] The good news is that such maldevelopment is unsustainable without massive foreign assistance. The bad news is that the United States has been and remains munificent in supplying that assistance. After the Cold War, however, Pakistan was left in the lurch. Only the threat of terrorism puts it back on the geopolitical map. Islamabad is compelled to stoke radical Islamism with one hand while fighting it with the other. It has brilliantly accomplished this, but the resulting chaos keeps FDI at bay and makes Pakistan all the more dependent on its geopolitical patron.

India could evade this cycle of dependency so long as its ruling classes felt secure in their neocolonial authority. By the 1990s, however, democracy had begun to take on dangerous substance. Meanwhile India's elites began to find their niche in a formative transnational capitalist class. Clearly their allegiance was less to India the nation than India the investment opportunity. Ironically India held its own throughout the Cold War, when the geopolitical going was so much tougher. Why raise the white flag now? The answer, quite simply, is that the nonaligned movement had never been about democratic India so much as about ruling-class interests. The long Nehruvian war against external colonialism ended when India's elites saw more profit in globalist alignment. Even before the BJP got into the act, the Congress Party inaugurated this globalist revolution from above. The BJP then got the upper hand by rooting globalization in the social bedrock of Hindutva.

The only hope for democratic India is a counterrevolution from below. This could have sweeping repercussions, for Indo-globalization will not be a simple clone of Washington-based neoliberalism. India will put its own stamp on the globalization process. The question is *which India* will do so. Under Manmohan Singh the Congress coalition is likely to be an even more potent instrument of globalization, for its nominal social reformism—like Western Third-Wayism—serves to defuse Left resistance. It must not be forgotten that the Congress Party has long been the darling of World Bank projects and the nemesis of the NVDP. Far from an egalitarian upset, the election of May 2004 augurs a return to elitist business as usual.

Notes

1. See W. Norman Brown, *The United States and India and Pakistan* (Cambridge, MA: Harvard University Press, 1955), 112.

2. Pankaj Mishra, "Murder in India," *The New York Review of Books* (August 15, 2002), <www.nybooks.com/articles/15636>.

3. Shiva Rao, "India Grapples with Freedom," (written in Madras, August 14, 1947), from the archives of *The Nation* (2001), <www.thenation.com/docPrint.mhml?I=archieve&s=19470823india>. It is only fair to note that Jinnah did not live long

enough to prove that judgment wrong. It is arguable that, despite his icy temperament, he was not the "evil genius" that Mountbatten described, or that the movie *Gandhi* so memorably depicted. The movie *Jinnah* tried to set the record straight, but ended up outraging Pakistan by casting Christopher Lee (famous for his Count Dracula roles) as the "Great Leader." The real Jinnah, as the film attests, supported women and religious minorities and looked with horror on the genocidal fanaticism of Hindus and Muslims alike. In retrospect it is clear that Jinnah's secular tolerance was cut from much the same mold as Nehru's. He was no Lincoln, but neither was he Count Dracula.

4. Amartya Sen, *Development as Freedom* (New York: Alfred A. Knopf, 1999), 180.

5. Sen, *Development as Freedom*, 181.

6. Qtd. in Sen, *Development as Freedom*, 182. Mao's remarkable candor had deep roots, reaching back to his democratic promises of 1945, and indeed to the political philosophy of one of the Communist Party's founding fathers, Chen Duxiu, twenty years earlier. See Arthur Waldron, "What Should the President Say at Tsinghua University?" *China Brief* (February 14, 2002), <www.jamestown.org/pubs/view/cwe_002_004_001.htm>.

7. Rob Jenkins, *Democratic Politics and Economic Reform in India* (Cambridge, U.K.: Cambridge University Press, 1999), 212.

8. Richard A. Matthew, "Environment, Population and Conflict: New Modalities of Threat and Vulnerability in South Asia," *Journal of International Affairs* 56, no. 1 (fall 2002): 245 (235–54).

9. Tariq Ali, *Can Pakistan Survive? The Death of a State* (New York: Verso, 1983), 50–51.

10. Deepa Ollapally, "Third World Nationalism and the United States after the Cold War," *Political Science Quarterly* 110, no. 3 (autumn 1995): 425 (417–34).

11. Pranab Bardhan, *The Political Economy of Development in India* (New York: Basil Blackwell, 1984), 71.

12. Satu P. Limaye, *U.S.-Indian Relations: The Pursuit of Accommodation* (Boulder, CO: Westview, 1993), 5.

13. Limaye, *U.S.-Indian Relations*, 6–8. The isolation that India would feel, especially after the fall of its de facto ally, the Soviet Union, would push it toward an active nuclear defense policy. See Steven P. Cohen, "India Rising," *Wilson Quarterly* (summer 2000), <wwics.si.edu/WQ/WQSELECT/INDIA.HTM>.

14. A measure of economic liberalization had been ventured even by Indira Gandhi, Nehru's daughter, and more was promised by her son Rajiv, but these early traces of globalization fell prey to insurmountable political obstacles, as both the Indian Left and Right balked at Gandhi's attempt to weaken the state in favor of the private sector. Rao, likewise, got cold feet after the Congress Party lost several key elections late in 1994. See Ollapally, "Third World Nationalism," 429; and on Rajiv Gandhi's failed liberalization efforts see Myron Weiner, *The Indian Paradox: Essays in Indian Politics* (New Delhi: Sage, 1989), 299.

15. Celia W. Dugger, "Indian Town's Seed Grew into the Taliban's Code," *New York Times* (February 23, 2002), <www.nytimes.com/2002/02/23/international/asia/23INDI.html>.

16. Ali, *Can Pakistan Survive?* 15–16.

17. Mushirul Hasan, "Partition: The Human Cost," *History Today* (September 1997), in *Britannica.com*, <www.britannica.com/magazine/print?content_id=32085>.

18. Hasan, "Partition: The Human Cost."

19. Qtd. in Pankaj Mishra, "A New, Nuclear India?" *The New York Review of Books* 45, no. 11 (June 25, 1998): 58 (55–64).

20. Mishra, "A New, Nuclear India?" 58.

21. Stephen P. Cohen, "India Rising," *The Wilson Quarterly* (summer 2000), <www.si.edu/WQ/WQSELECT/INDIA.HTM>.

22. Aron Ghosh, *Planning in India: The Challenge for the Nineties* (New Delhi: Sage, 1992), 14–15.

23. Christopher Candland, "Congress Decline and Party Pluralism in India," *Journal of International Affairs* 51, no. 1 (summer 1997): 31 and 33 (19–35).

24. Smithu Kothari, "Whose Independence? The Social Impact of Economic Reform in India," *Journal of International Affairs* 51, no. 1 (summer 1997): 92 (85–116).

25. Rajeev Bhargava, "India in the Face of Globalization," o*penDemocracy* (February 26, 2003), <www.opendemocracy.net/articles/debates/article.jsp?id=6+debateId= 91+articleId=1006>.

26. Arundhati Roy, "Fascism's Footprint in India," *The Nation* (September 30, 2002), <www.thenation.com/docprint.mhtml?i=20020930&s=roy>.

27. Smita Narula, "Overlooked Danger: The Security and Rights Implications of Hindu Nationalism in India," *Harvard Human Rights Journal* 16 (spring 2003): 41–42, and 54 (41–68).

28. Mishra, "A New, Nuclear India?" 62.

29. Globalists and other BJP affiliates counter that Gujarat has long been a hub of religious violence, and that large-scale rioting prior to 2002 actually declined after the BJP came to power. See "How Hindu an India?" *The Economist* (August 16, 2001), <www.economist.com/PrinterFriendly.cfm?Story_ID=744990&CFID=275149&CFT OKEN=2478485>.

30. Amitash Pal, "Bush Ignores India's Pogrom," *The Progressive* (July 2003), <www.progressive.org/july03/pal0703.html>.

31. Mishra, "A New, Nuclear India?" 64.

32. Pranab Bardhan, "Dominant Proprietary Classes and India's Democracy," in Atul Kohl, ed., *India's Democracy: An Analysis of Changing State-Society Relations* (Princeton, NJ: Princeton University Press, 1988), 215 (214–24).

33. Smithu Kothari, "Damming the Narmada and the Politics of Development," in William F. Fisher, ed., *Toward Sustainable Development* (Armonk, NY: M. E. Sharpe, 1995), 444 (420–44).

34. Barrington Moore Jr., *Social Origins of Dictatorship and Democracy: Lord and Peasant in the Making of the Modern World* (Boston: Beacon Press, 1966), 374.

35. William H. Thornton, *Fire on the Rim: The Cultural Dynamics of East/West Power Politics* (Lanham, MD: Rowman & Littlefield, 2002), 196–97.

36. Gail Omvelt, *Reinventing Revolution: New Social Movements and the Socialist Tradition in India* (Armonk, NY: M. E. Sharpe, 1993), 131.

37. Salman Rushdie, "The Most Dangerous Place in the World," *New York Times* (May 30, 2002), <www.nytimes.com/2002/05/30/opinion/30RUSH.html?pagewanted=print&position=...>.

38. Ahmed Rashid, "Pakistan on the Edge," *The New York Review of Books* (October 10, 2002), <www.nybooks.com/articles/15740>.

39. In spring 2000 the U.S. State Department concluded that South Asia had surpassed even the Middle East as the hub of world terrorism, but declined to mention that Pakistan was the epicenter of it all. See Jessica Stern, "Pakistan's Jihad Culture," *Foreign Affairs* 79, no. 6 (November/December 2000): 115 (115–26).

40. Kanti Bajpai, "An Indian 'War on Terrorism' against Pakistan?," *Dissent* (summer 2003), <www.dissentmagazine.org/menutest/articles/su03/bajpai.htm>.

41. K. Shankar Bajpai, "Untangling India and Pakistan," *Foreign Affairs* 82, no. 3 (May/June 2003): 117 (112–26). The Kashmir crisis has deep roots, reaching back to the 1947 partition, when the region was given the choice of joining India or Pakistan. Unfortunately the actual choice was made by a Hindu monarch, not by the Muslim majority. Pakistan responded by sending irregular "volunteers" to stir insurrection. Despite a cease-fire in 1948, this insurgency has continued, with Islamabad always claiming that militants operating out of Pakistan were outside its orbit of control.

42. See Stern, "Pakistan's Jihad Culture," 121.

43. Christopher de Bellaigue, "The Perils of Pakistan," *The New York Review of Books* 48, no. 18 (November 15, 2001): 44 (44–47); and William Easterly, "Clueless in Pakistan," *The Globalist* (November 29, 2001), <www.theglobalist.com/nor/gbs/2001/11-29-01.shtml>.

44. The timing of Pearl's abduction, a few weeks before Musharraf's visit to Washington, suggested to many that it was designed to embarrass the president, thereby punishing him for his recent "crackdown" on extremist groups. But in fact it served Musharraf's interest by reinforcing his image as a courageous moderate, holding the line against terrorist barbarism. On this standard interpretation see Husain Haqqan, "Trying to Create a New Pakistan," *New York Times* (Feb. 13, 2002), <www.nytimes.com/2002/02/13/ opinion/13HAQQ.html>.

45. There are several problems with this argument. First, the *Wall Street Journal* denies that Pearl was pursuing that angle. Second, as Ron Rosenbaum points out, Lévy tends to credit his "posthumous friend" Pearl with the fruits of his own investigation. See Ron Rosenbaum, "In Danny Pearl Book, Lévy Says Next 9/11 Brewing in Pakistan," *New York Observer* (September 13, 2003), <www2.observer.com/observer/pages/frontpage6.asp>.

46. See Amitabh Pal, "A Pacifist Uncovered," *The Progressive* (February 2002), <www.progressive.org/0901/pal0202.html>.

47. Yasheng Huang and Tarun Khanna, "Can India Overcome China?" *Foreign Policy* (September/October 2003), <www.foreignpolicy.com/story/printer.php?storyID=13774>.

48. Amrita Basu, "The dialectics of Hindu nationalism," in Atul Kohli, ed., *The Success of India's Democracy* (Cambridge, U.K.: Cambridge University Press, 2001), 163 (163–89).

49. Raff Carmen, *Autonomous Development—Humanizing the Landscape: An Excursion into Radical Thinking and Practice* (London: Zed Books, 1996), 33.

50. Chittaroopa Palit, "Monsoon Risings: Mega-Dam Resistance in the Narmada Valley," *New Left Review* (May/June 2003): 99 (81–100).

51. Benjamin Barber, *Jihad vs. McWorld: How Globalism and Tribalism Are Reshaping the World* (New York, Ballantine Books, 1995), 8.

52. Imran Khan, "Politics in Pakistan," *Resurgence* (downloaded September 19, 2002), <resurgence.gn. apc.org/articles/khan.htm>.

5

Politics of the Islamic Revival: Civil and Uncivil Islamism in Afghanistan and Central Asia

The Other Axis of Evil

AMERICA LAUNCHED ITS WAR ON TERRORISM in Afghanistan with willful forgetfulness of how it had once courted the Taliban, both as an ally in its new "great game" and as a guarantor of future oil flows in Central Asia. Only when those expectations proved unrealistic did Washington see fit to spotlight the Taliban's human rights record—a clear sign the courtship was over. The first public breach came in November 1997, when Secretary of State Madeleine Albright voiced outrage at Taliban gender atrocities. The geopolitical subtext was not hard to read, and to the Taliban it spelled betrayal. Infidelity in world affairs, as in personal affairs, carries a high price in their world. More than theological affinity, it was distrust of U.S. intentions that cemented the Taliban's relationship with their hired gun, Osama bin Laden.[1]

The problem was keeping this Saudi pluto-terrorist in line. When his al Qaeda network was implicated in the 1998 attacks on U.S. embassies in Kenya and Tanzania, the Taliban got more than it bargained for. The United States struck back with wild abandon: on August 20, 1998, it fired close to eighty cruise missiles (at $750,000 per shot) at "smart" targets in Afghanistan and Sudan (one ending up in Pakistan 400 miles off course).[2] Far more distressing, from the Taliban perspective, was the subsequent geopolitical reversal: America and Russia set aside their usual "great game" polarity to cosponsor a UN arms embargo against the Taliban, but not against its enemies to the north. Osama had produced the very insecurity that he was brought in to prevent.

This was as close as the United States ever came to backing the Taliban's arch-enemy, the United Front (alias Northern Alliance)[3] of Ahmed Shah Massoud. By 1999 Massoud was the only major figure standing in the Taliban's path, the others having fled into exile or having been bought off. To fully support him would have afforded almost certain victory over the Taliban *without U.S. military involvement*, and at a fraction of the cost of direct intervention. The reason this less invasive route was not taken has much to do with the rising tension between Islamism and Washington-directed globalization. While Washington prefers secular Kemalism to any Islamism, it is especially averse to the civil Islam that Massoud epitomized, for it represents something even more frightful from a globalist perspective than al Qaeda: the specter of autonomous development and hence geopolitical independence.

Fearful of America's developing accord with Massoud at home and Russia abroad, the Taliban sought a rapprochement with Washington. A meeting was scheduled in Pakistan on July 31, 2001, with Christina B. Rocca, the U.S. assistant secretary of state for South Asian affairs. Abdul Salam Zaeef, the Taliban's ambassador to Pakistan, stressed in a parallel interview that his government wanted continued friendship with America and hoped to resolve the al Qaeda problem through dialogue. To say the problem was negotiable was to say Osama was expendable. Zaeef pointed out that the Taliban and the United States shared a mutual enemy in Russia, and should remain allies. But he also admonished the Americans that it would be "their mistake" if they were "to join hands with our enemy."[4]

Only al Qaeda could give global force to that threat. Suffice it to say that the Taliban had not given sanctuary to Osama for the mere pleasure of his company. His presence was costing them, among other things, a seat in the UN.[5] He was a veritable weapon of mass destruction, but until that summer he was still a bargaining chip. By August, however, hopes for a negotiated solution had been dashed.[6] Both sides knew this was the dead end of Cold War geopolitics in the region. Without solid security guarantees in return, the Taliban had to reject Washington's demand that Osama be surrendered or at least expelled. The cost of this failed negotiation is unfathomable, for until then the Taliban was the only restraining force on bin Laden. It was a short hop from July 31 to September 11.

U.S. consternation at its lack of leverage was double barreled: aimed not only at Osama's Taliban hosts, but also at their Pakistani patrons.[7] The amity that had marked U.S.-Pakistani relations for decades was fast eroding. Paradoxically, however, 9/11 would restore that alliance with a vengeance. In an almost apologetic speech of September 19, 2001, General Pervez Musharraf (*President* Musharraf as of that June) told Pakistanis that this renewed cronyism with the American infidel was a matter of sheer survival, as the United

States had given him an ultimatum: join us or fight us. Clearly, though, the arrangement involved more carrot than stick. Nor would it be a mere temporary expedient. The idea was to position Pakistan as a permanent fortress in the new "world war on terrorism," much as it had served as a forward base in the war on communism. Accordingly, the Bush administration pledged a $3 billion aid package in 2003 as part of its "long-term commitment" to Musharraf's regime.

Oddly that commitment was given in full view of Pakistan's continuing aid to the Taliban. Could the world's sole superpower be so ill advised as to *accidentally* finance its avowed enemy? Some say no. From this vantage the real American objective has been to keep Afghanistan weak and destabilized so as to ensure permanent dependency and a pretext for ongoing U.S. (and Pakistani) involvement,[8] thus providing a base camp for expanded Central Asian operations. Clearly nation building has not been high on the American agenda, and some push the argument so far as to question the seriousness of the U.S. effort to snuff out the Taliban and al Qaeda.[9]

Russia, to be sure, looks with dark suspicion on all U.S. activity in the region. Its accord with Washington concerning the Taliban and other militant Islamisms is an exception to its more typical "great game" actions such as nuclear assistance to Iran and high-tech military sales to China.[10] These tactics would have been against Moscow's geopolitical interest if American expansionism had not been its paramount concern. An independent Afghanistan could relax regional tensions, but by this line of reasoning, that is exactly what the United States and Pakistan do *not* want. Their conjoint Afghan strategy has its roots in the "great game" of the 1980s. Zbigniew Brzezinski, President Carter's national security advisor, testifies that support for the Afghan Mujahedeen was not begun as a defensive reaction to Soviet aggression, but as a lure to draw the Russians into the Afghan equivalent of Vietnam.[11]

The ploy worked, but at an inordinate price. In a classic case of "blowback," this radical Islamic torpedo turned full circle on its sender. Bin Laden, after all, was one of the militants groomed by the U.S.-Arab-Pakistani axis.[12] Even Brzezinski can justify this cultural weapon of mass destruction only in terms of the coldest Cold War ends over means. It was a case of selective breeding, for extremists such as bin Laden were favored over moderate Islamists such as Massoud. Had funding been granted on the basis of battlefield results, Massoud would have taken the lion's share, as he was the commander most feared by the Soviets. Their seven attempts to invade his native Panjshir Valley all failed. Likewise, in their later resistance to the Taliban, other commanders such as Ismail Khan and Rashid Dostum were far less effective than the chronically underfunded Massoud.[13] By no accident the Alliance's last strongholds—the Shomali plains, Badakhshan Province, and the Panjshir Valley—were Massoud's home turf.

Since the geopolitical rationale for supporting radical Islamism died with the Cold War, U.S. support for the Taliban in the 1990s is impossible to explain without reference to corporate interest. After signing a mammoth oil contract with Turkmenistan in October 1995, Union Oil of California (Unocal) and Saudi Arabia's Delta Oil intended to pipe oil to Pakistan through a soon-to-be pacified Afghanistan. Unocal therefore welcomed the Taliban's capture of Kabul in September 1996 as a "positive development." By 1998, however, the stability that investors had expected was nowhere in sight, and in December Unocal withdrew from the operation."[14]

The Taliban was now worse than superfluous in corporate terms, for it stood in the way of any alternative source of stability, such as the present interim government. And since Pakistan's favoritism toward the Taliban had not abated, the residual Cold War bond between Washington and Islamabad was put under strain. Two cardinal facts prevented Pakistan from following the U.S. redirection. First, Afghan and Pakistani Pashtuns were too closely related, both ethnically and religiously, to permit such a rupture. And second, the fall of the Taliban would leave Pakistan surrounded by hostile nations: India, Iran, and now Afghanistan.[15]

Talibanization, Then and Now

Paradoxically it was 9/11 that restored the U.S.-Pakistan alliance, and indirectly siphoned U.S. aid back into the coffers of the Taliban and even al Qaeda. It is no secret that Quetta, the capital of Pakistan's Baluchistan Province, gives sanctuary to thousands of vagrant Taliban. Part of Baluchistan's governing coalition is the Jamiat-e-Ullema Islam (JUI) party. Suffice it to say that the government is no impediment to insurgency across the border. Ahmed Rashid quotes the provincial information minister as saying that the Taliban is the only legitimate government of Afghanistan. Taliban leaders give open press conferences,[16] and UN experts have testified that a host of Islamic militants are getting copious Pakistani support.[17]

It is well known, likewise, that Pakistan was the source of the world's most egregious WMD (weapons of mass destruction) cases. As a senior Washington official put it, "these guys are now three for three as supplier to the biggest proliferation problems we have": North Korea, Iran, and Libya.[18] Yet somehow Deputy Secretary of State Richard L. Armitage managed to be "thrilled" by the anti-terrorist efforts of Musharraf. Perhaps he was referring to the dictator's latest symbolic gesture: his promise to build a fence along parts of Pakistan's 1,520-mile border with Afghanistan, as if the Taliban cannot afford wire cutters, or will even need them where Pashtun guards man the border stations.

Afghans have difficulty understanding Washington's patience with their pro-Taliban ally, Pakistan, and many suspect duplicity. In Washington's defense it can be said that these contradictory policies are more likely the result of incompetence than nefarious design. While U.S. strategists are certainly not above destabilizing a Fourth World country with "wag the dog" equanimity, what is lacking is commercial motive. The Bush administration is in thrall to multinational interests that would not be well served by continuing civil strife in Afghanistan. Gore Vidal is surely right that the primary U.S. goal since the Cold War has been to make Afghanistan safe for American oil conglomerates;[19] and an Afghan civil war is hardly on that profit sheet.

Washington's corporate priorities were validated by recent Afghan appointments. It was surely no accident that a former Unocal employee, Hamid Karzai, was installed as president of the interim government, while another Unocal employee, Zalmay Khalilzad (later the U.S. ambassador) was sent as America's special envoy. Karzai is a Pashtun monarchist and early Taliban supporter, while Khalilzad was Unocal's point man in its pipeline negotiations and a de facto Washington lobbyist for the Taliban against its critics on the feminist and human rights front. At the height of this debate he penned a *Washington Post* op-ed article pressing for "reengagement" with the Taliban.

Washington's initial "engagement" traced to October 1996, when Unocal got its green light for a trans-Afghan pipeline. At that moment civilizational clash was nowhere in sight, and human rights was not an issue. As late as December 1997 Taliban representatives were still being regaled in Texas by Unocal. The regime's well-documented state terrorism and its notorious suppression of women's rights made no dent on these auspicious "engagements." In May *The Wall Street Journal* had joined the party by declaring the Taliban "the players most capable of achieving peace in Afghanistan."[20] That is to say the Taliban was the best security apparatus for vulnerable pipelines—Unocal's own Pinkerton police. *How* these advantages were secured was not a pressing consideration in corporate circles. Only when the Taliban proved unable to deliver the goods did other concerns, such as women's most rudimentary rights, suddenly take on importance as the rationale for a strategic reversal.

The Taliban made that policy shift easy by putting all women under de facto house arrest. Deprived of work and education, they were allowed outside only when wearing a burka (a full body veil that so impaired their vision that they often fell victim to moving vehicles), and only in the company of male relatives. Religious police hunted the streets for violators and dispensed summary beatings. Women caught wearing nail polish could have the tips of their thumbs cut off, but in Taliban terms that passed for lenience. Married adulterers could be stoned to death,[21] or savagely flogged if they were single.

Since all normal forms of recreation had been criminalized—books, music, parties, TV, children's toys, games, card playing, cameras, women's makeup, jewelry, stylish clothes, beard trimming, cigarettes, alcohol, newspapers and magazines, kite flying and parakeets, not to mention English practice with Christian missionaries—state terrorism increasingly took the form of entertainment. In Kabul there were "Friday circuses" where up to 30,000 men and boys would flock to the Olympic stadium to watch as women were beaten nearly to death for conversing with a nonrelative of the opposite sex, or to see public amputations performed on alleged thieves. But even as Amnesty International declared Afghanistan "a human rights catastrophe," American oil companies lobbied for its entry into the UN.[22]

The Taliban interpretation of sharia, or Islamic law—nurtured in Pakistan's Saudi-funded madrassas—was the strictest the Muslim world had ever known.[23] No room was left for the core Islamic values of peace and tolerance, not to mention the humanist discourse that flourished under Islam in the Middle Ages. True Islamism, and even true jihad, has a moral depth that could never countenance the slaughter of innocents, be they Muslim or non-Muslim. Except for its Arab funding, and the blessing of having enemies who spent half their time fighting each other, the Taliban could not have captured a single Afghan watering hole. In moral and spiritual terms the movement is to Islam what the Ku Klux Klan is to Christianity. Unlike the so-called "Afghan Arabs," who were virtually incorruptible fighters, most Taliban commanders could be bought.[24]

Militarily, however, the Taliban surprised even its Pakistani hosts in the winter of 1994. The Bhutto government backed it substantially—in part to blunt the power of Pakistan's secret police, the ISI; yet doubts persisted as to its abilities except as an adjunct force in the south. The ISI was still betting on their faithful puppet Gulbuddin Hekmatyar, America's favorite warlord and Massoud's inveterate enemy. Massoud had broken with him as early as 1973 over his use of terror tactics, which never concerned Washington. In early 1995 Hekmatyar was putting Kabul under siege, but he was not alone. The advance of the Taliban from the south caught him in the middle. In February 1995 the Taliban captured his headquarters, while President Burhanuddin Rabbani's troops under Massoud withdrew into Kabul.[25] They lost the city in September 1996, and by January 1997 had retreated into Massoud's Panjshir Valley,[26] which they would hold even as most of the country was lost in a long war of attrition.

Chronic drought turned out to be the Taliban's best ally, second to Pakistan. Their push north depended largely on ex-farmer mercenaries who had lost their crops and animals. With better funding, the Northern Alliance could simply have bought these agri-mercenaries away from the Taliban. As it was, the more affluent Taliban effectively *purchased* its control of 90 percent of Afghanistan by the summer of 1998.

The end seemed near to anyone unfamiliar with the generalship of Massoud. Robert Kaplan in *The Soldiers of God* compared it to the nonconventional prowess of Marshall Tito, Ho Chi Minh, and Che Guevara. What Massoud lacked was the material means to drive back the strategically inferior Taliban. Finally some support began to trickle in from regional sources. Four out of five Central Asian republics, along with Russia, Turkey, and India, now stood behind the Northern Alliance.[27] Pakistan's quest for geostrategic depth, as Brzezinski terms it,[28] was starting to unite Eurasia. Nonetheless the Taliban captured Taloqan, the capital of the Northern Alliance, on September 5, 2000; and in October, with 95 percent of the country under Taliban control, another major offensive was launched.

Massoud responded by moving his wife and children from Tajikistan to an Afghan base, thereby serving notice that, come what may, retreat was not an option for him. As Ahmed Rashid pointed out at the time, this Thermopylae-like stand was the "last buffer" between the Taliban and Central Asia: with "25,000 Russian troops and border guards on the . . . Tajik-Afghan frontier, a Massud withdrawal into Tajikistan will pit Moscow and Dushanbe directly against the Taliban."[29] Moreover, with winter snows just weeks away, 90,000 Afghan refugees were already massed in the mountains outside Tajikistan, and that figure could have risen to half a million if the Alliance had fallen.[30]

Shunning Massoud, as usual, Washington lavished assistance on Uzbekistan, its main strategic ally in the region after Pakistan—an odd combination, in that Uzbekistan is radically secularist while Pakistan has been undergoing its own Talibanization. But since there was no doubt that support would flow to the Alliance after 9/11, it was essential to al Qaeda that Massoud be eliminated. His assassination on 9/9 was not just a precursor of 9/11, but was part of the same operation. Until then Washington had ignored Massoud's warnings about the gathering terrorist storm in Afghanistan. Before 1998 it had even looked favorably upon the Taliban's Arab connections, which it saw as a useful counter to Iran. Even after the 1998 embassy attacks, the United States maintained a policy of denying support to any Afghan faction—meaning not a crumb for Massoud.

The Northern Alliance, minus Massoud, was a motley set of bricks with no mortar. This union of improbable allies—notably Tajiks, Uzbeks, and Hazaras—had one common bond: a determination to expel the Pakistani hegemony that cloaked itself in Taliban robes. That jihadic subterfuge was as alien to most Afghans as Soviet communism had been. Far from modeling their actions on Koranic scripture, the Taliban rescripted Islam, making the foot fit the shoe. A great religion was reduced to a penal code whose main concern was the length of a man's beard or a woman's burka. Even today, with the Taliban officially ousted, its reign of terror persists in much of the Pashtun sphere. Men traveling country roads in southeast Afghanistan are still having their noses cut off by Taliban insurgents for the crime of trimming their beards; and fundamentalist madrassas are back in action.[31]

Second Thoughts on the "Victory"

Far from extinguishing this quasi-jihadic fire, U.S. military operations have been accused by the UN of contributing to the climate of insecurity. The Taliban, it seems, did some things right. Mainly they reined in the warlords who prey relentlessly on locals. Not only did the United States give free rein to these predators, but often set them up as regional authorities. The lives of ordinary Afghans remain a lawless nightmare, with women subjected to much the same intimidation they suffered under the Taliban. Due process is almost nonexistent, and basic security is a luxury few enjoy. In just forty-eight hours in mid-August 2003, 115 died violent deaths, with another 100 critically injured.[32] Needless to say, democratic activists are especially vulnerable.

Since the Taliban's fall in late 2001, the Americans have convinced the Afghans that the Taliban is right: the foreigners are here to occupy, not to rebuild. With the central government exercising no control over most provinces, and with warlords on the government dole, many say things are actually worse after the Taliban's exit. In any case much is unchanged, such as the average annual income of $75. Western promises mock reality, while UN projects do little more than raise the cost of living. By May 2003 the Bush administration had provided a mere $2.5 million for women's programs, most of it going to construction firms, and none for rural education or job training. More than two decades of war and seven years of drought have left the country in ruins. With most livestock dead, and herders' mercenary services no longer needed, many have little choice but to join the drug trade. Meanwhile governmental collapse and massive displacements have left the country totally dependent upon outside aid.[33] Only the Bush administration could call this victory.

Even militarily the war was scarcely over when the Bush team declared it won, so as to pave the way for a long-awaited Iraq invasion. Afghanistan was left in a state of social meltdown, with international aid hampered by ongoing violence. Several vital NGOs, including the International Red Cross, the World Food Program, and Doctors Without Borders, were forced to pull out of the south. The denouement came in November 2003 when the UN refugee agency withdrew its workers from the south and east, suspending all aid to refugees returning from Pakistan to a virtual wasteland. Satellite imagery reveals unprecedented environmental trauma, exacerbated by severe shortages of fuel and building materials and continuing drought. Deforestation is compounded by illegal timber exports to Pakistan.

While doing little to ameliorate these conditions, Washington has the gall to complain about the narcotics trade that flourishes here, much as it condemned Massoud for doing nothing about drugs while the Northern Alliance was fighting for its life unassisted by the United States. At this point small farmers have little choice but to enter the only thriving sphere of economic activity. Poppy production doubled after 2002, and in 2003 furnished the second biggest opium harvest on record—providing over 75 percent of the world's poppy supply.[34] Previously this $2 billion cash crop was mainly for export. But increasingly Afghanistan is getting into the refining and distribution side of the business, serving an estimated 1 million Afghan addicts. Now only 15 percent of the country's output goes to the West.[35]

This figure is an expression of the desperation that was left to fester after the Cold War and again after the U.S. "victory" in 2001. Even the promise of "free and fair elections," along with a new constitution, cannot lift the defeatist pall that has settled over Afghanistan in the face of chronic insecurity and economic hopelessness. Afghans, moreover, are painfully aware that their American benefactor cares more about media images such as the Kabul to Kandahar highway (completed in 2003, with paving so thin as to carry an unintended symbolic meaning) than about rebuilding the Afghan nation.

Many who celebrated the Taliban's defeat are now having second thoughts. Public opinion about the new government is divided, to say the least. While the warlord Hekmatyar has transferred his loyalty to his erstwhile Taliban enemy,[36] some ex-Taliban stalwarts, such as the former deputy minister Abdul Hakeem Muneeb, have thrown their support to Karzai—precisely because he offers a backdoor version of the power structure they once sought from the Taliban. Call it Talibanization with a small 't.' That was fine for most of the 502 constitutional framers, including Muneeb. The majority were tribal elders with little more interest in progressive reform than the Taliban had.[37]

On Our Watch

It is women most of all who are stuck in the middle: unable for obvious reasons to accept even uncapitalized Talibanization, yet outraged by the "light footprint" policy whereby the U.S. and the UN end up supporting warlords who mimic the Taliban's patriarchic oppression.[38] The Taliban, after all, had seemed like saviors when they replaced these same Mujahedeen thugs in 1996. Now their appeal is rising once more, if only for the measure of security they could offer. This would mean severe repression for women, of course, but they already have that, and under the Taliban they would have less chance of being gang raped by U.S.-funded militia units. In most of the country the burka is still a woman's only "passport," and even in Kabul women find it necessary to wear a "chador" body cover (less cumbrous than a burka, but carrying much the same discriminatory weight) to avoid attacks by soldiers and police. Under the post-Taliban penal code women suspected of "moral crimes" are still arrested and given involuntary "chastity tests." A European Commission report points out that many such women end up behind bars for months without trial, while in Pashtun areas women can be bartered or sold—first wives being a popular exchange commodity.

It is not surprising, therefore, that women have led the fight for substantive democratic reform. For three days in early December 2003 a vanguard of 2,000 women from Kabul and at least ten provinces met to discuss appropriate responses to regressive elements in the country's proposed constitution. There were almost no burkas to be seen here, but also very little press coverage.[39] The event was a milestone nonetheless, for it signaled the rise of a grassroots movement that could offer hope for not only women but the whole nation. As things now stand there simply is no nation.

These efforts clearly paid off, for the final version of the constitution guaranteed 25 percent of the seats in Parliament to women—twice the number of earlier drafts.[40] On December 17 the convention got a full dose of this new medicine when a twenty-five-year-old social worker, Malalai Joya, risked never making twenty-six by voicing an unprecedented demand. Before they cut off her microphone, she called for liberation from the Mujahedeen warlords who control most of the country, and of course the convention as well. To their faces she called them "criminals" who should be tried in national and international courts.[41] She was threatened on the spot by the notorious Mujahedeen warlord Abdul Rabb al-Rasul Sayyaf, a Saudi-funded Wahhabi and presidential hopeful whose troops make a point of robbing homes and raping women on the very outskirts of Kabul.[42]

Not to be outdone by the Saudis, the United States does its part to fund and equip "good" (pro-U.S.) terrorists in their war against "bad" (anti-U.S.) ones. The warlord Hazrat Ali, for example, is a U.S. military favorite who has been identified by Human Rights Watch as one of the country's worst human rights violators. His fight with al Qaeda is purely a turf war. Indeed, as compared with Sayyaf or Ali, the Taliban and al Qaeda hold the moral high ground: they are perfectly willing to kill for their cause, but also to die for it. America's inability to register that distinction, or the even more significant distinction between civil and uncivil Islam, dooms its geopolitical ventures in the Muslim world.

A glaring case in point is its unconditional support of the terroristic warlord Ismail Khan, whose fiefdom claims suzerainty over five western provinces. Khan took power late in 2001 with full U.S. backing, and has used aid from both America and Iran to buttress his opposition to the interim government in Kabul. In April 2002 U.S. Secretary of Defense Donald Rumsfeld visited Khan and described him as "an appealing person" (precisely what he would say of President Bush). U.S. Special Forces still police the city of Herat on holidays as a favor to Khan, and as an unsubtle hint to Kabul that the region is off limits.[43] Human Rights Watch protests that all this is happening on the international community's watch. NGOs are simply helpless here, while the UN, taking its cues from the U.S., has reverted to its old habit of promoting stability over human rights.

In the absence of positive international pressure, it is little wonder that liberal democratic and human rights dissent was sidelined throughout the constitutional deliberations. After a year of heated negotiation, a draft constitution finally went for ratification by the Loya Jirga, or Grand Assembly, in December 2003. It had been scheduled for October, but the deteriorating security situation forced a delay. Likewise, ratification had been expected within ten days, but was dragged out for twenty-two days by ethnic strife that underscored the likelihood of renewed civil war regardless of the constitutional outcome. All major parties, however, could agree on the first proposed article: that Afghanistan is to be "an Islamic Republic." As under the Taliban, all laws "contrary to the sacred religion" will be banned.[44] This leaves most democratic rights, and gender equality in particular, in serious doubt. With full U.S. backing, Karzai and his Pashtun constituents have pushed for the strongest possible presidential powers, while former Alliance leaders such as Rabbani insisted on a parliamentary system that would disperse power.

The final draft was not quite so centrist or sexist as was expected, thanks largely to the entry of a third faction: women delegates, backed by ethnic Hazaras and Uzbeks. Womens' basic rights had been ignored by Karzai and his American keepers, but the double-minority Hazaras (Shia Muslims residing in a country that is 84 percent Sunni) have a tradition of being more open to women, as indicated by the percent of their female registered voters: 41 percent, as opposed to 7 percent in Pashtun areas. Zalmay Khalilzad lauds the American role in fostering democracy,[45] but the fact that women and minorities will have at least a nominal place in this government owes everything to local reformists who dared to speak out. Most were less inspired by any Western influence, let alone American influence, than by homegrown civil Islam, rooted in the traditions of Central Asia as opposed to Saudi Wahhabism and hence Talibanism.

Karzai, to be sure, charges that the followers of his nemesis Rabbani are the uncivil ones. But it must not be forgotten that Karzai was a strong supporter of the Taliban when it served his interest. His effective control over key constitutional committees prompted a December boycott of 200 non-Pashtun delegates from a crucial charter vote. Rabbani cogently argued that Karzai's program lays a foundation for future dictatorship. By backing the Karzai faction under these circumstances, the U.S. and the UN are once again compromising the democratic principles they claim to uphold. But in this case it hardly matters, since the constitution will have little application outside the capital. Like the road to Kandahar, the Loya Jirga amounted to a thinly paved media event. The central question is not, as Western pundits would have it, whether the new Afghan government will be secular or Islamic, but whether the Islamism it embraces will be civil or uncivil. With the exception of a small but dramatic gain on the part of women and minorities, the constitutional convention bore all the marks of Talibanization by other means.

Western media were so fixated on Iraq that few noticed the continued deterioration of post-Jirga Afghanistan. Even fewer recognized how U.S. military brutality served the recruiting needs of radical Islamism.[46] Meanwhile, like Chalabi in Iraq, Karzai began to show his true stripes. The one silver lining was that his weakness limited the scope of his corruption and ineptitude. But it also left the central government powerless to stanch the heavy fighting in Herat Province or to prevent the warlord Dostum from seizing control of the capital of Faryab Province in the north, thereby ousting a legally appointed governor. Travel in much of the country remained impossible without a military escort, and was inadvisable under any circumstances along most of the Pakistani border or in the no-man's-land north and east of Kandahar.

Karzai's answer to this crisis is to court what he dubs the "moderate" Taliban, though for women there is no obvious basis for such a distinction. The line between good and bad Taliban comes down to the question of who supports Karzai, not who opposes crimes against humanity. One of Karzai's good guys is none other than Abdul Sayyaf, whose militia, as mentioned before, is famous for mass rape and genocide. When one of Sayyaf's commanders, Abdullah Shah, was convicted of murder, he decided to go out in style: telling the whole story of who gave the orders, who knew about it, etc. Neither Karzai nor his American keepers wanted that story told. Nor did Mawlavi Fazl Hadi Shinwari, the hard-line cleric who at Sayyaf's behest had been appointed chief justice of the Supreme Court. Shinwari in turn installed a host of like-minded mullahs as judges across the country, all of whom hold the power to overrule any law they deem at odds with Islam. Even before the trial was over, Shinwari let it be known that he wanted Shah executed without delay, and we know from Amnesty International that the defendant was allowed no defense counsel or any chance to cross-examine witnesses, as if that could affect the verdict.

As Malalai Joya warned in her brave outburst during the Loya Jirga, Afghanistan is once more in the grip of the Mujahedeen. In the name of stability, America and its allies declare this arrangement a victory over terrorism, as if there is a single woman in Afghanistan who is free of terror. This is the state of affairs that the global community has pledged to underwrite with $4.4 billion in aid and low-cost loans, half of it from the United States, and with a projected $8.2 billion over the next three years. The Bush administration saw no need to attach conditions to this funding, for in its view the country was a success story long before Karzai's victory in the October 2004 presidential election. Let us end on that happy note. We have the word of a U.S. secretary of state that "In a few short years . . . Afghanistan has gone from being a failed state ruled by extremists and terrorists, to a free country with a growing economy and an emerging democracy."[47]

Islamism in Central Asia

American support for the Afghan Mujahedeen in the 1980s and the Taliban in the mid-1990s was at odds with its strong preference for Kemalist anti-Islamism. This animus was reinstated in full force by the "war on terror" that followed 9/11. More than ever the issue of Muslim politics was cast as a fire or ice contest between secular absolutism and radical Islamism: Ataturk or bin Laden. Graham Fuller sees this polarity as a serious misapprehension: "President Bush has repeatedly stressed that the war on terrorism is not a war on Islam. But by seeking to separate Islam from politics, the West ignores the reality that the two are intricately intertwined across a broad swath of the globe from Northern Africa to Southeast Asia." For Fuller the Manichaeism which Bush imposes on the Muslim world, in the name of being "with us or with the terrorists," is in the same spirit as bin Laden's concept of "a struggle between Islam and unbelief."[48]

But this binarism is nothing new. Geopolitical realists have always been wary of Islamic politics, while idealists have seen it as an impediment to democratic development. In fact, the reverse often holds: a lack of democratic development foments the reactionary Islamism which is then blamed for the country's political inertia, not to mention terrorism. A classic case of this "chicken and egg" causality was the Iranian Revolution. While the democratic thrust of the revolution was subverted by Ayatollah Khomeini, it was the prolonged state terrorism of the American implant, Shah Mohammed Reza Pahlevi, that paved the way for Khomeini.

Likewise, centrist repression has invited the rise of uncivil Islam throughout the post-Soviet sphere. Nowhere is this radical reflex more obvious than in Chechnya. It should be stressed that the Chechen separatism that took shape under Jokhar Dudayev in the early 1990s was motivated by nationalist rather than radical Islamic sentiments. Though Chechens were repelled by Dudayev's increasingly despotic rule, they preferred it to Russian rule. Their victory in the 1994–1996 war wrecked the country, however, and the resulting instability invited both warlordism and the militant radical Islamism that spilled over into Dagestan under the joint leadership of Shamil Basayev and the Afghan veteran Ibn ul-Khattab. Only at this point did Chechnya come under the shadow of the kind of jihadism that the Russians have falsely portrayed as the essence of Chechnyan insurgency.

This picture not only ignores the long history of Chechnyan resistance to the Romanovs and Soviets, but also the Sufi Islamic inspiration behind that separatism. Sufism provides a natural buffer against the kind of Islamic fundamentalism that one associates with Afghan Talibanism or Iranian theocracy. There is no denying that fundamentalist elements have played a key role in the current Chechnyan uprising, but, as Rajan Menon explains, those elements could not long survive the restoration of peace and stability: "What animates the Chechen struggle against Russia is not an imported Wahhabi coterie but a homegrown nationalism that is a product of the centuries-long struggle with Russia. Putin's war will only improve fundamentalist Islam's prospects in Chechnya; its brutalities will favor hard men who . . . favor neither secularism nor negotiations with Russia; theirs is a war of the faithful, and compromise is tantamount to faithlessness."[49]

A similar reflex is seen in Azerbaijan's current malaise, which is not so much a case of Islam defiling politics as politics (or the lack thereof) radicalizing Islam. There are many opposition parties here, yet their agendas (due in large part to their need for Western support) are often difficult to distinguish from that of the ruling New Azerbaijan Party (NAP). Until recently NAP was firmly under the grip of the ailing President Heidar Aliyev. On October 15, 2003, his son Ilham Aliyev, who had only recently been made the country's premier, easily won the presidential elections. He will doubtless perpetuate his father's policies, and the West will not protest this nepotism so long as the flow of Caspian oil and natural gas goes as scheduled.[50]

It is enough that the outward trappings of democratic process are on display. Indeed, the blatant fraudulence of the October election did not prevent the U.S. and the EU from instantly affirming the presidency of Aliyev II, their new crony. So, too, they looked on passively as 190 members of opposition parties were arrested in the week following the election. Hopes for a revote died away as the key geopolitical players—the United States, the EU, Turkey, and Russia—upheld the new regime.[51]

The Azerbaijani public, however, is losing hope in both its own political mechanisms and in the good intentions of the West. Many now feel that no matter which party prevails it is the Baku-Ceyhan pipeline that will win, not the people. Their desperate search for alternatives makes it almost certain that the Azerbaijan Islamic Party, which was banned in 1996, will be resurrected in some form. Although a mere 6 percent of those polled in a 1997 survey saw themselves as devout Muslims,[52] the absence of substantive democratic politics is creating the environment for an Islamic awakening, and there is little chance it will be the civil Islamic variety.

Islamism plays an even more decisive role in South Central Asia. The key question, however, is *which* Islamism. This is a prime issue in the making of the new Afghan constitution, which stops short of Taliban-style sharia but holds that no law can be contrary to Islam. So, too, judges can be selected for the supreme court who have training only in Koranic law. Afghanistan's chief justice, an Islamic hard-liner, answered questions on the subject by pointing to the Koran on his desk and saying, "This is the only law."[53]

Afghanistan, however, is hardly typical of Central Asia. Elsewhere in the region a civil Islamic compromise was far more promising after the Cold War. Unfortunately the same dictators who cracked the door on capitalism—such as Uzbekistan's Islam Karimov and Turkmenistan's Saparmurat Niyazov[54]—were determined to lock the door on Islam as a catalyst for democracy. Even Kyrgyzstan's Askar Akayev, who recognized the utility of Islam as a surrogate bonding agent in the absence of Soviet ideology,[55] ultimately slammed that door.

In the face of a regional Islamic revival, recycled Soviet leaders tried to adopt the persona of born-again Muslims, opening meetings and public speeches with passages from the Koran. Yet despite their feeble attempts at state-managed Islam, none of these states—with the exception of Tajikistan, whose political crisis forced it to legalize the popular Islamic Renaissance Party (IRP)—has come close to bridging the religious/secular gap. Most have neglected resurgent Islamic forms such as Sufism,[56] while banning political Islamism altogether. That ban, however, was only effective against moderate religious forms that could have served as a buffer against militant Islamism. Already by 1992 this foreign import was finding a home in the political underground of post-Soviet Asia.[57]

After seventy-four years of Soviet religious repression, it is understandable that the Muslim populations of Central Asia have lost sight of their own moderate traditions of Islam. Radical fundamentalist imports are quick to fill that void, abetted by regimes that are as tone deaf to religion in general as the Soviets were. These governments are at a vital crossroads. They can either accommodate civil Islamism, as Tajikistan finally did, or follow Uzbekistan in combating it utterly. In the absence of democratic political development, neither strategy is likely to work against radical Islamisms such as the HT (the Hizb ut-Tahrir al-Islami) or the IMU (Islamic Movement of Uzbekistan), which easily insinuate themselves where hope has been lost domestically.

On the surface, HT appears rather innocuous, having split with more radical Islamisms on the issue of violence. And compared to its fellow Wahhabisms, HT seems culturally porous. Ahmed Rashid observes that its success in the heart of Central Asia (it is the most popular form of Islamism in Uzbekistan, Kyrgyzstan, and Tajikistan) stems from its compromise position regarding modernity. Far from spurning all Western achievements, it incorporates some of them into its vision of a twenty-first-century caliphate. This relative openness should not, however, be confused with liberal tolerance. HT's strategy is to turn Western technologies against Western civilization.[58]

This veiled bellicosity becomes more overt in the movement's attitude toward non-Western competitors such as Sufism, Zoroastrianism, and Jadidism; and like all Wahhabisms HT is rabidly anti-Shia, going so far as to advocate the expulsion of all Shia Muslims from Central Asia.[59] That virtual declaration of civil war belies the organization's nonviolent claims. If HT is not a terrorist operation, it certainly is not a civil Islamic one, like the IRP. Some believe it is in fact the IMU's jihadic twin, rather like Sinn Finn and the Irish Republican Army.

Central Asian Cases in Point

That is certainly the view of the post-Soviet governments of Turkmenistan and Uzbekistan. The former has sometimes qualified its anti-Islamism diplomatically, but not domestically. Calling himself "Turkmenbashi" (father of all Turkmen), President Saparmurat Niyazov has all but deified himself, along with his mother, in patent opposition to Koranic precepts. Yet he never joined the anti-Taliban alliance of other Central Asian leaders. This exempted him from Taliban-inspired insurgency, despite the fact that he maintained good relations with the Taliban's arch-enemy, Russia.

The IRP never took hold in Turkmenistan, but its more virulent Islamist rival, the IMU, will not be so easily deflected in a land where grinding poverty and oppression—arguably the worst in Central Asia, with all political parties, meetings, and independent media flatly forbidden—coexist with largely untapped economic and political advantages, e.g., the seventh largest gas reserves in the world and the most ethnically homogeneous population in Central Asia.[60] Here secular and religious reformism are on an equal footing. Whereas Azerbaijan allows no *Islamic* opposition party, Turkmenistan allows no opposition whatsoever. Niyazov has earned the distinction of being listed by Freedom House as one of the world's eight worst tyrants.

Uzbekistan, meanwhile, finds favor with Washington by keeping its domestic and foreign anti-Islamism in perfect harmony. The neo-Soviet regime of Islam Karimov is the Bush administration's idea of a trustworthy ally. No religious practice is beyond suspicion here—except of course the government-sponsored version, comparable to the state-supervised Buddhism of Tibet under its present Chinese occupation. Lawrence Uzzell, president of the International Religious Freedom Watch, notes that it is not a healthy time to be either a devout Muslim or Christian in Uzbekistan. Simply to wear clothing indicative of Muslim piety can attract police attention.

The fall of the Taliban in Afghanistan should have relaxed these pressures, but the bottom line is that the government is as concerned about civil Islam as about its militant alternative. Karimov's conflation of the two, in the name of anti-terrorism, wins him U.S. support while smoke screening his general repression. One reason he gets away with this subterfuge is that the Uzbek population is not inclined to mix religion and politics. Even in the midst of the religious revival of the 1990s, a survey revealed that only 11 percent of Uzbeks thought an Islamic state desirable. While Karimov has personal reason to fear radical groups after an assassination attempt on him in February 1999, he has depended on that very militancy to justify his blanket crackdown on civil liberties.[61]

In 2000 the United States classified the IMU as a terrorist group, opening the door for increased cooperation between American and Uzbek security services. But from other quarters international pressure was building against the government's heinous policies. On September 1, 2001, the tenth anniversary of Uzbek independence, Karimov found it expedient to release 25,000 prisoners, and to reduce the sentences of another 25,000. Tellingly, the 7,000 held for membership in Islamic groups received no such clemency. The domestic question was how far this anti-Islamism could be pushed, for Uzbekistan had long been a bastion of Islamic culture and piety in Central Asia.[62] Equating anti-terrorism and anti-Islamism could backfire.

Indifferent to such cultural particulars, post-9/11 Washington has encouraged a shotgun approach to anti-terrorism. Thus Karimov has won support for what he would be doing anyway. It was not only for ethnic reasons that he supported the Uzbek warlord Dostam over Rabbani and Massoud in the

Afghan civil war. The key point was that the ruthless Dostam lacked all Islamic conviction.[63] Ironically, the Uzbek population's support for the government's religious policy is born out of its civil Islamic abhorrence of terrorism. So too this has cushioned the impact of Karimov's foreign policy. At a time when the U.S. entry into Afghanistan was inspiring riots throughout the Muslim world, American forces met little hostility here.

Beneath this placid surface, however, there are signs of growing unrest. Clearly it is not just religious appeal that advances the HT and IMU cause in Uzbekistan. In a country that has had no legal opposition since the early 1990s, radical Islamism is the only politically viable option. In that respect Karimov has been the IMU's best recruiting agent, and also the main reason for HT's drift away from its official tenet of nonviolent tactics.[64] The Taliban was of course pleased to fan these flames, in Kyrgyzstan as well as Uzbekistan.

The only real moderating influence on Karimov's regime is the United States, whose strategic backing is vital to the country's economy as well as its defense. Unfortunately U.S. criticism of the dictatorship has been mild to the point of endorsement. Since 1999 American Special Forces have been garrisoned in Tashkent to train the Uzbek army on how to better combat the IMU. But of course this knowledge can be applied against *any* armed resistance. Since nonviolent resistance to Karimov is almost impossible, Washington is in the morally derelict position of supporting a neo-Stalinist regime against any challenge whatsoever.

By contrast, the British ambassador, Craig Murray (soon to be ex-ambassador, thanks to his stridently unconventional style),[65] recently threw a bolt into the diplomatic gears at a function attended by ranking Uzbeks. Just after his U.S. counterpart gave his typical speech crediting Uzbek progress on human rights, Murray rose to blast the lack of such progress.[66] Still, much was left unsaid. Unconditional U.S. aid has given Karimov a new lease on oppression. Just days after 9/11, Washington was pressing Tashkent for landing and basing rights. Their price, in addition to hard cash, would be U.S. silence in the face of Karimov's human rights violations. Shortly after the Washington-Tashkent deal was announced on October 12, 2001, Dilip Hiro noted the irony that America's so-called "Enduring Freedom" campaign in Afghanistan was launched on the shoulders of two archetypal dictators—Musharraf and Karimov.[67]

The two differ significantly, however, in their religious politics. Musharraf cannot afford to equate anti-terrorism with anti-Islamism, whereas Karimov arrests people for attending unlicensed religious services, wearing religious attire, or even praying alone. Matt Bivens reports the case of a professor whose son was arrested on the charge of attending the wrong mosque. He confessed to being a terrorist after forty-three days of gruesome interrogation, during which time he had his fingernails torn out and pins inserted in his bleeding wounds. When he pointed out to the court that his confession was obviously coerced, the judge replied that "As long as it is written, it is so." He got six years. Had he been charged with possessing HT leaflets, it could have been twenty. The police keep HT fliers in stock to plant on those they happen to dislike, such as the human rights activist Ismail Adilov.[68]

The United States has implicitly recommended this "fortress Uzbekistan" role model to Central Asia, complete with a penal system that not only tortures prisoners but persecutes their families and friends.[69] While the war in Iraq is rationalized on the grounds of democracy promotion (now that the weapons of mass destruction argument has collapsed), Uzbekistan is trusted precisely because of its ersatz parliament, its dearth of independent media, and its anti-Islamist hard line. The message from Washington to Central Asia has been clear: to be on our gift list, do as Karimov does. The payback came in the weeks following the Iraq invasion, when Uzbekistan broke ranks with other Central Asian states by not reevaluating its U.S. ties.[70]

Only the growing success of the IMU induced Karimov to slightly relax his ban on secular opposition parties such as Erk and Birlik, so as to split the opposition.[71] This trace of tolerance was retracted in 2003. In the worst crackdown since 1999, political activists and any journalists worthy of the name were subjected to arrests, beatings, and a continuous barrage of intimidation. It began in May with the arrest of Ruslan Sharipov, a human rights advocate. To spare his mother and friends a similar fate, Sharipov confessed to charges of homosexuality. One of his defenders was nevertheless kidnapped and brutally beaten. In August a prominent journalist was arrested and beaten after heroin was planted in his car by the police, and meanwhile an Erk Party leader disappeared. Two others—a human rights leader and a BBC journalist—were attacked by a staged mob, as the police looked on approvingly.[72]

In effect, Washington looked on approvingly. Doubtless, in the midst of its new Iraq quagmire,[73] the Bush administration would have preferred that Karimov use more subtle means; but the end product of his domestic brutality was very much in line with the U.S. game plan.[74] Karimov has underscored his "fortress" mentality by laying land mines and erecting fences along Uzbekistan's borders with Kyrgyzstan and Tajikistan. None of this will deter radical Islamists, but it will very effectively split families and obstruct cross-border trade.[75] The dictator's aversion to these two countries is understandable: Kyrgyzstan has been Central Asia's model of general reformism, while Tajikistan has offered a prototype for civil Islamic inclusion. Both models are now at risk domestically, but Karimov is taking no chances.

At the time of its independence in the fall of 1991, Kyrgyzstan established its uniqueness among the old Soviet under-states of Central Asia by electing a noncommunist president, Askar Akayev, a former associate of the acclaimed Soviet physicist-turned-dissident Andrei Sakharov. Cut off from Soviet aid, and facing gargantuan economic problems, Akayev looked to the West for assistance. He drew applause in 1993 for becoming the first Central Asian leader to privatize his economy along the lines of IMF restructuration, and in 1998 he took Kyrgyzstan into the World Trade Organization. International acclaim, however, did not translate into multinational investment, and soon the country was also the regional leader in per capita debt.[76] Political unrest grew along with poverty, forcing Akayev to decide which meant more to him, the reforms he had inaugurated, or his hold on power.

That was easy enough. Akayev struck not only at progressive politics, but also at religious tolerance. Ironically this drew immediate international support from the United States, as well as Russia and China. As Akayev joined his neighbors in rigging elections and choking off dissent, U.S. Secretary of State Madeleine Albright arrived with promises of military assistance. The lesson was obvious: even in Kyrgyzstan, one of the least Islamized states of Central Asia, an Islamic threat must be conjured up to achieve the insider status that anti-communist authoritarians enjoyed during the Cold War. The name of the game, in this Cold War II scenario, is anti-terrorism, which for all practical purposes amounts to anti-Islamism. It was only when Akayev abandoned democratization that the IMU started to gain popularity here.[77] And only then did the West take Akayev fully under its wing.

The revelation that anti-Islamism is a geopolitical gold-mine is not comforting to countries that have experienced little Islamic resistance or have dealt with it successfully. Tajikistan looked like the prototypic success story after its 1992–1997 civil war, when the United Tajik Opposition (UTO) forced Islamic concessions from the post-Soviet government.[78] Those reforms seemed to assuage Muslim hopes for a democratic solution to their grievances. This posed an ideological conundrum for Tajikistan's neo-Stalinist neighbors by ushering in an even more dreadful threat than radical Islam. The specter of *civil* Islam now haunts all Central Asian regimes, not to mention their corporate cronies in the West. Though fighting continues with Muslim rebels under the UTO label, a 1997 accord guarantees the IRP a 30 percent share in government posts and representation.

At first President Imomali Rahmonov could not ignore this agreement, but after 9/11 the international climate allowed him to cheat more openly, blaming his recidivism on connections between the IRP and the IMU. Given the fact that secular reformism has no cultural roots in Tajikistan, and has declined in recent years, to clip the IRP's wings is to strike a blow against democratization as well. Much is at stake here for the whole region, since Tajikistan is the only Central Asian country that allows an Islamic party full political participation.[79] Without the government's IRP bargain, Muslim leaders could see militant resistance as their only viable alternative.

To ward off the threat of both civil and uncivil Islam, Central Asian regimes are resorting to the tactics of co-optation perfected by Mahathir in Malaysia and Suharto in Indonesia. Many experts believe the Tajik government is in league with the Tajik Council of Ulems in its decision to bar women from worshipping in mosques. As in Afghanistan, women are often the agents of democratic change. Barring them from mosques is a thinly disguised way of keeping them out of politics, since the mosque often doubles as a center of political activism.

So far Kazakhstan has not had to face the full brunt of the Islamic Revival. President Nursultan Nazarbayev has not needed the iron-fist anti-Islamism of a Niyazov or Karimov. Neither has he met the kind of secular democratic resistance that took Eduard Shevardnadze down, although the late 2004 democratic revolution in Ukraine did give a boost to the opposition, prompting Nazarbayev to dissolve the leading opposition party and to crack down on other reformists, for which actions he was rewarded with a generous gas deal from Russia's Putin. The opposition is stymied, for Kazakhstan's nomadic traditions render it more conservative and hence more culturally resistant to the IMU and other militant Islamisms.[80] But even here the attraction of radical Islamism is enhanced by political repression. A moderate opposition party, the Democratic Choice of Kazakhstan (DCK), was formed in November 2001, but its leaders have been subjected to continued abuse.[81] The government would not be the only winner in a DCK defeat. Militant Islamism would also profit, and the two victors would benefit from each other. Like other neo-Stalinist leaders of the region, Nazarbayev is coming to depend on the threat of radical Islamism as a cover for ruthless practices.

The value of this camouflage is obvious in the case of Georgia's recent "velvet revolution," where Shevardnadze did not have radical Islamism as an excuse for "emergency" measures. Nor could he expect to be propped up by the United States, as other oil magnates have been, since he had allowed Russia's energy giants to pull the strings in that sector. He got little in return for indenturing himself to Moscow. The belated arrival of dozens of Russian special operations units in Thilisi could not save him from massive risings in the streets in November 2003.[82]

There is less chance of a potent secular challenge in Kazakhstan. To inoculate himself against religious reformism, Nazarbayev makes a show of his own ornamental religiosity. In September 2003 he sponsored the Congress of World and Traditional National Religions, where well-screened Islamic representatives from Saudi Arabia, Egypt, Indonesia, Iran, and Pakistan were joined by an assortment of Buddhist and Christian delegates. Substantial funding has been offered by Iran to promote more such meetings, in keeping with President Khatami's belief in the importance of a dialogue of civilizations.[83] Nazarbayev's religious congress, however, is a staged dialogue whose whole point—like the "air-conditioned Islam" of Egypt's bourgeois salons—is its silence on the issue of political Islamism.

Turkey after Kemalism

Conversely, the Islamic revival that is sweeping most of Eurasia has a pronounced grassroots dimension. Even in Turkey, the birthplace of Kemalism, pure secularism has lost much of its allure after decades of economic dysfunction. Many unemployed Turkish youth are turning to Islam, while Iranian youth seem to be moving in the opposite direction. What the two have in common is opposition to the status quo.

This shift was marked by the sweeping victory of Turkey's Justice and Development Party (AKP) in the November 2002 legislative elections. The AKP's moderate stance is suggested by its dual impact: its triumph has hurt both the Islamic old guard of Necmettin Erbakan's Welfare Party and the secular establishment of the military and judiciary, which banned Welfare after its strong electoral showing of 1995. Under Recep Tayyip Erdogan, the AKP represents a new breed of Islamism: culturally conservative without being fundamentalist, and reformist without being ideologically strident. As such it can muster a much broader political base.

Secularists, of course, accuse the AKP of being a Muslim Trojan horse; but the party is clearly more interested in ties with the West, and specifically with the EU, than in courting Muslim nations, as Erbakan did.[84] Granted, like most germinal democratic movements, the AKP is a mixed bag. Its conservatism is more ingrained than its still untested liberalism. Two important tests will be its treatment of the Kurds and its handling of the Cyprus issue. It helps that Turkey knows it is being judged by Europe on a more liberal democratic yardstick than the United States ever applied. This confounds those in Central Asia, such as Karimov,[85] who revere Kemalist étatism.

For now Turkey has turned away from militarist secularism as well as panTurkism.[86] Recent terrorist attacks by Islamic extremists underscore, by way of contrast, the civil quality of the AKP, but these could trigger an anti-Islamist response on the part of the military and even the general public. This reactionary reflex—conditioned by fifteen years of war against separatist Kurds—is exactly what Islamic militants want, since it could sabotage the reform movement and drive a wedge between Europe and Turkey. For its part, Europe should remember that Islam itself is not the problem. During the Inquisition, countless Jews fled Europe to take refuge in the far more tolerant Ottoman Empire. Jews and Muslims have peacefully coexisted in Turkey since the fifteenth century. Hence the AKP's embrace of civil Islam could revive a tradition whose liberal roots are at least as deep as Europe's.

The United States, unfortunately, has evaluated the AKP and civil Islam in general by a very different standard: the post-9/11 loyalty test. Things got off to a bad start on March 1, 2003, when the AKP-dominated legislature joined Mexico and Chile in defying their superpower ally over Iraq. To Washington's dismay, U.S. forces were denied basing rights by this erstwhile client state. Writing in the *New York Times*, William Safire declared the AKP "Saddam's best friend," as if the post-9/11 world offered but two choices: Bush or Saddam. Deputy Secretary of Defense Paul Wolfowitz went further: denouncing the Turkish military for its failure to overturn this legislative decision.[87]

What Turkey's recalcitrance actually indicates is that civil Islam is conducive to unexpurgated democracy. The problem—as realists such as Kissinger have known all along—is with democracy itself, which is not nearly so tractable or predictable as a good military junta. As of February 2003 these upstart democrats were asking $92 billion for their support, whereas the Americans drew the line at $24 billion.[88] This put even the more astute American empire builders in a bind. They knew that the best defense against radical Islamism is civil Islam, which can also be a roadmap for democratic obstinacy.

So too it pulls the rug out from under the U.S. attempt to promote Turkey as a model of secularity, the antithesis of the Iranian model. In fact, Turkey's civil Islamic synthesis renders it a better bridge between East and West than Kemalism ever was. After eight decades, Ataturk's anti-Islamist barricade is breaking down, but Turkey will have to almost reinvent itself if it is to serve as a prototype for democratization in the Muslim world.[89]

One of the major obstacles to that project is the resistance of militant Islamism to what it sees as the AKP's treasonous tilt toward Europe. The November 2003 terrorist attacks in Istanbul not only sank Erdogan's hopes for a smooth economic recovery (if only because of the damage it will do to the Turkish tourist industry, the source of a third of the nation's foreign currency) but trapped him in a no-man's-land between military secularism and "more Islamic than thou" radicalism. Should he feel compelled to court the military for security reasons, this could injure his standing with the EU, and definitely it would compromise the new Turkish model of civil Islam in Central Asia.

Turkish authorities claim that Hizbullah, the terrorist organization thought to be behind the bombings (which has no known links to the Lebanese organization of the same name), has al Qaeda links. That may be, but it should be noted that this conclusion serves both the domestic and diplomatic interests of the government, which is in the embarrassing position of having employed Hizbullah in its long war with Kurdish nationalists. Turkish security forces turned on their hired monster after it was no longer needed, and now Hizbullah appears to be repaying that betrayal as well as Erdogan's departure from his anti-Western campaign promises.[90]

As Amir Taheri points out, the Islamist undertow is an old story in Turkey. On the secular side it traces to Prime Minister Adnan Menderes, who played the Islamic card and was hanged in 1960 after a military coup. This sword cuts both ways, however. When Prime Minister Suley Demirel played a similar card in the 1970s, he was hounded by Muslims who found him insufficiently Islamic. The deciding factor may now be the relationship of Turkish Islamism and liberalism. In 1996, Erbakan's Rifah (Welfare) Party entered a right-wing coalition that alienated the very constituents on the liberal Left who would be needed as allies against an inevitable military challenge. It remains to be seen if Erdogan can do a better job of keeping moderate Islamism and liberalism under the same roof. The current wave of terrorism is putting that already tenuous union under strain, and Taheri's prognosis is grim. The AKP's survival hinges on whether it can keep its liberal house in order in the face of militant Islamism, which got a huge boost from the U.S. invasion of Iraq.

Iran's Democratic Impasse: The Limits of Radical Moderation

Civil Islam in Turkey cannot win for losing: its political survival depends on such a heavy dilution of its religious content that its Islamic credentials come into question. Indonesia and Iran may be the only two countries where civil Islam might prosper without compromising itself in this way. From different sides, democratic Islamism is foiled in both cases—in Indonesia by military secularism and in Iran by Shia dogmatism. Breaking that deadlock will not be easy, but it helps that in these two cases reform has only the government to fight, not the nation's political culture. It should not be forgotten that Iranian theocracy was grafted onto a democratic revolution, much as the Bolsheviks stole the Russian Revolution from the Mencheviks.

Khomeini brought better organization to the revolution, and unlike secular activists he could issue Koranic fatwas or declare enemies mortad (excommunicated). At first he professed solidarity with other resistance factions, mainly targeting the Shah, the United States, and Israel in his speeches. This tactic afforded rare oppositional unity, as the Shia mullahs who rallied to his cause had been set up by the Shah himself as a barrier to the political Left.[91] Likewise Khomeini gained middle-class support, even among junior military officers, by promising liberation for all Iranians. This inclusivity won out in the short run, but was likely to backfire once his deceit became obvious. What spared him a counterrevolution was Saddam Hussein's attack on Iran in 1980. The ensuing eight-year war drained reformist zeal and cast resistance in an unpatriotic light.

It also pitted two vast propaganda machines against each other: Baathist pan-Arabism and Iranian pan-Islamism.[92] After a poor initial showing—due in no small part to Khomeini's purge of the professional army in favor of his Islamic Revolutionary Guard, or *Sepah*—the tide began to turn early in 1982 as Sepah gained military experience. After eighteen months the Iraqis were expelled and a successful counteroffensive was launched. This fueled nationalist as well as pan-Islamist sentiments, stanching resistance to the theocratic takeover.

With the Iranians on the road to victory, and the world's oil at issue, the Reagan administration threw its support behind Saddam. The tide turned once more as Iraq acquired better weaponry and war materials, including U.S.-supplied dual-use technology that Iraq predictably used to produce chemical and biological weapons.[93] No less important were the diplomatic signals both superpowers sent Iraq that its increasing use of chemical weapons, on its own Kurdish citizens as well as Iranians, would not have serious international repercussions.[94] For once the superpowers agreed on something: that an Iranian victory was against their mutual interest. After Iraq won major victories in 1988, Iran accepted a UN-brokered cease-fire. By then even Khomeini's ardent supporters came to doubt his leadership, but under conditions of bare survival no group was in a position to oppose him openly.

Nevertheless the dismal outcome of the war—which for all its suffering had no real victor—sustained a tempered reformism in the form of civil Islam. On the surface this religious current seems to run counter to the cultural demographics of youth: with over half of Iran's 65 million population under twenty-five, the ostensive drift has been toward agnosticism as well as closer ties with the United States. But unlike Turkey's deep-rooted secular tradition, this nascent secularity is mainly reactive:[95] dependent upon theocratic excesses in much the same way that an American youth counterculture was once dependent upon the Vietnam War. Only civil religion can generate the staying power to finish the job.[96]

The reelection of President Mohammad Khatami in 2001 by a large margin, coupled with a new reformist majority in Parliament, raised hopes that a velvet revolution was at hand. Disillusionment set in, however, as the president's helplessness became obvious. By September 2003 Khatami himself had admitted defeat. Clearly the real rulers were inside the unelected Council of Guardians and the judiciary. Voter apathy is understandable, given the council's power to reject any candidate and void all election results. There is simply no "legal" way to depose the theocrats. Some form of non-velvet resistance is necessary, yet the public balks at this thought after the indelible trauma of a revolution gone wrong.

Iranian reformists are caught in an oxymoronic quest for radical moderation. Student protest is too rash and fleeting,[97] while gradualism is too easily monitored and crushed by the council. Nor can outside powers do much. Any such input, especially from the United States, will be seen as invasive. As Whit Mason observes, President Bush all but saved the theocrats in January 2002 by declaring Iran part of his infamous "Axis of Evil." In response, hundreds of thousands of Iranians of all political stripes poured out in February to celebrate the republic's twenty-third anniversary.[98] By July, when Bush called on Iranians to seek "reform from below," he had more than lost his audience.[99]

Nor was this exhortation necessary in a country which since 1890 has had more rebellions and revolutions than any Muslim nation.[100] Early in the twentieth century the Iranians had a constitution and an elected parliament. This development was axed by the Pahlavi dynasty that took over in 1921 under British auspices. Democratization resumed after World War II, only to be jettisoned once more in 1953 through a CIA-engineered coup, after which the United States rushed through a grant-in-aid package of $45 million to secure the royalist regime. Clearly Eisenhower and his henchman John Foster Dulles did not share Truman's reluctance to topple recalcitrant governments[101]— even democratic ones (ten months later he did it again in Guatemala).

Despite their understandable reserve, Iranians are now saying (if only through their refusal to vote) that nothing short of real democracy will suffice. The question is what the target will be when moderation starts to wear thin. The latest wave of reformism was ignited in July 2003 by the brutal death of a Canadian photo journalist, Zahra Kazemi, at the hands of governmental thugs. Iran watchers were shocked by the brazen reaction of reformists. First, an investigation ordered by Khatami revealed that Kazemi did not die of a stroke, as earlier announced, but rather from blows inflicted on her during interrogation. Calls for further investigation followed, not only in reformist media but in an open session of Parliament.[102]

One of Kazemi's defenders, 2003 Nobel laureate Shirin Ebadi, occupies the middle ground in a two-front war on reform. On the one hand she castigates U.S. and Israeli double standards on human rights, while on the other she deplores Iran's theocratic incubus. Like President Khatami she upholds the complementarity of Islam and democracy—that being a central tenet of all civil

Islam. Though most Iranian reformists share this conviction,[103] they are divided over which is the greater evil, the theocratic devil they know or the globalist devil they fear even more, having met its precursor in the forced Westernization of the Shah's White Revolution. In that sense Khomeini's was a counterrevolution—"an aberration to counter an aberration," as Robert Kaplan puts it. For most Iranians its one redeeming feature was that it gave them back something of their autonomy and self-respect.[104] The Bush administration has clumsily reactivated that national reflex, once more turning resistance energies against Washington.

For the moment, reformism seems to be in retreat, but for Ayatollah Moussavi Tabrizi its success is marked by its imprint on parts of the theocracy itself.[105] Tabrizi stands with a host of progressive-minded clerics, such as Grand Ayatollah Saanei (former head of the judiciary under Khomeini), Abdollah Nouri (the former interior minister under Khatami), Grand Ayatollah Ali Hossein Montazeri (a leading critic of Khomeini's successor Ali Khamenei), and Mohsen Kadivar (a pro-democratic theologian imprisoned for his Koranic opposition to theocratic rule).[106] Even nonprogressives recognize that sooner or later a real revolution will erupt if reform is not forthcoming. But whether Iranian democracy comes the soft or hard way, it will not come by way of a made-in-Washington implant such as Baghdad is now suffering.

Conclusion

The driving force behind this implant strategy has been an almost indiscriminate anti-Islamism, which in the present Muslim context is tantamount to anti-democratism. Reza Aslan points out that Americans have difficulty grasping the centrality or even the possibility of civil Islamic democracy, even as they accept without question the religious foundations of the Israeli state. This double standard is hard to fathom in view of the fact that America itself began as something of a religious democracy.

There is, to be sure, real danger that Islamist democracy could take a reactionary turn, but there is no less danger that today's corporate funding of U.S. politics could surrender American institutions to the dictates of a transnational corporate class. The two dangers are dialectically linked, for global corporatism is well aware that its foremost enemy is Islamism, and vice versa. That is why Washington invested so much in the Shah, and, failing that, in Saddam Hussein. And that is why it can unabashedly support a neo-Stalinist such as Karimov. Unless U.S. policymakers can come to grips with Islamic reform politics, it is a safe bet they will soon be asking, "Who lost Central Asia?"

Notes

1. On Washington's post-Taliban designs see Patrick Martin, "Oil Company Adviser Named US Representative to Afghanistan," *World Socialist Web Site* (January 3, 2002), <www.wsws.org/articles/2002/jan2002/oil-j03.shtml>.

2. Chalmers Johnson, *Blowback: The Costs and Consequences of American Empire* (New York: Henry Holt, 2000), 10.

3. The term "Northern Alliance" was born of Pakistani propaganda, which sought to portray Massoud's resistance as nothing more than the rise of disgruntled ethnic minorities. In fact, it was the Taliban that deserved this "minority" criticism. The Taliban's popularity never went deep, even among Pashtuns, many of whom turned against it in November 2001 as the alliance closed in on Kandahar. See Michael E. O'Hanlons, "A Flawed Masterpiece," *Foreign Affairs* 81, no. 3 (May/June 2002): 53 (47–63).

4. Kathy Gannon, "Taliban Seeks Friendship with U.S.," *The Nando Times*, from the Associated Press (July 31, 2001), <www.nandotimes.com/world/story/53212p-787383c.html>.

5. Ahmed Rashid, "On the Spot," *The Far Eastern Economic Review* (October 19, 2000), <www.feer.com/ _0010_19/p28region.html>.

6. Of course, as the American press tells it, it was the United States that sought a negotiated solution and the Taliban which rebuffed it: "U.S. attempts to negotiate with the Taliban earlier this year to have it expel bin Laden failed. . . ." See Bob Woodward and Vernon Loeb, "CIA's Covert War on bin Laden," *Washington Post* (September 14, 2001): A01.

7. Bin Laden was introduced to the Taliban in 1996 by Pakistan's ISI, which later refused to assist in his capture. See Ahmed Rashid, *Taliban: Militant Islam, Oil and Fundamentalism in Central Asia* (New Haven, CN: Yale University Press, 2000), 180–81.

8. E.g., Matthew Riemer, "Prioritizing Pakistan at the Expense of Afghanistan," *Power and Interest News Report* (September 4, 2003), <www.pinr.com/report.php?ac=view_printable&report_id=86&language_id=1>.

9. In *Bin Laden, la verite interdite*, journalist Guillaume Dasquie and former French intelligence officer Jean-Charles Brisard spotlight the robust courtship of President Bush and the Taliban. John O'Neill, the FBI's former director of anti-terrorism, is quoted as charging deliberate U.S. State Department interference with the hunt for Osama bin Laden. See Marjorie Cohen, "The Deadly Pipeline War: U.S. Afghan Policy Driven by Oil Interests," *Jurist* (December 7, 2001), <//jurist.law.pitt.edu/forum/forumnew41.php. More likely the State Department simply differed with the tactics being employed. The hard truth, as Syed Saleem Shahzad puts it, is that U.S. intelligence has no idea what is happening within Taliban or al Qaeda ranks. See Shahzad, "US Shooting in the Dark in Afghanistan," *Asia Times* (June 28, 2003), <www.atimes.com/atimes/Central_Asia/EF28Ag01.html>.

10. Erich Marquardt, "Taking the Initiative: Washington in Central Asia," *Power and Interest News Report* (September 18, 2003), <www.pinr.com/report.php?ac=view_printable&report_id=93&language_id=1>.

11. The Soviet invasion took place on December 24, 1979, yet President Carter had already authorized aid to the Afghan opposition on July 3. See "Afghan Islamism Was Made in Washington: Interview with Zbigniew Brzezinski. . . ." *Emperor's Clothes* (from *Le Nouvel Observateur* interview of January 15–21, 1998, p. 76; translated by Bill Blum), <emperors-clothes.com/interviews/brz.htm>.

12. Johnson, *Blowback*, 10–11.

13. Both were former enemies of Massoud. The famously unscrupulous Dostum, a Uzbek, had been a commander under the communist regime, while Khan had better credentials but had been defeated by the Taliban in 1996. See Antonio Giustozzi, "Afghanistan: The Problems of Creating a New Afghan Army," New Nations special report (2003) from *Newnations.com*.

14. Suresh Jaura, "Afghanistan Oil and USA: The Importance of Afghanistan to the New Great Game," *South Asian Outlook: An Independent e-Monthly* (December 2001), <www.southasianoutlook.com/sao_back_issues/december_2001/af_oil_usa.htm>.

15. Norimitsu Onishi, "Gains by Northern Alliance Mean Losses by Pakistan," *New York Times* (November 13, 2001), <www.nytimes.com/2001/11/13/international/asia/13BEAC.html>.

16. Ahmed Rashid, "Taliban Stepping Up Attacks against Targets in Afghanistan," *Eurasianet.org* (July 28, 2003), <www.eurasianet.org/departments/insight/articles/eav072803_pr.shtml>.

17. Ahmed Rashid, "Islamabad's Lingering Support for Islamic Extremists Threatens Pakistan-Afghanistan Ties," *Eurasianet.org* (July 23, 2003), <www.eurasianet.org/departments/insight/articles/eav072803a_pr.shtml>.

18. Patrick E. Tyler and David E. Sanger, "Pakistan Called Libyans' Source of Atom Design," *New York Times* (January 6, 2004), <www.nytimes.com/2004/01/06/international/middleeast/06NUKE.html>.

19. Gore Vidal, *Dreaming War: Blood for Oil and the Cheney-Bush Junta* (New York: Thunder Mouth Press/Nation Books, 2002), 20.

20. Vidal, *Dreaming War*, 40–41.

21. Pankaj Mishra, "The Afghan Tragedy," *The New York Review of Books* (January 17, 2002), <www.nybooks.com/articles/15113>.

22. Jan Goodwin, "Buried Alive: Afghan Women under the Taliban," *On the Issue* (February 27, 1998), <www.echonyc.com/~onissues/su98goodwin.html>.

23. Rashid, *Taliban*, 26 and 29.

24. See Tim Weiner, "Afghan Arabs Said to Lead Taliban's Fight," *New York Times* (November 10, 2001), <www.nytimes.com/2001/11/10/international/asia/10ARAB.html>.

25. Rashid, *Taliban*, 34.

26. Rashid, *Taliban*, 53. The world remained largely indifferent. Roaring '90s America had long since turned the channel from events in Afghanistan, and later that year the Asian Crash cornered the market on Asian anxieties. Massoud's plight got more attention in France than in the United States, where his determined resistance was a thorn in the side of the stability the corporate world expected in return for its pro-Taliban lobbying efforts.

27. Ahmed Rashid, *Jihad: The Rise of Militant Islam in Central Asia* (New Haven, CT: Yale University Press, 2002), 5.

28. Zbigniew Brzezinski, *The Grand Chessboard: American Primacy and Its Geostrategic Imperatives* (New York: Basic Books, 1997), 139.

29. Rashid, "On the Spot."

30. Rashid, "On the Spot."

31. Inside Pakistan they were never out of action, despite President Musharraf's promise of January 2002 to register all madrassas and to monitor the political activities of both madrassas and mosques. Two years later, no such action had been taken, and the clergy was assured that it would not be. See Samina Ahmed, "Pakistan's Unkept Promise: The Untamed Madrasas," *International Herald Tribune* (January 26, 2004), <www.iht.com/cgi-bin/generic.cgi?template=articleprint.tmplh&ArticleId=126492>.

32. "Two Days of Armed Struggle in Afghanistan Leaves 115 Dead," *Afghan.com* (August 16, 2003), <www.Afghan.com/?af=printnews+sid=36417>.

33. Two and a half million Afghan refugees have returned from Pakistan and Iran, while another 500,000 people are displaced internally. See "U.N. Refugee Agency Pulls Staff from Afghanistan," *New York Times* (November 18, 2003), <www.nytimes.com/aponline/international/AP-Afghan-UN-Withdrawal.html>.

34. Carlotta Gall and Amy Waldman, "Afghanistan Faces a Test in Democracy," *New York Times* (December 15, 2003), <www.nytimes.com/2003/12/15/international/asia/15AFGH.html>; also Nicholas D. Kristof, "Seizing Failure in Afghanistan," *The International Herald Tribune* (November 17, 2003), <www.iht.com/cgi-bin/generic.cgi?template=articleprint.tmplh&ArticleId=117841>; and "Publisher's Overview December 03," at www.Newnations.com. Today's opium production level is thirty-six times higher than in the Taliban's last year in power, that being an indication of how badly the Taliban wanted a reconciliation with Washington. On the present poppy boom see "Afghan Poppy Crop Leaping," *MSNBC News* (November 28, 2003), <www.msnbc.com/news/999130.asp?ocv=CB10>.

35. H. D. S. Greenway, "Afghan Narcotics Add to Woes," *Boston Globe* (January 22, 2004), <www.bostonglobe.com/news/globe/editorial_opinion/oped/articles/2004/01/22/afghan_narcotics_add_to_woes/>

36. Ahmed Rashid, "Afghanistan: Pashtun Push," *The Far Eastern Economic Review* (September 19, 2002), <www.feer.com/articles/2002/0209_19/p022region.html>.

37. See "Afghanistan's Long Journey," *The Economist* (December 17, 2003), <economist.com/agenda/PrinterFriendly.cfm?Story_ID=2281858>.

38. "All Our Hopes Are Crushed: Violence and Repression in Western Afghanistan," *Human Rights Watch* 14, no. 7 (November 2002): 6 (1–52).

39. Victoria Hobson and Constance Borde, "Mobilizing in the Land of the Burka," *International Herald Tribune* (December 18, 2003), <www.iht.com/cgi-bin/generic.cgi?template=articleprint.tmplh&Article=121864>.

40. Ahmed Rashid, "Rebuilding Afghanistan," *The Nation* (January 26, 2004), <www.thenation.com/ docprint.mhtml?i=20040126&s=rashid>.

41. Eric de Laverne, "Une femme défie les moudjahidin," *Libération* (January 5, 2004), <www.liberation.fr/imprimer.php?Article=169082>; and Amy Waldman and Carlotta Gall, "A Young Afghan Dares to Mention the Unmentionable," *New York*

Times (December 18, 2003), <www.nytimes.com/2003/12/18/international/asia/18AFGH.html>.

42. Ahmed Rashid, "The Mess in Afghanistan," *The New York Review of Books* 51, no. 2 (February 12, 2004), <www.nybooks.com/articles/16897>.

43. Julien Bousac, "Afghanistan: Emirate of Herat." Clearly the United States is also playing the old British game of divide and conquer. In Iraq, for example, the British played Kurdish and Shia tribal powers off against their Sunni proxy, King Faisal. See Martin Walker, "The Making of Modern Iraq," *The Wilson Quarterly* (spring 2002), <wwics.si.edu/index.cfm?fuseaction=wq.essay&essay_id=32217>.

44. "Afghan Draft Constitution Worries Civil-Society Advocates," *Eurasianet.org* (November 14, 2003), <www.eurasia.net.org/departments/rights/articles/eav111403_pr.shtml>.

45. Zalmay Khalilzad, "Afghanistan's Milestone," *Washington Post* (January 6, 2004): A17.

46. Zia Sarhadi, "Post-Jirga Politicking in Afghanistan Confirms Problems Facing US," *Muslimedia International* (February 2004), <www.muslimedia.com/afg-postjirga.htm>.

47. Qtd. in Christopher Marquis, "Led by U.S., Nations Pledge Billions to Revive Afghanistan," *New York Times* (April 1, 2004), <www.nytimes.com/2004/04/01/international/asia/01DONO.html>. This optimism fits a pattern. From an early stage in Powell's career he mastered the art of whitewash, and in Vietnam he played a key role in the coverup of the pattern of atrocities associated with the My Lai massacre. He ardently defended "drain-the-sea" tactics whereby villages suspected of supporting the Viet Cong were torched, and never wavered in his depiction of U.S. and South Vietnamese military relations as "excellent." See Robert Parry and Norman Soloman, "Behind Colin Powell's Legend—My Lai," *The Consortium* (1996), <www.consortiumnews.com/archive/colin3.html>.

48. Graham E. Fuller, "The Future of Political Islam," *Foreign Affairs* 81, no. 2 (March/April 2002): 49 and 59 (48–60).

49. Rajan Menon, "Russia's Quagmire: On Ending the Standoff in Chechnya," *Boston Review* (summer 2004), <http://bostonreview.net/BR29.3/menon.html>.

50. "Azerbaijan," *Newnations.com* monthly report, update No. 274 (October 27, 2003), <www.newnations.com/headlines/az.php>.

51. Fariz Ismailzade, "Disillusionment Defines Azerbaijan's Opposition," *Eurasianet.org* (November 13, 2003), <www.eurasianet.org/departments/insight/articles/eav111303_pr.shtml>.

52. Daan van der Schriek, "Little to Lose: Opposition in Azerbaijan," *Eurasianet.org* (February 3, 2003), <www.eurasianet.org/departments/rights/articles/eva020303_pr.shtml>.

53. See Preeta D. Bansal and Felice D. Gaer, "Silenced Again in Kabul," *New York Times* (October 1, 2003), <www.nytimes.com/2003/10/01/opinion/01BANS.html>.

54. Shafiqul Islam, "Capitalism on the Silk Route," in Michael Mandelbaum, ed., *Central Asia and the World: Kazakhstan, Uzbekistan, Tajikistan, Kyrgyzstan, and Turkmenistan* (New York: Council on Foreign Relations Press, 1994), 168–69 (147–76).

55. V. F. Kovalskii, "Democratic Declarations and Political Realities," in Alexei Vassiliev, ed., *Central Asia: Political and Economic Challenges in the Post-Soviet Era* (London: Saqi Books, 2001), 239 (235–51).

56. This post-Soviet revival marks the regeneration of Persian traditions in Tajikistan, Uzbekistan, and Azerbaijan. See Jehangir Pocha, "Iran's Other Religion," *Boston Review: A Political and Literary Review* (summer 2003), <bostonreview.net/BR28.3/pocha.html>.

57. Rashid, *Jihad*, 55–56.

58. Rashid, *Jihad*, 115 and 120–21.

59. Rashid, *Jihad*, 122–23.

60. Rashid, *Jihad*, 74, 77, and 102.

61. Ted Weihman, "Uzbek Crackdown Deepens Diplomatic Dilemma for United States," *Eurasianet.org* (September 10, 2003), <www.eurasianet.org/departments/rights/articles/eva091003_pr.shtml>.

62. Rustam Mukhamedov, "Can Islam Be a Strong Opposition Force in Uzbekistan?" *Central Asia-Caucasus Analyst* (October 22, 2003), <www.cacianalyst.org/view_article.php?articleid=1840>.

63. However, after the Taliban took Kabul and advanced northward, Karimov relaxed his opposition to Massoud. See Zalmay Khalilzad, "Anarchy in Afghanistan," *Journal of International Affairs* 51, no. 1 (summer 1997): 51 (37–56).

64. Alisher Khamidov, "Hizb-ut Tahrir Faces Internal Split in Central Asia," *Eurasianet.org* (October 21, 2003), <www.eurasianet.org/departments/insight/articles/eav202103_pr.shtml>.

65. Nick Paton Walsh, "The Envoy Who Said Too Much," *Guardian* (July 15, 2004), <www.guardian.co.uk/print/0,3858,4971166-103680,00.html>.

66. David Sterne, "British Envoy's Speech Reverberates in Uzbekistan," *Eurasianet.org* (January 14, 2003), <www.eurasianet.org/departments/rights/articles/eav011403_pr.shtml>. In fact, even the U.S. State Department has made this point in its annual human rights report. See Bruce Pannier, "Central Asia: State Department Sees Little Improvement in Rights Situation," *Eurasianet.org* (April 5, 2003), <www.eurasianet.org/departments/rights/articles/eav040503_pr.shtml>.

67. Dilip Hiro, "Bush's Uzbek Bargain," *The Nation* (October 17, 2001), <www.thenation.com/docPrint. mhtml?i=special&s=hiro20011017>.

68. Adilov was released after two years due to U.S. State Department pressure, proving what a modicum of human rights engagement can accomplish. See Matt Bivens, "Uzbekistan's Human Rights Problem," *The Nation* (2001), <www.thenation.com/docPrint.mhtml?I=special&s=birens20011030>.

69. This has provoked hunger strikes among prisoners, such as those at the infamous Yaslyk prison in the Karakalpakstan Desert, which is heavily used for political and religious prisoners. See "Prisoners at Notorious Uzbek Prison Declare Hunger Strike," *Central Asia-Caucasus Analyst* (October 27, 2003), <www.cacianalyst.org/view_article.php?articleid=1886>.

70. Konstantin Parshin, "Iraq War Prompts Most Central Asian Leaders to Reevaluate US Ties," *Eurasianet* (April 4, 2003), <www.eurasianet.org/departments/insight/articles/eav040403_pr.shtml>.

71. Erica Marat, "The Erk Protest Sets a Precedent for Karimov to Revise Relations with Political Opposition," *Central Asian Caucasus Analyst* (November 5, 2003): 9 (9–10).

72. Weihman, "Uzbek Crackdown Deepens Diplomatic Dilemma for United States."

73. International pressure forced Washington to roll back its foreign aid pledge to Uzbekistan as of July 13, 2004, but just two days later Elizabeth Jones, the assistant secretary of state for European and Eurasian affairs, arrived in Tashkent to mollify Karimov. See Yuri Yegorov, "Washington Pushes Karimov Closer to Moscow," *Eurasia Daily Monitor* 1, no. 57 (July 22, 2004), <jamestown.org/publications_details.php?volume_id=401&issue_id=3024&article_id=2368291>.

74. In all fairness it should be mentioned that the State Department has often been at odds (though not often enough, and all too timidly) with the Pentagon over human rights in Central Asia and especially Uzbekistan.

75. Pauline Jones Luong and Erika Weinthal, "New Friends, New Fears in Central Asia," *Foreign Affairs* 81, no. 2 (March/April 2002): 65 (61–70).

76. Rashid, *Jihad*, 68–69.

77. Alisher Khamidov, "Kyrgyzstan: Organized Opposition and Civil Unrest," *Eurasianet.org* (December 16, 2002), <www.eurasia.org/departments/rights/articles/eav121602_pr.shtml>.

78. Nargis Zokirova, "Tajikistan: No Girls Allowed," *Transitions Online* (October 2004), <www.tol.cz/ look/TOL/printf.tpl?IdLanguage=1&IdPublication=4&NrIssue=85&Nr…>.

79. Alexei Igushev, "Tajikistan: Governing Opposition," *Eurasianet.org* (January 6, 2003), <www.eurasianet.org/departments/rights/articles/eav010603_pr.shtml>.

80. HT has found some acceptance in southern Kazakhstan, but it is the long settled Fergana Valley—subsuming parts of Uzbekistan, Tajikistan, and Kyrgyzstan—that has been most prone to the jihadic firestorm from the south. On Kazakh religious conservatism see "Kazakstan," *Newnations.com* update No. 274 (October 27, 2003), <www.newnations.com/headlines/kz.php>.

81. Aidar Kusainov [a pseudonym made necessary by the threat of government reprisals], "Nazarbayev Presses Crackdown against Political Opponents," *Eurasianet.org* (July 27, 2002), <www.eurasianet.org/departments/rights/articles/eav040202.shtml>.

82. Alexander Rondeli, "Georgia: A Rough Road from the 'Velvet Revolution,'" *openDemocracy* (December 4, 2003), <www.opendemocracy.net/debates/article-3-33-1619.jsp>.

86. *Newnations.com* monthly report on Kazakhstan, update no. 274 (October 10, 2003), <www.newnations.com/headlines/kz.php>.

84. Jean-Christopher Peuch, "Turkey: What Remains of Political Islam?" *Eurasianet.org* (January 18, 2003), <www.eurasianet.org/departments/insight/articles/eav011203_pr.shtml>. This is not to say that the AKP has entirely shed the radical Islamist propensities of the Welfare Party. The foreign minister, an AKP stalwart, has lent support to Milli Görüs, a known militant group in Germany. See Daniel Pipes, "The Islamic Republic of Turkey?" *National Post* (August 7, 2003), <www.national-post.com/components/printstory/printstory.asp?id=0c517c2b-028a-4efa-…>. On

Erbakan's Islamist foreign policy see Fawaz A. Gerges, *America and Political Islam: Clash of Cultures or Clash of Interests?* (Cambridge, U.K.: Cambridge University Press, 1999), 209.

85. Paul Kubricek, *Nations, State, and Economy in Central Asia: Does Ataturk Provide a Model?* The Donald Treadgold Papers in Russian, East European, and Central Asian Studies; Jackson School of International Studies, University of Washington, No. 14 (August 1997), 8.

86. On the latter see Mehrdad Haghayeg, *Islam and Politics in Central Asia* (New York: St. Martin's Press, 1996), 183.

87. Noam Chomsky, "Dictators R Us," *AlterNet* (December 21, 2003): <www.alternet.org/story.html? StoryID=17435>.

88. A bonus was thrown in, however: the Turkish army would be let loose on the oil fields of northern Iraq, so as to prevent the Kurds from thinking too concretely about independence. See David Ignatius, "The Turkish Card," *Washington Post* (September 16, 2003): A19.

89. See Stephen Black, "Turkish Political Leaders Face Perilous Political Situation," *Eurasianet.org* (June 26, 2003), <www.eurasianet.org/departments/insight/articles/eav062603_pr.shtml>.

90. "An Islamist Facing Islamic Terrorism," *The Economist* (November 27, 2003), <economist.com/world/Europe/PrinterFriendly.cfm?Story_ID=2250501>; and "Turkey Breaks Up Al Qaeda Cell behind Blasts," *New York Times* (December 26, 2003), <www.nytimes.com/reuters/international-security-turkey.html>.

91. Abbas Milani, "A Revolution Betrayed," *Hoover Digest* (fall 2003), <www-hoover.standford.edu/publications/digest/034/milani.html>.

92. Mohssen Massarrat, "The Ideological Contest of the Iran-Iraq War: Pan-Islamism versus Pan-Arabism," in Hooshang Amirahmad and Nader Entessar, eds., *Iran and the Arab World* (New York: St. Martin's Press, 1993), 29 (28–41).

93. Robert Parry, "Missing U.S.-Iraq History," *In These Times* (December 16, 2003), <www.inthesetimes.com/print.php?id=498_0_1_0>.

94. Reagon's Secretary of State George Shultz and his deputy Donald Rumsfeld, later defense secretary under Bush II, worked hard early in 1984 to reassure the Iraqis that the U.S. did not share the UN's concern over Iraq's continuous use of chemical weapons against Kurds as well as Iranians. See Christopher Marquis, "Rumsfeld Made Iraq Overture in '84 despite Chemical Raids," *New York Times* (December 23, 2003), <www.nytimes.com/2003/12/23/international/middleeast/23RUMS.html>.

95. Nasser Hadian, "US Policy toward Iran Should Promote Civil Society," *Eurasianet.org* (September 17, 2003), <www.eurasianet.org/departments/insight/articles/eav091703_pr.shtml>.

96. Combining elements of Islamism and Zoroastrianism, Iranian civil religion reconciles freedom (*Azadi*) with a religious conception of the state. The force of this amalgam can also be glimpsed in Kurdish religious politics, where there has been an equally pronounced Zoroastrian influence. See David Menashri, *Post-Revolutionary Politics in Iran: Religion, Security and Power* (London: Frank Class, 2001), 33. It is no accident that the Kurdish zone of northern Iraq has produced the most democratic government in the Arab world.

97. Michel Bôle-Richard, "Les étudiants iraniens s'attaquent à la toute-puissance des mullahs," *Le Monde* (December 18, 2002), <www.lemonde.fr/imprimer_article_ref/0,5987,3201—302607,00.html>.

98. Whit Mason, "Iran's Simmering Discontent," *World Policy Journal* 29, no. 1 (spring 2002): 79 (71–80).

99. He had also done much to discredit reformists "from above," such as President Khatami, whose input was weakened vis-à-vis hard-liners on issues such as IAEA (International Atomic Energy Agency) inspections. See "Iran's Nuclear Menance," *The International Herald Tribune* editorial (November 26, 2003), <www.iht.com/cgi-bin/generic.cgi?template=ariticleprint.tmplh&AricleId=119019>.

100. Indeed, only one or two Third World countries have had a more active revolutionary history. See Nikki R. Keddie, "Why Has Iran Been Revolutionary?" in Hooshang Amirahmadi and Nader Entessar, eds., *Reconstruction and Regional Diplomacy in the Persian Gulf* (London: Routledge, 1992), 19 (19–32).

101. See William Blum, "Iran's 1953: Making It Safe for the King of Kings," excerpted from Blum's *Killing Hope* (Monroe, ME: Common Courage Press, 1995), <www.thirdworldtraveler.com/Blum/Iran_KH.html>.

102. Ladane Nasseri, "A Death in Iran," *The Nation* (September 22, 2003), <www.thenation.com/docprint. mhtml?I=20031006&s=nasseri>.

103. This is denied by one of the most vocal opponents of the civil Islam thesis—none other than Reza Pahlavi, the son of the deposed Shah. Like President Bush, Pahlavi collapses moderate and extremist Islamism into a monolithic militancy that is anathema to democratic reform. In his view Islamism of all stripes is the contemporary equivalent of Nazism. Those who see Khatami as a moderate Islamist are as deluded, he asserts, as those who mistook Ribbentrop for a moderate Nazi. And by implication the same can be said for all civil Islamists, Kazemi included. See Adel Darwish's "My Vision," an account of an interview with Pahlavi in *Mideast News* (February 2002), <mehrdad5.vwh.net/articles/men202.htm>.

104. Robert D. Kaplan, *The Ends of the Earth: . . . A Journey to the Frontiers of Anarchy* (New York: Vintage Books, 1996), 182.

105. Scott Peterson, "In Iran, Hopes for Democracy Dwindle," *The Christian Science Monitor* (December 18, 2003), <www.csmonitor.com/2003/1218/p01s04-wome.htm>.

106. Sanam Vakili, "Iran's Fragile Fault Lines," *Policy Review* 121 (October 2003), <www.policyreview.org/oct03/vakil.html>.

6

Proxy Power: Iraq and the Roots of Arab Resistance

The British Art of Proxyism

THE IRANIAN REVOLUTION OF 1979 WAS just the most glaring point on an arc of unrest reaching from North Africa to Pakistan. Already radical Islamism was starting to rival communism as the West's worst nightmare,[1] and it struck even greater anxiety in Arab leaders. They rightly sensed that the new fundamentalism was not so much a theological departure as a declaration of war on corruption,[2] which of course meant them. One of them, however, stood to profit enormously from the mounting tension: the new Iraqi president, Saddam Hussein, had the luck of sitting on the geocultural front line of Iran's Shia challenge to Sunni power structures. This could be compared to the benefits reaped during the Cold War by Japan, Korea, Pakistan, Turkey, and finally China on the geopolitical edge of the Soviet Union.

Saddam wasted no time in converting this locational advantage into a fulsome claim on pan-Arab leadership, even as he turned that advantage into a horror story for non-Sunni Iraqis. The West looked the other way as this outcast majority (roughly 60 percent Shiites and 20 percent Kurds)[3] came under a reign of terror every bit as gruesome as that suffered by dissidents in Iran.[4] A popular children's song marked the implosion of Iraqi Baathism into Saddamism: "We are Iraq and its name is Saddam/We are love and its name is Saddam/We are a people and its name is Saddam/We are the Baath and its name is Saddam."[5] The Baath Party, modeled on Nazism, had found its Hitler. As Turi Munthe puts it, the messenger had become the message.[6]

The West's role in the making of Saddamism fits a pattern reaching back to Iraq's national origins. In 1918 the British military and its obliging civil commission (so like the Governing Council set up by the United States in post-Saddam Iraq) filled the void left by the defeated Ottoman Empire. Against their Sunni Ottoman rulers, the Shiites began to hone the oppositional nationalism that defines their politics to this day. This put them at the forefront of the rebellion against the British in 1920, after the country's promised independence was denied. No one familiar with Britain's colonial history would be surprised that Iraq's "self-determination" papers turned out to be a bill of perpetual British rights.[7] The League of Nations backed this extortion by declaring Iraq a mandate of the United Kingdom.

More even than the revolt against the Turks, the new Arab rising showed signs of broad popular backing in its blurring of lines between Sunni and Shiite, tribal nomad and town dweller. The British would cure that soon enough. Meanwhile they struck back with the kind of "shock and awe" tactics, including aerial bombardment, that American forces would emulate in their Iraq gambit of 2003. Such brutality strips bare the sham of a civilizing or democratizing mission. T. E. Lawrence (no stranger to colonial horror) charged that his government was even "worse than the old Turkish systems. They . . . killed a yearly average of two hundred Arabs in maintaining peace. We have killed about ten thousand Arabs in this rising this summer."[8]

Lawrence could almost have been talking about the Americans eighty-three years later when he wrote that "the people of England have been led . . . into a trap from which it will be hard to escape with dignity and honour. They have been tricked into it by a steady withholding of information. . . . We are today not far from a disaster."[9] And like the present American reconstruction, Britain's efforts were economically strained. It has been estimated that this revolt cost the British, in addition to the lives of 2,200 troops, three times as much as the entire Arab rising against the Turks. *The Times* (not known for liberal stances) protested in July 1921 that the government was lavishing funds on Mesopotamia while ignoring dire domestic needs such as education and housing for the poor.[10] Throughout the West this was a time of anti-liberal restructuration, not unlike the neoconservative priorities that the Bush II administration unleashed on America and the world after 9/11.[11]

In both cases imperial ambitions collided with stark fiscal realities. While Lawrence was spotlighting a moral disaster, the British were mainly concerned about the cost factor. The lesson they took from the Iraq uprising was that naturally contentious Arabs could be handled more economically by less overt means. Hereafter British power in the Middle East would be exercised, like American power today, by way of Arab proxies. Prince Faisal, Britain's trusty ally in its war on the Turks, was implanted as Iraq's hereditary monarch in

1921—much as Washington tried to implant the infamous Iraqi expatriate Ahmed Chalabi as its neocolonial agent, followed after his fall by the ex-CIA operative Ayad Allawi.

The idea—implemented by Churchill (intent on redeeming his imperialist credentials after his Gallipoli fiasco) at the Cairo Conference of March 1921— was to have a Mesopotamian branch of the British Empire on the cheap. Britain would control fiscal and judicial administration, as well as military matters, with the bill passed on to the natives themselves in the form of oil revenues.[12] Faisal and his Hashemites could rule Iraq any way they pleased, so long as it did not conflict with British interests.[13] The beauty of it was that Faisal, as a Sunni, would need ongoing British assistance to keep the Shiite majority in line. This dependency prevailed behind the scenes for a quarter of a century after Iraq's de jure independence in 1932.[14] No wonder the Americans adopted the British model, while never mentioning it publicly. Instead they talked of replicating their postwar policies in Germany and Japan. The Iraqis, however, instantly recognized the 1920s prototype, and smelled a rat in Chalabi.

The same divisive strategy that the British utilized in India, setting Muslims against Hindus, would here be used to turn up the heat between Sunnis and Shiites. Previously these groups had managed to coexist in relative harmony, despite a theological rivalry reaching back to the seventh century. It helped that the Ottomans had achieved a higher degree of religious tolerance than any empire since ancient times.[15] And even the British legacy of contention has not made Iraqi Shiism the kind of puristic Islamism that took shape in Iran or Pakistan. Most of the country's Shiites have avoided not only the pan-Arabism of Saddam but also the pan-Islamism of their fellow Shiite, the Ayatollah Khomeini, who regarded national and ethnic politics as a Western trick to divide and conquer the Islamic world.[16] Much as Lenin erred in expecting the German working classes to turn against their capitalist oppressors, Khomeini erred in expecting Iraqi Shiites to rise against their Sunni overlords.[17] Both lacked an awareness of the resistance capacity of nationalism.

The Shiites finally rose against Saddam in 1991, egged on by false promises of U.S. assistance. Tens of thousands would pay with their lives for Washington's cold feet, while thousands more would suffer prolonged affliction or death from the "Gulf War Syndrome" that the allies dumped on southern Iraq in the form of depleted uranium (DU) shells and bombs. The official House report on the Gulf War concluded that "the performance of U.S. equipment . . . in Operation Desert Storm exceeded even the most optimistic expectations."[18] That was written in 1992, on the assumption that the military's "performance" record was a closed book. But, as was the case with Agent Orange in Vietnam, the official end of the war was hardly the end of the death toll—and once again most of the victims would be innocent civilians. Even knowing DU was a factory for cancer, kidney disease, and chronic respiratory problems,[19] the U.S. military used it unstintingly in the 2003 invasion.

It is uncanny that pro-invasion hawks such as Dick Cheney and Paul Wolfowitz expected cheers in the streets from southern Iraqis. They did get half a miracle, however, as Shiite communities remained for the most part nonviolent, unlike their Sunni counterparts north of Baghdad. Though wary, Shiite clerics showed extraordinary patience in the face of Washington's manifest imperialism. At best U.S. policy was torn between its glowing democratic objectives and its intimate association with authoritarians such as Israel's Ariel Sharon and Egypt's Mohamed Hosni Mubarak. So too in Iraq, America's democratic commitment collides with its desire to keep firm control of any future government, not to mention Iraqi oil.[20] This strategic schizophrenia puts the United States in the odd position of contesting the patently democratic Shiite decree, issued by the Grand Ayatollah Ali al-Sistani, that no national constitution will be accepted which has not been ratified by a directly elected body.[21]

The British were less conflicted imperialists, yet even they were not immune to Gandhi's ultimate weapon: his ability to make them see themselves as they were. The same tactic might work on today's Americans if only they could be forced to see the damage they do in the name of liberation. Unfortunately the self-censorship of U.S. media precludes such self-recognition. The standard American question therefore remains, in fleeting moments of interest, "Why do they hate us?"

New Set of Dominoes

There is reason to doubt whether either approach—the Shiite demand for democratic immediacy or the American insistence upon neocolonial procrastination and proxyism—can deliver a cohesive state.[22] Ethnic and religious strife runs deep, casting doubt on the viability of Iraq as a nation. That in turn casts doubt on the stability of the whole region. The silver lining is that some degree of instability is a prerequisite for reform. In both Iran and Iraq, a sweeping cultural reformation is taking shape within the Shiite camp. Call it the Iranian Revolution in reverse, complete with the theological and political resurgence of Najaf, Iraq (home of the shrine of Ali, the first imam of Shia Islam).

It was from here that Khomeini lobbed his critical salvos at the Shah of Iran through the 1960s and 1970s. He swore revenge for himself and other Shiites after his expulsion from Iraq in 1977, but lost military credibility after he executed most of the officers of the once formidable Iranian army.

Thus, ironically, he ended up boosting Saddam's regional power and prestige, which was further assisted by inflated oil prices after the Iranian Revolution.

If Saddam was Shia Islam's worst enemy from without, Khomeini was its worst from within. Iranian theocracy destroyed the sacred/secular dialectic that traditional Shiism afforded. Khomeini's revolutionary premise was that individual salvation was impossible within a corrupt system.[23] It followed, as Azar Nafisi stresses in *Reading Lolita in Tehran*, that the first task of an Islamic state is to erase the lines between the personal and the political. Like the "new man" of Leninist eschatology, the ayatollahs were out to recast the people of Iran in their own image.[24]

This coincided with the shift of Shiism's geocultural center from Najaf to Qom, Iran. Sunni power structures were put on full alert in Saudi Arabia, Bahrain, Kuwait, and Iraq, while Western oil cartels were apoplectic. A new kind of domino theory took shape in Washington as fear of communism lost ground to the new demon of jihadic Islamism, though during the 1980s the two nightmares would coexist. Finally even Michel Foucault had to admit that something was awry. He had rushed to Tehran in 1978 to enjoy what he took to be the revolutionary antithesis of crass, Western materialism. This romance came to a bitter end as the mullahs set about liquidating thousands of innocent Iranians, and publicly hanging gay men, including Foucault's lover.

Saddam would soon be drafted as the secular defender of American interests, first by President Carter's pugnacious national security advisor, Zbigniew Brzezinski, and then more programmatically by the Reagan administration.[25] Saddam felt secure enough in this function to invade Iran in defiance of international law, to flagrantly engage in chemical warfare against Iranians and Kurds, and to wage total war on dissent inside Iraq—all the while being courted by the United States and the West in general. Brzezinski met Saddam in July 1980, effectively giving him a green light for the invasion of Iran two months later. And in the spring of 1982, with Iran on the brink of victory, Reagan broke official neutrality to tip the balance in Iraq's favor.

First, though, Iraq had to be taken off the State Department's list of countries supporting terrorism.[26] This led to the June 1982 national security directive that released billions in aid and military supplies to the flagging dictator. The CIA was directed to service Saddam's military needs, e.g., to provide him with the cluster bombs and armor penetrators he would require to block Iran's thrust, including its notorious "human waves."[27] Equally important was the diplomatic assurance given Saddam concerning his rising use of chemical weapons, which forced Tehran to reciprocate.[28]

Hundreds of millions of dollars worth of dual-use (military-friendly) technology were furnished to Iraq, and in the late 1980s billions in U.S. government export credits were extended,[29] such that by the time of the Gulf War the United States was left holding $2 billion in defaulted Iraqi debt. Declassified documents now reveal that current Defense Secretary Donald Rumsfeld, then a special envoy for the Reagan administration, paid friendly visits on Saddam in 1983 and 1984—the latter specifically to reassure the dictator that his use of chemical weapons would not pose an obstacle to cordial relations with America (incredibly this fact did not deter Rumsfeld and other Bush II administrators from citing Saddam's use of poison gas as one of their reasons for deposing him).

Reagan's secretary of state, George Schultz, pushed for unconditional support for Iraq (which not surprisingly would become a prime customer of the Bechtel Corporation that Shultz headed).[30] One security expert, Joseph Coffey, was marching in step when he concluded in 1989 that Saddam was the best security guarantee for states like Kuwait(!).[31] The Bush I administration made still more improved relations with Iraq a cornerstone of its Middle East policy, despite the fact that the end of the Iran-Iraq War had removed any strategic excuse for this relationship.

When questions were raised concerning Saddam's human rights violations and his use of chemical weapons, Secretary of State James Baker intervened personally to reaffirm the pro-Iraq stance of the Reagan years. The working assumption behind this blunder was that Shiite Islamism is an undifferentiated anachronism, being the same in Iran, Iraq, or wherever. Notice the striking similarity to the early Cold War notion of undifferentiated communism. As the Cold War receded, this surrogate monolith was already on hand to fill the adversarial void. It was this new set of dominoes that inspired U.S. strategists to betray the Iraqi Shiites who rose against Saddam after the Gulf War. So too it inspired the distrust of Shiite democratism that blighted U.S./Iraqi relations after the 2003 invasion.

Green Light

Saddam might have continued to profit from Washington Shia-phobia had he not begun to swallow his own party line. Like a magician who starts to believe in magic, he internalized one of the central myths of Saddamism: that his power rested primarily on pan-Arab leadership rather than strongman services rendered to international oil conglomerates.[32] The paradox of Iraqi power, in Kenneth Pollack's view, is that any Iraq strong enough to counter Iran would also be capable of overrunning Kuwait and threatening Saudi Arabia. To the West that translates as a threat to one of the world's most critical oil pumps, on which the health of the global economy depends.[33]

The end of the Iran-Iraq War had already put Kuwait and Saudi Arabia in jeopardy, and the eclipse of Soviet power raised Iraq's status among Arab "orphans of perestroika."[34] In February 1990 Saddam called for renewed pan-Arabism under his auspices to counter U.S. unipolarity. Tensions in the Middle East reached the boiling point that spring, as Bush-administration rhetoric concerning a new global order (read pax Americana) ran aground on the issue of justice for Palestinians. Arabs reasonably took this as the canary in their mine shaft. Losing patience with Egypt's pro-Western tilt, the Palestinian Liberation Organization (PLO) shifted its diplomatic fealty to Iraq, while others looked to Saddam as an effective balancing agent against Saudi Arabia. Yemen went so far as to side with Iraq during the Gulf War.[35]

What Saddam now needed was a way to showcase his rising status in a fairly low-risk manner. Kuwait looked inviting after it made itself a pariah within OPEC by brashly exceeding its mandated productions limits. Like other Arab states it had made huge loans to Iraq during the war with Iran, even as it reaped windfall profits by taking over most of Iraq's oil production quota. Most of these creditor states forgave their loans to Iraq after the war, but Kuwait demanded payment in full for the $22 billion it had extended.

Kuwait's violation of OPEC production agreements began the very day after the August 1988 cease-fire, thereby depressing world oil prices and costing Iraq an estimated $7 billion per year at a time when it badly needed capital for reconstruction. In March 1989 Kuwait proposed a further production expansion of 50 percent. When OPEC rejected this proposal, Kuwait broke ranks entirely and *doubled* its production. Soon the United Arab Emirates followed Kuwait's lead, all but destroying Iraq's postwar recovery plans. Meanwhile, Kuwait added insult to injury by slant drilling under Iraqi oil fields.

There is no mystery, then, as to why Iraq would want to invade Kuwait. The pressing question is why Washington misled both sides as to the likely consequences of their actions. Sources close to Kuwaiti leaders have confirmed that the United States and Britain let Kuwait know how pleased they were to have OPEC undermined.[36] Suffice it to say that Kuwait was made to feel secure in its otherwise suicidal conduct. Taken alone, America's destabilizing impact on the region's delicate power balance might seem like hard-hitting but shrewd geopolitics. It takes on a truly sinister character, however, when coupled with the simultaneous assurances given to Iraq that the United States would remain neutral in the event of a war. Just five days before Saddam's invasion, Ambassador April Glaspie told him that Washington "took no position" on the conflict.[37]

That was Saddam's green light, just as Brzezinski's visit had been in 1980. He could reasonably infer that at least a temporary occupation would be tolerated.[38] Some believe it was Iraq's sizeable debt which inspired the invasion, but Saddam certainly knew that a permanent occupation—voiding all debts by nullifying the creditor—was an unrealistic prospect. More plausibly the idea was to use Kuwait as a bargaining chip in return for better loan terms and/or some tangible pan-Arab benefit, such as Israel's evacuation of the West Bank and Gaza. To retreat on those terms would have been be a veritable victory, much as Nasser's military defeat in the 1956 Suez Crisis was transformed into a political triumph.[39]

Saddam had every reason to assume that profitable negotiation would follow, as Washington had only recently made it clear that it wanted stronger economic and military relations with him. A national security directive to that effect had been signed by President Bush on October 2, 1989, stating that "normal relations between the United States and Iraq would serve our long-term interests." Just a year later Bush was refusing to negotiate and calling Saddam "the butcher of Bagdad."[40]

Too late Saddam discovered that the United States, minus Soviet competition, was capable of operating on his own moral plane. Consider, for example, the power politics surrounding the investigation of the 1988 downing of Flight 103 over Lockerbie, Scotland. British and U.S. investigators were in hot pursuit of leads indicating that the plot had been hatched as an act of revenge for the downing of an Iranian civilian airliner by the U.S. military in the summer of 1988. Preliminary evidence suggested that the grisly task of payback was carried out by terrorists based in Syria. But as the Bush administration faced the challenge of garnering Arab support against Saddam, Syria was put off limits. As of April 1989 the investigation abruptly shifted its target from Iran and Syria to Libya. Syria reciprocated by providing troops for the Gulf War coalition.[41]

Finding himself isolated, Saddam had little choice but to play his ultimate pan-Arab card: firing Scud missiles on Israel so as to "Zionize" the war. The idea was to win back by force of mass appeal the Arab states, including most of the Arab League, that had turned against him.[42] This would transform the conflict into a glorious civilizational clash, with Saddam cast as part Saladin and part Nasser. Deputy Secretary of State Larry Eagleburger rushed to Jerusalem to offer whatever it took to keep Israel on the sidelines.[43] The Bush team managed to preserve its coalition on paper, but at the level of the "Arab street," outside the gated community of the New World Order, the forces of global jihad were massing.

America's military triumph was thus delusive. What Gabriel Kolko says of the Vietnam War applies equally to the Gulf War, which was no more a struggle between armies than between profoundly different images of history and human existence. In the view of North Vietnam's General Giap, war is not reducible to military matters. In the final analysis it is a contest of philosophies. The Bush I administration was right, then, to insist that the Gulf War was not just about oil; but neither was it about freedom and democracy. It exuded the globalist hubris of "the West against the Rest." The only real winner in this culture war was Wahhabi Islamism, which thereafter was on the march not only in the Middle East, but in Central, South, and even Southeast Asia. More than ever the Arab states had to deal with this devil of their own making.

Operation Desert Storm, the first major military operation of the post–Cold War era, put Sunni leaders in a double bind, for they well knew that Saddam's weakness spelled Shiite strength.[44] Distrust of the United States had grown steadily for half a century,[45] and crested with the end of the Cold War, as Arab distrust of both superpowers came to be focused on just one. The prospect of America's post–Cold War unipolarity became Saddam's calling card in the Arab world, such that his ignominious defeat in the Gulf War would be quietly lamented even by America's Arab allies. It did not help that President Bush openly heralded the coalition's goal of establishing a beachhead for the New World Order.[46] Arabs were not taken in by this oilman's claim that his latter-day Crusade was launched in the spirit of freedom and democracy.

Post–Gulf War Islamism

Washington's post–Gulf War policies belied such humanitarian claims. Far more punishment was visited on Iraq than Germany and Japan had received after World War II. Granted, the no-fly zones that America and Britain enforced protected Kurds in the north, but neither this defensive umbrella nor years of economic sanctions (which cost the lives, by conservative estimate, of tens of thousands of Iraqi children)[47]—would have been necessary if popular rebellion against Saddam had received half the assistance it was led to expect by the Bush administration. Even after his blitzkrieg on Kuwait, Saddam was considered the "lesser evil" as compared to a de facto Shiite merger between Iraq and Iran. That possibility, however, was almost as remote as the chance of Vietnam under Ho Chi Minh willingly submitting to rule by China.

The brutality of postwar sanctions on Iraq suggests that the Gulf War was being continued by other means. Unfortunately the target was more the general public than the Baathist power elite. If this policy was designed to encourage rebellion, its goal was certainly not *popular* uprising, for the Shiites were not provided even the minimal tools for insurrection. Clearly what Washington wanted was rebellion within rather than against the Sunni power structure, i.e., Washington hoped for an in-house regime change rather than the kind of democratic revolution that would empower Shia Islamism.

The stated justification for ongoing sanctions would be Iraq's WMD (weapons of mass destruction), but that threat had lost credibility by the late 1990s. Even Condoleezza Rice, Bush's future national security advisor, asserted in Clinton's last year in office that Saddam possessed no WMD stockpile.[48] Unquestionably Saddam had pursued such a program in the 1980s, but that was with the full knowledge and tacit approval of the United States and other Western powers. Presumably Washington's approval did not extend to nuclear weaponry, but this qualifier was based more on practical politics than principle; for no such limit was applied in the case of Pakistan, which was foolishly considered a tractable vassal state that could be trusted not to indulge in nuclear proliferation. Now, for geopolitical rather than humanitarian reasons, Washington was ready to clip Saddam's wings.

The end of the Cold War had left the Arab world more vulnerable than ever, as the Gulf War amply illustrated: around 100,000 Iraqis perished, as opposed to 148 U.S. battle casualties. In retrospect it is obvious that the Soviets had played something of a moderating role in the region, lending support to a client state when it came under threat, but withholding support when it threatened the power balance.[49] U.S. actions were also held in check, for to counter the Soviets the Americans had to placate Arab regimes. The Gulf War served notice that, absent that Cold War balance, the United States was now the region's loose cannon. While early globalists dismissed power politics as a historical artifact, Arabs knew globalization to be a euphemism for Western empowerment and its converse, Arab impotence.[50] This view is reflected in recent comments by Yemen's President Ali Abdullah Saleh, who draws a sharp distinction between democratization, which he supposedly favors, and U.S.-Israeli practice, which he rightly deplores.[51] Even before the fateful scandal broke in spring 2004 concerning torture at Abu Ghraib prison, America had exchanged the moral high ground of soft power for a geopolitics of sheer force.[52]

As the British learned the hard way after the First World War, Arabs will not yield to undisguised coercion. Three remedies have been advanced for the regional imbalance: (1) the overt pan-Arabism that Saddam vented on Kuwait, (2) the covert pan-Islamism that Osama bin Laden cultivated after the Gulf War, and (3) the search for new geopolitical alliances to contravene U.S. hyperpower. This third strategy was discernable in the Sino-Arabic cosponsorship of Pakistan's nuclear arsenal. As China's petroleum needs mushroomed, a natural partner was found in the Arab world's thirst for WMD technology.[53]

This could be the wave of the future, in which case al Qaeda–type resistance will be reduced to an interim balancing act.

Radical Islamism is nonetheless a dire threat to U.S. hegemony in terms of image deflation. That a small band of malcontents could strike a blow on the scale of Pearl Harbor cuts the world's sole superpower down a notch. There is the real danger, moreover, that today's cycle of terrorism and counterterrorism has no brake, for the Cold War control mechanism of mutually assured destruction is unavailable. Compromise and negotiation are ruled out when one's enemy exists only as a maze of rhizoid cell structures with no convincing chain of command.

The real enemy is not so much an institution as a sociocultural animus: an anti-Western reflex that is especially virulent in the case of militant Wahhabism. The United States itself helped to nurture this lethal strain of Islamism by propping up its Saudi patrons for decades, while they in turn fostered the most rabid religious extremism on earth.[54] Finally America joined them in the funding, training, and equipping of Wahhabi-inspired insurgents against the Soviets in Afghanistan. Insurgency, of course, is renamed terrorism when it turns on its Western host. The irony of this U.S.-funded jihad was not widely appreciated until 9/11, when it was revealed that fifteen of the nineteen hijackers were Saudi nationals, and after about 200 Saudis were captured fighting in Afghanistan with al Qaeda and the Taliban.

Although the paramilitary milieu that brought Osama bin Laden to prominence had no deactivation mechanism, it did not have to become a global weapon of mass destruction. By his own testimony it was the Gulf War, and the thought of Western troops treading on sacred Arab soil, that turned Osama against his Saudi and American patrons. That meant breaking with mainstream Wahhabism, which remained loyal to its benefactor, the Saudi royal junta. Osama's apostasy forced his flight from Saudi Arabia to the Sudan in 1991. His primary enemy, however, was not the Saudi ruling class as such, but the secular commercialism it embraced.

By the same token Osama spurned the efforts of some of his subordinates to put him in contact with a far more consistent secularist, Saddam Hussein. The feeling was of course mutual: even in hiding, after his fall, Saddam cautioned his supporters to be wary of both domestic fundamentalists and foreign (i.e., al Qaeda) fighters entering Iraq. He never relinquished the secular rancor that once endeared him to the West, when his special contribution to Baathism had been to purge it of its Shia content, purifying the secular politics that once cut across ethnic and sectarian lines.[55]

If the chasm dividing these competing Arabisms was not so wide as that between Baghdad and Tehran, it was still vast. Perhaps the only thing that could bring the two camps together would be the prospect of Western troops

garrisoned on Arab soil. The irony is that the U.S. invasion was partly justified—by true believers such as Douglas Feith, the undersecretary of defense
for policy—on the ground that al Qaeda was enmeshed in what Secretary of
State Colin Powell called, in his February 5, 2003, address to the UN Security
Council, a "sinister nexus" with Saddam. In fact it was the invasion itself that
invited that unlikely fusion.

Likewise it was the post–Gulf War establishment of a UN "safe haven" in
northern Iraq that invited lawless elements into the area. The Kurdish Islamic
group Ansar al-Islam, which is known to have al Qaeda ties, found sanctuary
here until it took heavy losses after the American invasion. For Powell to point
to this remote outpost as proof of a full-fledged alliance between Saddam and
Osama was more than a simple intelligence error. He well knew that any such
al Qaeda/Baath linkage was forged on the anvil of U.S. policies.[56] Even Iraq's
own Sunni Wahhabism was suppressed during the Saddam era, though it is
staging a comeback thanks to the fall of secular Baathism.

With Friends like These

Prior to the so-called Iraqi intifada of spring 2004—which witnessed a Sunni-
Shiite convergence in the face of a common enemy—Iraq's Wahhabi rebound
was at once anti-Shiite and anti-American. Saudis blame America for the Shiite resurgence, but Shia democratization has its own internal dynamic. Consider the case of Sheik Hussein Fadlallah, who was once the spiritual leader of
Hezbollah fighters in Lebanon, but has emerged as a leading progressive. He
was, indeed, one of the first clerics to unequivocally condemn the attacks of
9/11. Washington's blanket suspicion of Shiism misses an opportunity for dialogue with such leaders, and contributes to the civil Islamic void that both
Sunni and Shiite extremists are now filling. The chance that Iraq might afford
an exception to the cultural implosion of both regional camps—centered in
Saudi Arabia and Iran, respectively—is fading fast.

In Saudi Arabia that reactionary impulse is grounded in the political symbiosis of Wahhabism and the extended royal family, although these 10,000-
odd princes are hardly of one mind. Against the puritanical *Tawhid* ideology
of Prince Nayef and Prince Sultan (the interior and defense ministers, respectively),[57] relative reformists such as Crown Prince Abdullah and Sheikh Abdul
Aziz al-Sheikh back a *Taqarub* agenda of improved relations between Sunni
and Shia Muslims as well as Muslims and non-Muslims. Even Aziz, however,
is now putting a distance from the country's secular-minded liberals. Meanwhile Sultan, who has worked assiduously to block the extension of women's
educational opportunities, is determined to thwart any chance that the ap-

pointed Shura Council could evolve into an elected legislature[58] (an action Washington will not be inclined to protest, given the council's strong condemnation of U.S. actions in Iraq).[59]

From a Tawhid perspective the Gulf War and the 2003 invasion of Iraq involve more than a geocorporate power grab. They also evince an American strategy to play the old British game in reverse. Rather than planting a Sunni island in a sea of Shiism, the Americans are seen as insinuating Shia and Zionist insurgency into the Sunni heartland. To be fair, these suspicions are not without some factual basis. It is now known that the United States seriously considered seizing Middle Eastern oil fields three decades ago during the Arab oil embargo, and neoconservative ideologues such as Richard Perle and David Frum (inventor of the term "Axis of Evil") make no secret of their wish to "liberate" Saudi Arabia's Eastern Province, Al Hasa, from the Sunni-dominated nation. Two cardinal facts bear noting: first, Al Hasa is mainly populated by Shiites, and second, this is where most Saudi oil is located.[60]

Those twin facts explain oil magnate Jim Oberwetter's sudden interest in religious freedom in Saudi Arabia, after he was nominated by President Bush to be the new ambassador to Saudi Arabia.[61] The president himself seems only selectively to have shed his skepticism about neo-Wilsonian tampering in other countries' affairs. He is testing the water in those areas that happen to be oil saturated. His idealist conversion would take on more credibility if he were to show equal concern for, say, religious freedom in Tibet.

Like all recent administrations, Bush Jr.'s has been tough on Shiism. But, as if to prove he is not a total bigot, he shows much tolerance for the religion of his Sunni friends in the Saudi ruling class. This bond is virtually a Bush family tradition, given Bush Sr.'s cozy relations with Saudi members of the Carlyle Group, including several bin Laden family members.[62] This soft spot was unfortunate in view of the defining event of Bush II's presidency, for it was Saudi Wahhabism, not Afghan Talibanism or Iraqi Saddamism, that bred the mentality of 9/11's suicide bombers. Any effective war on terrorism must come to terms with that fact. Somehow Riyadh must be induced to cut its ties not only with Osama bin Laden, but with the strain of Islamism that produced him. That task will be every bit as daunting as was the Cold War challenge of getting the Soviet Union to jettison communism.[63]

Resistance in a New Key

It would help if Washington, while waging war on Islamic terrorism at the NGO level, would also confront the issue of Zionist state terrorism. Its assumption has been that the real Palestinian problem is not the Israeli occupation, but only the resistance to the occupation. The cost of that misconception can hardly be over-stated. Among other things, it forfeits the influence Washington might have on Arab progressives, who understandably feel betrayed by the West. America has become synonymous with grievous oppression on the part of both Arab states and Israel. In the words of a recent Beirut editorial, any local citizen "who suggests that a Middle Eastern leader has done something wrong is likely to be pressured or imprisoned and perhaps even liquidated."[64]

Islam became the obligatory medium of resistance, since it alone afforded the necessary organization for concerted action. With the advent of new information media, however, public discourse is moving beyond the mosque. Critics charge al-Jazeera, the twenty-four-hour news channel operating out of Qatar, with catering to noxious causes, and undeniably the channel's $100 million a year funding by the Qatar government comes with strings attached. Nonetheless these media are having a catalytic effect on the Arab street as a grassroots force of resistance.[65]

Mindful that they are living on the edge of social and political upheaval, regional elites were doubtless relieved at the eleventh hour cancellation of the March Arab League summit in Tunis, where made-in-America reform would have been the inescapable axis of discussion. Arab regimes would not relish a direct confrontation with the United States at this time, but they were equally fearful of looking like pawns in the "Greater Middle East Initiative" that Washington was about to launch through the G-8.[66] As a preemptive measure, Egypt fostered its own carefully screened conference in mid-March. But attending Arab intellectuals and NGOs gave Cairo more than it bargained for. The resulting Alexandria Statement called for sweeping constitutional reforms to guarantee a host of basic rights such as free speech and free elections. Taking warning, Arab leaders seized upon the fallout from the Abu Ghraib prison scandal in Iraq to reconvene the Tunis summit in May, this time turning the focus away from democracy to more innocuous issues such as modernization and development.

Washington, too, would hope for far less potent reformism. It is no more ready to accept Islamic democracy today than it was in 1992 when it lent tacit approval to the military overthrow of Algeria's democratically elected and therefore Islamist parliament—an action that tore the country apart and cost 100,000 lives by 1997.[67] Washington's vaunted initiative—informed by such renowned anti-Islamists as Bernard Lewis and Samuel Huntington—is an attempt to preempt the new wave of Islamist democratization. A more subtle variant of this less-is-best slant on Islamism is ventured by Gilles Kepel, who tempers Huntington's pessimism with a strong dose of end-of-history élan: the confident prediction that political Islamism (which he tends to equate with militant Islamism) is a dying cause. Kepel's point, as Olivier Da Lage reads it, is that the only alternative to Western liberal democracy is Islamic re-trenchment, a reactionary reflex that is doomed from the start.[68]

Conversely, speaking in his capacity as chairman of the Egyptian National Human Rights Commission, former UN Secretary-General Boutros-Ghali points out the deep roots of native Islamic reformism—a paradigm that was broad enough to easily absorb the Western-inspired rationalism of Mahmoud Azmi, the Egyptian diplomat who helped author the UN's Universal Declaration of Human Rights.[69] The question is how the civil Islamic current that subsumed Azmi could have been so successfully subverted by Egypt's ruling National Democratic Party, which for almost a quarter of a century has used the country's emergency law to censor the press, to suppress opposing parties, and to drastically curtail civil liberties. A big part of the answer is the $50 billion that the United States has pumped in since 1975. Egypt's proxy fee was permanently secured when it made peace with Israel in 1979.

Throughout the Middle East it was political machination, rather than any inherent qualities of Islam, that provided a breeding ground for jihadic Islamism. The trick was to keep dissent turned outward. Fearing Islamist reform more than Wahhabi extremism, Saudi elites long denied the existence of al Qaeda operations in their midst. But in May 2003 Riyadh was shaken out of its lethargy by three suicide bombings that killed 25 and wounded almost 200. The fact that most of these casualties were foreigners did little to buffer the revelation that the government was losing control. Only a few days before, officials had declared al Qaeda "weak and nonexistent" here, which was to say "not our problem." Finally Islamic reformists such as Sulaiman al Hattian and former religious zealot Mansour Nogidan were getting some long overdue attention.[70]

U.S. policies, however, cut against this reformist grain. It says much about the Bush "anti-terrorist" strategy that, despite a Saudi crackdown, al Qaeda commands more public support now than before the May bombings. Though this sympathy rarely extends to domestic insurrection, it warmly embraces jihad in Iraq and elsewhere. A major suicide bombing in April 2004 underscored the severity of the crisis, as police surveillance of al Qaeda served only to shift insurgency from centrally organized strikes to almost random violence on less protected targets. In the next week a bomb attack in Syria and a foiled plot in Jordan testified to the fact that this new militancy—the first of its kind to strike Syria in two decades—was much more than a local security problem.

Any solution, accordingly, must be sought on an international level. This would have been a good time for Washington to grant that it too had played a part in the making of "Islamic" terrorism. In the 1960s the United States joined hands with King Faisal in fostering Islamic fundamentalism as a counterweight to both Nasserism and the Left.[71] And in the 1980s it again conspired with the Saudis to fund the Afghan jihadism that metamorphosed into al Qaeda. A healthy sense of mutual error might have laid a foundation for mutual trust.

It was not to be. The U.S. invasion of Iraq destroyed what little trust existed between Arabs and Americans, and in April 2004 the Bush administration's endorsement of Sharon's plans for Palestine removed all ambiguity concerning U.S. priorities. With the Iraq occupation looking more and more like a re-colonization project, the United States found itself backed into much the same corner that Israel had occupied in Lebanon. In desperation the military turned almost exclusively to force of arms as a fast-drying cement for proxy statehood. The fear was that Iraq would break into three hostile camps: the Shiites in the south, the Kurds in the north, and the Sunnis in the embattled middle, with the Shiites bowing to Iran as well as Mecca. But increasingly that fear is matched by the even more dreadful prospect of a Sunni/Shiite united front.[72] The Americans had insisted on a unified Iraq, and now that wish was coming back to haunt in the form of pan-sectarian resistance. This irony was compounded when Washington turned to Iran for assistance in curbing the Shiite rising.

Washington had collided with what Samuel Huntington terms the "democratic paradox": the rebound of democratic populism against the West. It took a full year for the fact to sink in that "victory" in Iraq would not follow the postwar script of Germany and Japan. By the end of April 2004, just over a year after the official end of combat operations, U.S. fatalities had reached 734.[73] The administration's bellicose response to this predicament made matters even worse, as the Sunni uprising in Falluja was joined by the formidable Shiite militia of the cleric Muqtada al-Sadr.

Conclusion

How, one wonders, did the Bush team expect a model democratic transition in this of all places? A glance at other Arab experiments with democracy suggests the dim prospects of Iraq's even more volatile ethnic mix. While neighboring Kuwait possesses many of the procedural prerequisites for democracy, women are still denied the vote, as is a huge *bidoon* (stateless) population, and opposition parties are nonexistent. Granted, a more glittering image is cast by "democratic" sheikdoms such as the United Arab Emirates, where all the allurements of globalization are on display—e.g., Dubailand, a $5 billion Disney clone now under construction.[74] Here consumers are encouraged to forget their cultural location, along with any thought of resistance to the system that provides these wonders.

Iraqis, however, are not likely to welcome a Najafland or Fallujaland any-time soon. Instead of globalist proxihood, they want democracy on their terms, and now rather than later. The first U.S. administrator of Iraq, Jay Gar-ner, was sacked for agreeing with the Iraqis on this point. It was essential for his superiors that Iraqi industries be privatized before the Iraqis were given a democratic voice in the matter. As Garner told the BBC, this plan had been drawn up in late 2001. That patently undemocratic strategem put Americans in the awkward position of having to refuse the very thing the invasion was supposed to be about, once the WMD excuse evaporated. The administra-tion's real priorities shined through in Bush's national security talks, where the focus was more on "free market" objectives than on democracy. The key point is conveyed in an *Al-Mada* cartoon showing an encounter between an Iraqi looter leaving a building and a Western official about to enter. The looter tells the administrator, "Don't bother. We privatized it before you."[75]

Exposed for what it is, the occupation is reduced to unvarnished imperial-ism. Most Americans would balk at this role if they were to face it directly, but their media have so far spared them that burden. If they ever start to get the message—perhaps through photographs of returning coffins,[76] or a full ac-count of the sexual torture of Iraqi prisoners—the neoconservative agenda for the Middle East will collapse. With democratic imperialism revealed as a sham, dissident voices of Middle Eastern reform might finally get the help they need.

A good example of such noninvasive engagement is the $1 million that Sen-ator Patrick Leahy has tagged for Egyptian NGOs in the foreign appropria-tions bill. Unfortunately that is a miniscule figure beside the $2 billion the United States bestows on Egypt each year with little or no reform conditions attached. Ducking behind state sovereignty rights, President Mubarak does not bother hiding his intention to set up his son Gamal as his successor. With the economy failing and opposition mounting, Mubarak is determined not only to retain his whole panoply of "emergency" powers, but to push through new laws to control the very NGOs that Leahy is trying to promote. While these organizations are a thorn in Mubarak's side, real change is not likely until U.S. proxy funding is either cancelled or repackaged as a democratic im-perative.

President Bush was right when he spoke, in November 2003, of a "freedom deficit" across the region. What he failed to mention was that a prime source of that deficit has been Washington's massive support for reactionaries such as Mubarak and Sharon. So too the United States has generously funded radical Islamism as a geopolitical weapon. The rise of al Qaeda has much more to do with U.S. policy than with Islam per se.[77] While religious culture certainly af-fects politics, political tactics also impact culture. Thus the most pernicious "civilizational clash" is not between Islam and the West, but between antithetical political camps on both sides. In Washington this pits paleo-liberalism against neoglobalism (i.e., the post-9/11 melding of neoliberalism and neoconservativism), while Islamists are split between reformism and jihad.

Washington policy has seldom taken the progressive side in this Islamic culture war, and after 9/11 it came down even harder on reformism by adopting the blanket anti-Islamism that is Israel's trademark. This conflation of civil and uncivil Islam helps to turn the cultural backwater of jihad into a torrent of popular resistance. Kepel may be correct that Islamic militancy was on the wane by the 1990s in terms of its social base. But, as Benjamin Barber stresses, jihad was by then being recommissioned by way of reaction to globalization. And that was before radical Islamism had received the greatest blessing Allah could bestow: a president who saw scant value in the global outpouring of sympathy and goodwill that followed 9/11.

In peddling its own Initiative, the Bush administration did much for the cause of radical Islamism. Words from Washington were so discredited that regional reformers came to fear any public display of support from the Americans. Perhaps in that sense it was just as well that the administration ignored the reform potential of civil Islam. Even Western progressives tend to make this mistake. Most, as Amitai Etzioni observes, see civil society and religion as antithetical.[78] Americans are even suspicious of more secular NGO projects such as Egypt's Ibn Khaldun Center, run by the prototypic moderate Saad Eddin Ibrahim. In the three years of his imprisonment, prior to his release in June 2003, Professor Ibrahim's efforts gained a broad following at home and abroad. He is quick to point out, however, that his position has deep regional roots. It revives the liberal tradition that thrived in many parts of the Arab world for at least a century before the Israeli victory of 1948 and the geocultural inroads of the Cold War.

There was hope that the end of the Cold War would invite less intrusive American policies. But the U.S. war on terrorism once again provides a no-questions-asked support system for what Ibrahim calls "Despots' Alley": the string of autocracies that line the old Silk Road from Beijing to North Africa.[79] It is along this indelibly Muslim swath that two key questions of current political development are at issue: First, can democracy be compatible with Islamic culture? And second, can Washington-directed globalization be resisted by anything short of jihad?

To answer these questions in the negative is to join those strange bedfellows, Margaret Thatcher and Osama bin Laden, in their shared conviction that "There Is No Alternative" to current global capitalism—none, that is, except bin Laden's equally totalistic imperative of global jihad. As Barber put it in the mid-1990s, at the height of "TINAesque" triumphalism, McWorld and

Jihad are in fact symbiotic twins. Both are implacably at war with the civil foundations of democratic society,[80] and each sustains the other. It follows that Islamic terrorism is less threatened by the neoconservative hawks surrounding Bush than by civil Islamic reformists.

This is an easy position to take, because Ibrahim is so manifestly pro-Western. A harder but equally important argument is that our support for democratization, to be authentic, must reach beyond the confines of American interests. It must bypass, that is, the Bushian ("for us or against us") litmus test for who the good guys are. As in Algeria before, the paramount question in today's Iraq is how far our commitment to democracy extends. If it stretches no farther than our proxy power, then we have not advanced one inch beyond the British ethics of the 1920s.

Indeed, in terms of political legitimacy, our erstwhile proxy Chalabi[81]—abetted by the infamous John Negroponte, Bush's ambassador (as of June 30, 2004) to Iraq[82]—is at the opposite end of the spectrum from Britain's original proxy, Faisal, who earned pan-Arab respect through real and perilous resistance. Americans are far more hypocritical in their effort to convince the Iraqis, the world, and themselves that theirs was a democratically inspired invasion. The message we are sending the Iraqis, and by implication the whole Islamic world, is that we encourage democracy only where it does our bidding and elects our proxies. Any other course of action will be branded "terrorism."

What the Iraqis in turn are telling us is that this is not 1920. Their rising intifada is not so much inspired by Islamic cultural retrenchment as by the civil Islamic demand that the democracy they adopt must be theirs, not ours. Just ten weeks before the nominal return of Iraq's self-rule on June 30, 2004, there was still no clarity as to the powers that the new government would hold—except that they would be minimal. It was hardly a surprise when the Bush administration let it be known that on issues of vital interest to America, such as foreign military operations on Iraqi soil, the new leadership would have no authority whatsoever. The question is how long and to what degree the Iraqis will be willing to accept this proxihood.

Notes

1. Moscow, too, was discomfited by this new radicalism. See Mohammed Ayoob, "Oil, Arabism, and Islam: The Persian Gulf in World Politics," in Mohammed Ayoob, ed., *The Middle East in World Politics* (London: Australian Institute of International Affairs, 1981), 130 (118–35). This anxiety would reach its apex in the thought of "confrontationalists" such Bernard Lewis, Gilles Kepel, and Samuel Huntington, who see not only radical Islamism but Islam per se as incompatible

with Western values such as democracy. See Fawaz A. Gerges, *America: Clash of Cultures or Clash of Interests?* (Cambridge, U.K.: Cambridge University Press, 1999), 21–23. While most confrontationalists have tended to hail from the Right, the Left was no less disturbed by the Iranian challenge. Islamism in general had no place on the base/superstructure grid of causality that the Left shared with developmental modernists. On their rude cultural awakening see Peter Gran, "Studies of Anglo-American Political Economy: Democracy, Orientalism, and the Left," in Hisham Sharabi, ed., *Theory, Politics and the Arab World: Critical Responses* (New York: Routledge, 1990), 247 (228–54).

2. Nasr Hamid Abu Zeid, "The Modernization of Islam or the Islamization of Modernity," in Roel Meijer, ed., *Cosmopolitanism, Identity and Authenticity in the Middle East* (London: Routledge Curzon, 1999), 83 (71–86).

3. Some estimates put this Shiite figure as high as 70 percent, which lends credibility to the view that the Shia community has every right to expect, at the minimum, a Shiite president. Some, such as the Ayatollah Muhammad Yacoubi, go much farther—demanding a formal political role for the Shia clergy. See Susan Sachs, "Iraqi Shiites Enter Era of Inclusion, Not Exclusion," *New York Times* (December 21, 2003), <www.nytimes.com/2003/12/21/international/middleeast/21SHII.html>.

4. It should be noted that Arab nations looked on with mute indifference as this horror story unfolded—a fact that drives a wedge between post-Saddam Iraq and its Arab neighbors. See Fawaz A. Gerges, "Rudderless in the Storm: Arab Politics Before and After the Iraq War," *Dissent* (winter 2004), <www.dissentmagazine.org/menutest.articles/wi04/gerges.htm>.

5. Turi Munthe, "Saddam's Islamist Legacy," *openDemocracy* (June 10, 2003), <www.opendemocracy.net/debates/article-2-95-1523.jsp>. Saddamism consummated the party's earlier implosion into a regional and familial power structure at the time of its rise to power in 1968, following the eclipse of Nasserism after the June 1967 war. Under Ahmad Hasan al Bakr and Saddam the party purged all competing groups, and Bakr's failing health left Saddam increasingly in command by the mid-1970s. He became president in July 1979.

6. Munthe, "Saddam's Islamist Legacy." Even in the 1920s Sati al-Husri, the architect of Iraq's educational policies under Faisal, grafted the ideas of Herder and Fichte into his classic Arab nationalism. This seemingly innocuous import set the stage for more radical Germanophilia after Iraq got its formal independence in 1932. Since its establishment in 1922, Iraq's relative internal autonomy made it the natural hub of Arab nationalism. See Bassam Tibi, *Arab Nationalism: A Critical Enquiry*, translated and edited by Marion Farouk-Sluglett and Peter Sluglett (London: Macmillan Press, 1981, second edition), 120–21.

7. See T. E. Lawrence, "A Report on Mesopotamia by T. E. Lawrence," *Sunday Times* (August 22, 1920), <www.lib.byu.edu/~rdh/wwwi/1918/mesopo.html>.

8. T. E. Lawrence, "A Report on Mesopotamia by T. E. Lawrence."

9. T. E. Lawrence, "A Report on Mesopotamia by T. E. Lawrence."

10. Simon Bromley, *Rethinking Middle East Politics: State Formation and Development* (Cambridge, U.K.: Polity Press, 1994), 75–76.

11. See Abbott Gleason, "The Hard Road to Fascism: Today's Antiliberal Revolt Looks a Lot like 1920s Europe," *Boston Review* (summer 2003), <bostonreview.net/BR28.3/gleason.html>.

12. Bromley, *Rethinking Middle East Politics*, 79.

13. See Joshua C. Baylson, *Territorial Allocation by Imperial Rivalry: The Human Legacy in the Near East* (Chicago: University of Chicago, 1987), 110.

14. Roy R. Anderson, Robert F. Seibert, and Jon G. Wagner, *Politics and Change in the Middle East: Sources of Conflict and Accommodation*, 3rd ed. (Englewood Cliffs, NJ: Prentice Hall, 1990), 82.

15. Justin McCarthy, *The Ottoman Turks: An Introductory History to 1923* (Boston: Longman, 1997), 345.

16. Charles G. MacDonald, "The Kurdish Question in the 1980s," in Milton J. Esman and Itamar Rabinovitch, eds., *Ethnicity, Pluralism, and the State in the Middle East* (Ithaca, NY: Cornell University Press, 1988), 245 (233–52).

17. David Rieff, "The Shiite Surge," *New York Times* (February 1, 2004), <www.nytimes.com/2004/ 02/01/magazine/01SHIITE.html>.

18. Representatives Les Aspin and William Dickenson [House Armed Services Committee], *Defense for a New Era: Lessons of the Persian Gulf War* (Washington: Brassey's—a Division of Maxwell Macmillan, 1992), 16–17.

19. Seymour M. Hersh, *Against All Enemies—Gulf War Syndrome: The War between America's Ailing Veterans and Their Government* (New York: The Ballantine Publishing Group, 1998), 93–94. The military itself requires its personnel to wear special insulated clothing when working around DU sites, removing all doubt that it understands the risks involved with battlefields where DU shells and bullets remain radioactive almost indefinitely. See "Where the Trail Should Lead," *The Christian Science Monitor* (April 30, 1999), <www.csmonitor.com/durable/1999/04/30/fp10s2-csm.shtml>.

20. On the incompatibility of these objectives see Slavoj Zizek, "Iraq's False Promises," *Foreign Policy* (January/February 2004): 44 (42–49).

21. Dilip Hiro, "Sectarianism in Iraq," *The Nation* (February 2, 2004), <www.thenation.com/docprint.mhtml?i=20040202&s=hiro>.

22. Adel Malek, "Iraq . . . United or Divided?" *Al-Hayat* (January 18, 2004), <dar-alhayat.net/www.actions/print2.php>.

23. Ali Reza Sheikholeslami, "From Religious Accommodation to Religious Revolution: The Transformation of Shi'ism in Iran," in Ali Banuazizi and Myron Weiner, eds., *The State, Religion, and Ethnic Politics: Afghanistan, Iran, and Pakistan* (Syracuse, NY: Syracuse University Press, 1986), 249 (227–55).

24. See Cheryl Miller, "Theorists and Mullahs," *Policy Review* 119 (June 2003), <www.policyreview.org/jun03/nafis_print.html>.

25. William Hartlung, "Guns as Bread-and-Butter," *The Bulletin of the Atomic Scientists* (September 1992), <www.bullatomsci.org/issues/1992/s92/s92.reviews.html>.

26. "Irangate: Saddam Hussein, U.S. Policy and the Prelude to the Persian Gulf War, 1980–1994," *Digital National Security Archive* (2003), <nsarchive.chadwyck.com/iges-sayx.htm>.

27. "The Teicher Affidavit: Iraqgate" [a sworn declaration of NSC official Howard Teicher for the United States District Court, Southern District of Florida, dated January 31,

1995], <www.webcom.com/~lpease/collections/hidden/teicher.htm>. The Teicher affidavit was filed in support of charges brought by the Justice Department against the military contractor Teledyne Industries for selling cluster bombs to Iraq by way of Chile. It offered powerful testimony that the CIA assumed responsibility in the 1980s for making key weapons and war materials available to Iraq. Unfortunately the Teledyne trial got little press coverage, coinciding as it did with the O. J. Simpson trial. Nor did the Clinton administration show any real interest in the issue. In his 1992 presidential race, Clinton made frequent reference to the Republican "tilt" toward Iraq, and promised a full investigation, while vice presidential candidate Gore called this scandal "worse than Watergate." But by 1993 the new administration was clearly adopting the GOP tilt, and finally it sought to bury the issue entirely with the January 1995 Hogan report, a Warren Commission–type whitewash which denied all U.S. involvement in weapons procurement for Iraq. See "Teicher"; and "'Spider's Web': United States Illegally Armed Saddam Hussein," *APFN.com* (November 16, 2002), <www.apfn.org/APFN/IRAQGATE.HTM>; see also Robert Perry, "Iraqgate: Confession and Cover-Up" <www.fair.org/extra/9505/iraqgate.html>.

28. Gawdat Bahgat, "Proliferation of Weapons of Mass Destruction: Iraq and Iran," *Journal of Social, Political, and Economic Studies* 28, no. 4 (winter 2003): 424 (423–49).

29. Hartlung, "Guns as Bread-and-Butter." UN inspection teams searching Iraq for WMD in the 1990s commonly found these dual-use imports from the United States and other Western countries at inactive WMD production sites. See "Irangate: Saddam Hussein, U.S. Policy and the Prelude to the Persian Gulf War, 1980–1994."

30. Schultz was Bechtel's chief executive before joining the Reagan administration and is currently one of its directors. Bechtel's special relationship with Saddam did not prevent it from getting major reconstruction contracts in Iraq following the invasion. See Robert Scheer, "U.S. Winked at Hussein's Evil," *Common Dreams Newscenter,* from the *Los Angeles Times* (December 30, 2003), <www.commondreams.org/cgi-bin/print.cgi?file=/views03/1230-07.htm>.

31. Joseph I. Coffey, "Conclusions and Recommendations," in Joseph I. Coffey and Gianni Bonvicinni, eds., *The Atlantic Alliance and the Middle East* (London: Macmillan, 1989), 295 (268–307).

32. But twelve of the Arab League's twenty-one members gave at least nominal support to the Western alliance against Saddam. See John L. Esposito, "Political Islam and Gulf Security," in John L. Esposito, ed., *Political Islam: Revolution, Radicalism, or Reform?* (Boulder, CO: Lynne Rienner, 1997), 53 (53–74).

33. Kenneth M. Pollack, "Securing the Gulf," *Foreign Affairs* 82, no. 4 (July/August 2003): 3–4 (2–16).

34. Gideon Gera, "Middle Eastern Responses to the Sea Change in Eastern Europe," in David H. Goldberg and Paul Marantz, eds., *The Decline of the Soviet Union and the Transformation of the Middle East* (Boulder, CO: Westview Press, 1994), 186–88 (183–91).

35. Patrick E. Tyler, "Yemen, an Uneasy Ally, Proves Adept at Playing Off Old Rivals," *New York Times* (December 19, 2002), <www.nytimes.com/2002/12/19/international/middleeast/19YEME.html>.

36. David Campbell, *Politics without Principle: Sovereignty, Ethics and the Narratives of the Gulf War* (Boulder, CO: Lynne Rienner, 1993), 44–45.

37. This supposed neutrality was confirmed by Assistant Secretary of State John Kelly, see Campbell, *Politics without Principle*, 45. See also Ron Paul, "Texan Congressman Speaks of 'Forbidden Truth,'" in "'Spider's Web': United States Illegally Armed Saddam Hussein," <www.apfn.org/APFN/IRAQGATE.HTM>.

38. Paul Krugman, "The Wars of the Texas Succession," *The New York Review of Books* 51, no. 3 (February 26, 2004), <nybooks.com/articles/16911>.

39. Bassim Tibi, *Conflict and War in the Middle East, 1967–91: Regional Dynamic and the Superpowers*, translation by Clark Krojzl (New York: St. Martin's Press, 1993), 66 and 177.

40. "Iraqgate Scandal Documents," in "'Spider's Web': United States Illegally Armed Saddam Hussein."

41. Isabel Hilton, "Maybe None of Them Are Terrorists," *The Guardian* (March 31, 2004), <www.guardian.co.uk/alqaida/story/0,12469,1182509,00.html>.

42. Lawrence Freedman and Efraim Karsh, *The Gulf Conflict—1990–91: Diplomacy and War in the New World Order* (Princeton, NJ: Princeton University Press, 1993), 100.

43. Alan R. Taylor, *The Superpowers of the Middle East* (Syracuse, NY: Syracuse University Press, 1991), 110–12.

44. What they probably did not yet recognize was that the new Shia Islamism would be more dangerous to them than Khomeini's had been, since his had challenged their secular dictatorship with a theological dictatorship, whereas post-Saddam Shiism contained the germ of something far more radical: a civil and potentially democratic Islamism.

45. Prior to World War II the United States had been the most trusted Western nation in the Middle East. However erroneously, American philosophy and policy alike had been seen as anti-imperialistic. By 1945 that pristine image was already tarnished. See Tareq Y. Ismael, *International Relations of the Contemporary Middle East: A Study in World Politics* (Syracuse, NY: Syracuse University Press, 1986), 135.

46. Roger Owen, *State, Power and Politics in the Making of the Modern Middle East*, 2nd ed. (London: Routledge, 1992), 105.

47. Left critics typically cite the figure of half a million. This is certainly inflated, since many other factors besides sanctions contributed to Iraq's high child mortality during the 1990s. But that is not to say, as *The New Republic* has argued, that Saddam alone is responsible for the crisis. Matt Welch makes a cogent case for the conservative "over 100,000" figure, which is more than sufficient to classify coalition policies as genocidal. See Welch's "The Truth about Sanctions against Iraq," *Policy* 18, no. 2 (winter 2002), 8–12.

48. Tariq Ali, "Re-Colonizing Iraq," *New Left Review* (May/June 2003): 7 (5–19). Later, of course, she changed her position to conform with Bush-administration needs. Her new position rested on the dreadfully flawed assumption that Saddam would not trouble to hide what he did not have; ergo, he *definitely* had weapons of mass destruction. Never mind that Bush consistently depicted Saddam as "a madman." The possibility that Saddam was bluffing does not seem to have crossed Rice's mind—unless her change of mind was a bluff. Saddam's cohorts would later say that he kept up the pretense in order to impress Arab neighbors. See Maureen Dawd, "The Mirror Has Two

Faces," *New York Times* (February 1, 2004), <www.nytimes.com/2004/02/01/opinion/01DOWD.html>.

49. E.g., the Soviets—contrary to the dark suspicions of Nixon and Kissinger—worked to restrain the Syrian invasion of Jordan in 1970, but they let it be known that a U.S.-Israeli attack on Syria would meet stiff Soviet opposition. See Benjamin Miller, "Perspectives on Superpower Crisis Management and Conflict Resolution in the Arab-Israeli Conflict," in George W. Breslauer, ed., *Soviet Strategy in the Middle East* (Boston: Unwin Hyman, 1990), 260 (247–84).

50. On this pervasive sense of powerlessness, see Gerges, "Rudderless in the Storm: Arab Politics Before and After the Iraq War."

51. "Other Comment: Change in the Middle East," from *Dar Al-Hayat*, in the *International Herald Tribune* (January 15, 2004), <www.iht.com/cgi-bin/generic.cgi?template=articleprint.tmplh&ArticleId=125014>.

52. Abu Ghraib was just one small island of horror in a veritable archipelago of prison camps that the CIA uses for torture by proxy throughout the world. See Stephen Grey, "America's Gulag," *New Statesman* (May 17, 2004), <www.newstatesman.com/site.php3?newTemplate=NSArticle_NS7newDiplayURN=200405170016>.

53. Gal Luft, "U.S., China Are on Collision Course over Oil," *Los Angeles Times* (February 2, 2004), <www.latimes.com/news/opinion/commentary/la-oe-luft2feb02,1,370578.story>.

54. Recently Washington has shown equal dedication to protecting its Saudi partners from the exposure of their involvement in 9/11 and other opprobrious engagements such as Pakistan's WMD proliferation, whose money trail led back to the Saudis. See Greg Palast, "Muzzling Michael, Muzzling Me," from *The Observer* (May 6, 2004), archived <gregpalast.com/printerfriendly.cfm?artid=329>.

55. Jonathan Steele, "Why the U.S. Is Running Scared." *Guardian* (January 19, 2004), <www.guardian.co.uk/Iraq/Story/0,2763,1126178,00.html>; and Tariq Ali, "How Far Will the US Go to Maintain Its Illegitimate Primacy in Iraq?" *Dissident Voice* (February 18, 2004), <www.dissidentvoice.org/Feb04/ Ali0218.htm>.

56. *New York Times* columnist William Safire makes the same mistake with his interpretation of an intercepted message to Ansar as the "smoking gun" to corroborate Bush-administration claims of a Saddam/Osama linkage. What it actually signifies is the ability of U.S. foreign policy to drive usually antithetic enemies together. See William Safire, "Found: A Smoking Gun," *New York Times* (February 11, 2004), <www.nytimes.com/2004/02/11/opinion/11SAFI.html>.

57. Nayef commands the infamous secret police, while Sultan is known to have close ties with the bin Laden family. Both are backed by the most radical Wahhabi imams. See Michael Scott Doran, "The Saudi Paradox," *Foreign Affairs* 83, no. 1 (January/February 2004): 35 and 43 (35–51); and William Safire, "The Split in the Saudi Royal Family," *New York Times* (September 12, 2002), <www.nytimes.com/2002/09/12/opinion/12AFI.html>.

58. "The Limits of Reform," *The Economist* (March 25, 2004), <//economist.com/world/africa/PrinterFriendly.cfm?Story_ID=2545948>. Ironically it is the al Qaeda phenomenon that provides the best public relations for Abdullah, especially in the

wake of terrorist attacks inside Saudi Arabia in May and November 2003. If the former bombing got the public's rapt attention, the latter turned many toward reform, as nearly all the victims were Arabs. Bin Laden's popularity fell thereafter, while secular reformists were joined by a growing number of nonviolent Islamists. See "Adapt or Die," *The Economist* (March 4, 2004), <economist.com/world/africa/Printer Friendly.Cfm?Story_ID=2482168>.

59. "Saudi Shura Council Deplores US Practices in Iraq," *Arabic New.Com* (April 13, 2004), <www.arabicnews.com/ansub/Daily/Day/040413/2004041309.html>.

60. Ashraf Fahim, "'Liberating' Saudi's Shi'ites (and Their Oil)," *Asia Times* (March 18, 2004), <www.atimes.com/atimes/Middle_East/FC18Ak03.html>.

61. "Saudi Arabia Cannot Stay a Family-Owned Business," *Houston Chronicle* (November 24, 2003), <www.chron.com/cs/CDA/printstory.hts/editorial/2247657>.

62. See Eric Leser, "L'empire Carlyle," *Le Monde* (April 29, 2004), <www.lemonde.fr/web/imprimer_article/0,1-0@2-3230,36-362942,0.html>.

63. Leser, "L'empire Carlyle."

64. "Other Comment," *Daily Star* (Beirut) editorial reprinted in the *International Herald Tribune* (February 3, 2004), <www.iht.com/cgi-bin/generic.cgi?template=articleprint.tmplh&ArticleId=127856>.

65. See Marc Lynch, "Taking Arabs Seriously," *Foreign Affairs* 82, no. 5 (September/October 2003): 84 (81–94).

66. It lost much of its firepower after word of it was leaked in February by the liberal Arab newspaper *Al-Hayat* in London. See Maggie Mitchell Salem, "Where the Greater Middle East Plan Went Awry," *Arab News* (April 2004), <www.arabnews.com/?page=7&section=0&article=42658&d=7&m=4&y=2004>; and Gilbert Achcar, "Greater Middle East: The US Plan," *Le Monde diplomatique* (April 2004), <mondediplo. com/2004/04/04world>. Arabs need no forensic analysis to recognize the American and Israeli fingerprints on such multilateral directives. See Gamal Essam El-Din, "Reform and Reformulating," *Al-Ahram Weekly*, No. 678 (February 19–24, 2004), <weekly.ahram.org.eg/2004/678/eg3.htm>.

67. Gilles Kepel, *Jihad: The Trail of Political Islam*, translation by Anthony F. Roberts (Cambridge, MA: The Belknap Press of Harvard University Press, 2002), 254.

68. Olivier Da Lage, "Éche de l'islam politique?" *Le Monde diplomatique* (July 2000), <www.monde-diplomatique.fr/2000/07/DA_LAGE/14050>; and Kepel, *Jihad: The Trail of Political Islam*, 371–76.

69. Boutros Boutros-Ghali, "Egypt's Path to Rights . . .," *Washington Post* (April 7, 2004): A31.

70. Sulaiman al Hattian, "Saudi Arabia Must Alter Its Culture of Fanaticism," *International Herald Tribune*, from the *New York Times* (May 16, 2003), <www.iht.com/cgi-bin/generic.cgi?template=articleprint. tmplh&ArticleId=96429>.

71. Contradictorily, the United States backed Egypt's Sadat in his effort to totally secularize his nation's politics following his highly unpopular peace treaty with Israel. He made a mockery of Egyptian democracy by staging a 99.9 percent public approval rating on his April 1979 referendum concerning the peace treaty. See Lawrence Wright, "The Man behind Bin Laden," *The New Yorker* (September 16, 2002), <www.newyorker.com/fact/content/?020916fa_fact2>.

72. The best compromise, from a Kurdish perspective, would be a loose federalism that keeps the three orders under one roof but at a safe remove from one another. The Kurdish leader Aschalair Talabani points out that historically there has never been an Iraqi national identity. Nor will there be one anytime soon. See "Es wird eine Föderation im Irak geben—interview mit Kurdenführer Talabani," *Kurdishinfo.com* (February 17, 2004), <www.spiegel.de/politik/ausland/0,1518,286653,00.html>.

73. "OIF/OEF Casualty Update [as of April 30, 2004]," *U.S. Department of Defense Press Resources,* <www.defenselink.mil/news/Apr2004/d20040430cas.pdf>.

74. Stanley A. Weiss, "Sheiks Give Modernity a Try," *International Herald Tribune* (April 15, 2004), <www.iht.com/cgi-bin/generic.cgi?template=articleprint.tmplh& ArticleId=515016>.

75. Republished in the *Iraqi Press Monitor* No. 61 (April 21, 2004), <www.wpr.net/ archive/ipm/ipm_061.html>.

76. Since 1991 the Pentagon has enforced a ban on photographs of returning caskets. In April 2004 a cargo worker was summarily fired by Maytag Aircraft for providing such a photo to *The Seattle Times.* See Hal Bernton, "Woman Loses Her Job over Coffins Photo," *The Seattle Times* (April 22, 2004), <seattletimes.nwsource.com/cgi-bin/ PrintStory.pl?document_id=2001909527&zsectio…>.

77. Against the anti-Islamic grain of Bernard Lewis and Fouad Ajami, Mahmood Mamdani has provided a useful corrective with his emphasis on the machinations of America's late–Cold War proxy conflicts. John Esposito points out, however, that this simply reverses the myopia of standard anti-Islamism. The real source of Huntingtonesque civilizational clash is not religion or politics alone, but both combined. See Hugh Eakin, "When U.S. Aided Insurgents, Did It Breed Future Terrorists?" *New York Times* (April 10, 2004), <www.nytimes.com/2004/04/10/arts/10MAMD.html>.

78. Amitai Etzioni, "Religious Civil Society Is Antidote to Anarchy in Iraq and Afghanistan," *The Christian Science Monitor* (April 1, 2004), <www.csmonitor.com/ 2004/0401/p09s01-coop.htm>. Bushites, of course, only consider them antithetical in the case of non-Christian religion.

79. Saad Eddin Ibrahim, "Reviving Middle Eastern Liberalism," *Journal of Democracy* 14, no. 4 (October 2003): 9 (5–10).

80. Benjamin R. Barber, *Jihad vs. McWorld: How Globalism and Tribalism Are Reshaping the World* (New York: Ballantine Books, 1995), 6.

81. In May 20, 2004, the Bush administration booted out its star proxy by ordering a raid on Chalabi's home. This could redound to Chalabi's interest, however, by validating his otherwise weak credentials as an Iraqi patriot.

82. As the U.S. ambassador to Honduras in the 1980s, Negroponte was instrumental in covering up the activities of Honduran death squads that tortured and killed hundreds as part of Reagan's war on the Nicaraguan Sandinistas. See Matthew Rothschild, "Negroponte, a Torturer's Friend," *The Progressive* (April 20, 2004), <www.progressive.org/webex04/wx042004.html>.

7

The Neoglobalization of Iraq: Empire and Resistance in a New Key

Selling a Quagmire

WHATEVER ELSE ONE MAY THINK OF HIM, G. W. Bush must be credited with extraordinary sales skills. Like a real estate agent who manages to sell inaccessible lots in a swamp, Bush managed to keep his ratings up while selling America a quagmire. Even as his administration ignored the real perils of Saudi Wahhabism (or actively camouflaged them, as film director Michael Moore would have it), it miscast Saddam as the mother of global terrorism. The decision to invade Iraq was put beyond debate by Saddam's mythic stockpile of weapons of mass destruction (WMD). Thomas Powers dubs this "the least ambiguous case of misreading of secret intelligence information in American history."[1]

"Misreading" is too generous a word for it, given the pressure the White House applied to the intelligence community to extract desired results. The National Intelligence Estimate (NIE) of October 1, 2002, more than met those desires, and a week later Congress voted for war.[2] The question is how much the administration's slant on Iraq was inspired by ideological prepossessions as opposed to economic calculation. It is no secret that Bush II was in thrall from the first to Reagan-era power brokers, but neither Reagan nor Bush I allowed neoconservatives to utterly dictate foreign policy.[3] In the wake of 9/11, these pseudo-Reaganites threw out the ideal of global community in favor of "shock and awe" unilateralism. Indeed, according to a real Reaganite, Clyde Prestowitz, they threw out conservatism as well.

The neocons had in Bush II a president who knew very little of foreign affairs and even less about the Middle East. On the verge of the invasion, Iraqi advisers who met Bush in the Oval Office were struck by his vast ignorance of the problems facing the coming occupation. The president was unaware, for example, that Iraqi Muslims were grievously divided along sectarian lines. Patently he had not been engaged in any serious planning concerning the war's aftermath. We now know that he summarily dismissed two crucial intelligence reports of January 2003 from the National Intelligence Council. These predicted that an invasion would not only ignite a firestorm in Iraq, but would fuel Islamist terrorism throughout the world. The administration centered its case around Iraq's acquisition of aluminum tubes that according to Condoleezza Rice, Bush's national security advisor, were only suitable for nuclear weapons development. She gave that statement in an interview of September 2002, yet in 2001 she had been informed by the Energy Department that these tubes were suitable only for conventional, small artillery purposes.[4]

What is even more disturbing is how the major media bought the White House script. Few hard questions were put to the Bush Doctrine or its test run in Iraq. Nor was much attention given to how a president who had campaigned on a pledge of foreign policy humility and a rejection of nation building could saddle the United States with the total reconstruction of Iraq as well as Afghanistan.[5] Instead of pursuing the question of whether the invasion was necessary, the media had been "full of quite detailed discussions of the merits of a preliminary bombing campaign, versus a big tank operation through the desert, versus an 'inside-out' approach of parachuting troops right into Baghdad. . . ."[6] The war itself was never much of an issue.

One reason for this journalistic hiatus was the advance "intelligence" barrage of Ahmed Chalabi's Iraqi National Congress (INC), much of which was paid for by U.S. taxpayers via operations such as the Information Collection Program. Funds provided by the Iraq Liberation Act purchased the services of the public relations firm Burson-Marsteller to promote the INC agenda. Dozens of INC-inspired stories ran in major American media after 9/11, validating the president's prior determination to raise Saddam over Osama as the global terrorist-in-chief. Since the post–Gulf War era the State Department and the CIA—which favored the Iraqi National Accord (INA) of Ayad Allawi, a former Baathist and CIA minion[7]—had expressed grave doubts about the INC spin factory; but the neocons focused their doubts on the CIA and State Department. The White House fatefully sided with the neocons, funneling $33 million into INC coffers between March 2000 and May 2003.

On 9/12/01 Jim Hoagland, chief foreign correspondent for the *Washington Post*, led the charge under the title "What about Iraq?" Blame was laid on the

CIA for not giving credence to the INC's insistence that Iraq had a hand in 9/11. And on December 20 Judith Miller of the *New York Times* put the INC version of Saddam's WMD threat on the paper's front page under the head-line "Iraqi Tells of Renovations at Sites for Chemical and Nuclear Arms." Not one of these alleged sites, which were said to lie under hospitals or within palace walls, was ever located.[8]

Nevertheless Vice President Cheney stuck to his double-barreled mantra concerning Saddam's WMD and his ties to al Qaeda, more than hinting that Iraq was somehow responsible for 9/11.[9] When none of these claims found empirical support, the official reason for the invasion shifted to the civiliza-tional task—consistent with Bernard Lewis's diagnosis of modern Islamic cul-ture as morally and politically moribund—of removing a genocidal tyrant and establishing a showcase democracy in the Middle East.[10] 9/11 united Lewis and Bush in the neocon determination to set Muslims straight.[11] Neoglobalism (the art and practice of armed globalization) was now on the march.

But why start with Iraq? Some wayward progressives advanced humani-tarian justifications from the first,[12] but Bush found it more arresting to build his case around the imaginary smoking gun of WMD. Oil was hardly mentioned, nor was the geopolitical utility that Iraq could have as a U.S. for-ward base, comparable to Germany after World War II. For Gabriel Kolko that was the clincher: the invasion was essentially a Cold War rerun. Much as the establishment of NATO in 1949 had been aimed at Europe as well as the U.S.S.R., America's preemptive strike on Iraq had more to do with resid-ual Cold War ambitions than with post-9/11 security needs.[13] Iraq, in effect, was NATO II.[14]

To sell this geopolitical atavism would require a credible global foe. Neo-cons such as Richard Perle found that perfect adversary in jihadic Islam. What Perle did not mention is that Islam has harbored this jihadic ambition since the seventh century. Nor was it mentioned that Saddam Hussein, as an arch-secularist, was the natural enemy of Perle's chosen enemy. These were trifling details for the personal disciple of a leader who answers directly to God, and therefore does not "nuance." What mattered for Bush and his neocon planners was their strategic Trinity: getting to Jerusalem by way of Baghdad,[15] paying for the trip with Iraqi oil, and doing it all in the name of democratization.

Even the Bush team must have known that Iraq was grossly unfit as a dem-ocratic base camp. Accordingly, massive and protracted U.S. military involve-ment would be necessary, and this very presence would discredit any demo-cratic project. It is common knowledge that Sunnis by and large detest Shiites as much as they do Israelis. And the feeling is certainly mutual. Both groups, moreover, share a deep and fully reciprocated antipathy toward the Kurds. The paradox is that these entrenched animosities only enhance Iraq's geopolitical appeal, just as they did for the British in the 1920s. What better place could there be for divide-and-conquer tactics?

For the neocons, then, negatives became positives, and the perfect man to reap them was Perle's friend Chalabi. It was no secret in the intelligence community that Chalabi and his INC cohorts were in the misinformation business, but from a neocolonial vantage this character defect was just another positive: Like his arch-rival Allawi, Chalabi was reliable insofar as he could be bought. Many journalists were aware of his weakness as an intelligence source, but few broke silence on the matter.[16] Little concern was voiced over known facts such as the 1989 collapse of Chalabi's Middle East banking empire or his sentence in absentia by Jordan to twenty years in prison on thirty-one charges of embezzlement, theft, and illegal speculation. Throughout the Middle East the mere mention of his name evoked contempt, but at the American Enterprise Institute (AEI) he was hailed as nothing less than the "George Washington of Iraq."

That was far more important for Chalabi's career development than what the Iraqis thought. He was wheeled in as the chief power broker on the Iraqi Governing Council, especially in the areas of finance and appointments. Not surprisingly his relatives and cronies began raking in the best contracts and positions. Since 1998 the Pentagon had paid him and the INC $340,000 per month to be lied to about Iraq.[17] Under Bush this "intelligence" was evaluated almost exclusively by the Pentagon's neoconservative think tank, the Office of Special Plans, whose findings were passed directly to the White House. The CIA was not even allowed to interview INC informants without special permission from the Pentagon.[18]

Chalabi had every reason to expect his personal power to mushroom after the Coalition Provisional Authority (CPA) relinquished its authority. Seen in this light, Sistani's case for a directly elected provisional government took on a democratic aura,[19] while Chalabi looked more and more like America's erstwhile proxy, the Shah of Iran, complete with his 440,000-strong military and Savak terror police. The Bush administration's concern was that the Iraqis might reject this Karzai-like implant in favor of their own brand of democracy. It did not intend to give them that opportunity.

Washington's dread of Shia empowerment came wrapped in the orientalist notion that democracy is a distinctly Western institution which has little chance of emerging elsewhere. In 1992 Colin Powell spelled out the standard assumption that there was no chance of a homegrown "Jeffersonian" democrat stepping forth in Iraq. Removing Saddam, he argued, would simply make room for somebody else of the same ilk, though putting up new statues and wall portraits might take some time.[20] It is certainly true that thirty years of

Baath Party rule allowed no individual or group to gain experience in democratic leadership, but what Powell missed was the democratic propensity of civil Islam.

Many in the president's inner circle—such as Perle and David Frum, co-authors of the apocalyptic *An End to Evil*—were even more rabidly anti-Islamic than Powell. In 2002, for example, the Bush administration was willing to bestow $500 million on a bloody but secular dictatorship in Uzbekistan. In all fairness, this orientation did not originate with Bush II idealogues. Muslims have strong historical reason to construe U.S. calls for democracy as a cover for imperialistic designs on their world. What distinguishes neocon orientalism is the utter contradiction between its anti-Islamist premises and its "democratic" project. If Islam per se deserves such disdain, the process of imposing democracy on *any* Muslim country would be so costly and prolonged that the stated American mission would be doomed from the start. In fact, the neocons are not ardent promoters of democratic export to the entire Muslim world, but only that part of it which happens to sit on top of the world's major oil reserves.

Shiism and the Search for Legitimacy

Rising anarchy in Iraq forced the Bush administration into an election-year reversal: an urgent appeal for UN intervention. Much as Britain once fell prey to Churchill's lethal underestimation of the need for ground forces in the Dardanelles in 1915, the Bush team grievously "misread" the number and type of troops that would be needed for minimum security in Iraq.[21] Berlin and Paris were willing in principle to endorse a renewed UN role,[22] but there was more than a whiff of moral hazard in bailing Washington out from quagmires of its own making, thus creating what Tariq Ali calls the United Nations of America. The UN would thereby give its ex post facto blessing to operations it had no part in conceiving or shaping. Ali contends that Boutros-Ghali was dismissed as the UN secretary-general for daring to contrast the West's solicitude toward Bosnia with its virtual indifference toward ever greater tragedies unfolding in Africa.[23] As he sees it, Kofi Annan got his job as a reward for services rendered to the Clinton administration, and not surprisingly he stood ready to rubber-stamp U.S. unilateralism.[24] In fact he ended up declaring America's actions against Iraq illegal, and faulting the United States for not working with the UN.

The UN withdrew from Iraq in October 2003 after the death of about two dozen employees, including the highly regarded chief UN representative Sergio Vieira de Mello. Now the organization is being pressed to return to an even more combustible Iraq. It would have helped, of course, if the UN had been granted a formative role from the start, and if postwar policy could have claimed the kind of broad international support that postwar operations enjoyed in Afghanistan.[25] In a belated bid for legitimacy, Secretary of Defense Donald Rumsfeld—who was for striking Iraq rather than Afghanistan after 9/11, on the surreal ground that "there aren't any good targets in Afghanistan"[26]—also urged NATO to join the fray by assuming command of British and Polish troops south of Bagdad.[27] It is unrealistic, however, to suppose that any external organization can implant legitimacy here. That has to be a domestic product, and certainly an Islamic one. America's anti-Islamism might have meshed with postcolonial secularism of the 1950s and 1960s, but is woefully out of line with political realities in today's Iraq.[28]

Surprisingly, the division of mosque and state gets considerable support from Sistani, whose influence could be decisive in bridging the gap between Iraqi and American preferences. Part of Sistani's attraction for Shiites is his proven autonomy: He never yielded to Saddam or the Iranian ayatollahs. But by the same token he resisted the dictates of the Americans, who oddly see themselves as facilitating democracy even against the popular will of the Iraqis. This dam will soon break, for as Fareed Zakaria notes, the occupation can survive pockets of insurgency but not a dozen protest marches "with thousands chanting 'colonialists go home!'"[29] On a single day in January 2004 about 100,000 (including many Sunnis) protested in Baghdad in support of Sistani, while smaller groups demanded the execution of Saddam.

The democratic dynamic at work here should be obvious. If Shiism contains some rabidly undemocratic elements, so did the American constitution at the time of its framing. Even Pentagon analysts should have discerned that the Hawza—the powerful but amorphous Shiite political authority—was not initially hostile to America's stated objectives. Accordingly it pressed its demands by strictly nonviolent means: demonstrations, strike threats, and simple noncooperation. It was no accident that Shiite areas south of Baghdad were relatively peaceful during the early occupation, while the Sunni Triangle north and west of the capital was racked by violence reminiscent of Mogadishu. The Hawza restored a semblance of domestic order after Saddam's fall. American strategists had scarcely considered the need for postinvasion security at vital sites such as hospitals, where Hawza volunteers stepped in as de facto security guards. In sum, the Shiites spared the Americans the nightmare of complete anarchy.

Already the Hawza has a democratic dimension, in that Shiites choose their own ayatollahs. Unlike the Sunnis, who are sworn to obey their rulers even when they turn out to be tyrants, Shiites owe no fealty to worldly powers gone bad.[30] Only his earned popularity makes Sistani the "supreme" ayatollah. So too it makes him the bane of American strategists who want to empty the word "democracy" of its less convenient (e.g., anti-American) meaning. Certainly there was nothing democratic about the American policy of handpicking delegates to the constitutional assembly. By contrast, Sistani has reached out to Sunni and Christian minorities and insisted on a "full and free" Iraqi vote.[31]

After muzzling this democratic voice, and that of civil Islam in general, the Coalition had only itself to blame for the unrest that exploded in the south. Too often U.S. troops used tactics associated with Zionist state terrorism in Palestine. Predictably this inspired more insurrection. No longer could it be said that the south, unlike the "Sunni Triangle," was calm and supportive.[32] The tide had turned so decisively that even moderates within Sunni and Shia ranks could not afford overt cooperation with the Coalition or its proxies. American intransigence raised the status of reactionaries like Sheik Hareth al-Dhari on the Sunni side and Muqtada al-Sadr on the Shia side. Even the transitional government under Allawi would be forced to appease the hard-liners it was supposed to crush. Success was downgraded to simply avoiding civil war, while U.S. hopes of turning Allawi into an Iraqi Mubarak evaporated.[33]

Cheating the Kurds, as Usual

The Kurds have been America's only consistent supporters in Iraq, but they too recoil from American proxyism. The "safe haven" they have enjoyed since the Gulf War has been a rare exception to their general treatment. Only after a million Kurds fled into Turkey and Iran did U.S.-directed forces finally offer them protection. This was at the behest of the Turks, who feared waves of unruly refugees.

It is surprising, given their history, that the Kurds are not more hostile toward the West and America in particular. In 1920 the United States joined Britain and other world powers in promising them their own state in the Treaty of Sèvres. The next year the British decided that oil-rich Kirkuk was better kept for themselves, as part of the mandate they would wrench from the League of Nations. To make sure the disgruntled Kurds were in no position to do anything about it, Britain saw to it that they were dispersed among several states, especially Turkey and Iraq, which would keep these fractious tribes in line.[34]

That would be no small task, as the Kurds were heir to a legendary fighting spirit (their ancestors did more damage to Alexander the Great's army than the Persians had). It was no accident that during the 1930s the Iraqi army succeeded in destroying the military capabilities of all the region's tribes *other than the Kurds.*[35] Even today, under U.S. auspices, the non-Kurdish zone is ger-rymandered to include Kirkuk, which Saddam did his best to Arabize in the 1980s. Pan-Arabism was a Baathist euphemism for terroristic pacification, a weeding process which was applied most aggressively to the Kurds.[36]

Early in the 1970s America briefly departed from the British script. For that moment Henry Kissinger encouraged the Kurds to rebel, only to abandon them to the Shah with his infamous words that "Covert action should not be confused with missionary work." To be sure, the surviving Kurdish insurgents could not confuse the two. Nor can they forget that the United States was avidly courting Saddam before and after his chemical weapons attacks on them during the Iran-Iraq War. At the town of Halabja alone (close to the later mountain stronghold of the Taliban-style Ansar al-Islam fundamentalist re-sistance) 5,000 Kurds were killed on March 16, 1988, and hundreds more were slaughtered on the road by Iraqi air attacks. The death toll approached 200,000, with hundreds of villages completely destroyed.

Washington encouraged the Kurds and Shiites to rebel after the Gulf War, only to betray them once again in their hour of need. Partly out of fear of a divided Iraq, and partly as a favor to the Turks, signals were sent to Saddam that he would have a free hand to crush both rebellions.[37] The United States stood by as Iraqi helicopter gunships used the Kurds for live target practice, much as the British RAF had bombed them in the 1920s and early 1930s—such that the Kurdish rebel leader, Sheikh Mahmud, was jokingly called the "Director of RAF Training."[38]

This goes far to explain why most Kurds, despite their hatred of Saddam, had grave misgivings about the 2003 invasion. Later U.S. attitudes did little to allay those fears. In February 2003 Bush's special envoy, Zalmay Khalilzad, in-formed Kurdish leaders that Turkish troops would be deployed in the Kurdish zone for "humanitarian" purposes—Turkish humanitarianism being, for Kurds, an oxymoron bordering on black humor. It was added that Kurdish self-government was to be terminated, and hundreds of thousands of Kurdish refugees would not be allowed to reclaim their homes. Only by comparison with Saddam could the bearer of such grim tidings be called a friend. One must wonder why the Kurdish reaction against the Americans was not more like Osama's.

Geopolitically, the answer is one of simple default: the end of the Cold War deprived the Kurds of their "northern card."[39] With every state in the region at their throats, they had little choice but to cast their lot with the United States. And given their loathing for Saddam, any present enemy of his came with a good recommendation. Thus the vast majority of Kurds still manage to view the Americans as liberators. They simply ask that the new Iraq should have a federal system to ensure their minority rights. At one point the Iraqi

Governing Council, in which the Kurds had five votes, approved this arrangement, which would have put Washington in a position of embarrassed opposition to its own political creation.[40] Fortunately for the Americans, the Shiites soon reversed this decision.

Some observers believe federalism would make for sectarianism, but sectarianism is already an entrenched reality in Iraq.[41] A failure to face this fact could make for civil war. The best hope for peace is through compromise: the Shiites must relax some of their creedal demands, the Kurds must yield some degree of their autonomy, and the Sunnis must agree on a democratic process that locks in Shiite gains but keeps themselves in the game.[42] Unfortunately Washington will not budge on this issue. Indeed, it let the interim constitution (the Transitional Administration Law, or TAL) quietly expire at the time of the vaunted transfer of sovereignty, and it was only the TAL that had kept the Kurds in the hypothetical state of "Iraq." Under it they were guaranteed some protection against Shiite domination. By refusing to recognize ethnic rights and boundaries, L. Paul Bremer (the first chief of civilian operations) thought he was strengthening the bonds of Iraqi identity. In fact he was writing the epitaph for a would-be nation.[43]

By any reckoning the Kurds deserved a better deal. It is a telling fact that no U.S. soldiers were killed in Iraqi Kurdistan in the early "postvictory" war. So too this zone remained largely terrorist free until February 2004, when terrorist bombings cost the Kurds one of their best negotiators, Abdul Rahman. It was precisely for fear of a terrorist influx that they had protested the dismantling of border controls in April 2003. Meanwhile Bremer pressed the Kurds to give up still more power in the spheres of taxation, Kirkuk oil, and military autonomy;[44] and, to top it off, $4 billion promised to the Kurds from UN oil-for-food funds was slipped into the CPA budget.

On the surface, Allawi's refusal to honor TAL terms was yet another blow to the Kurds. Technically Washington had no authority under international law to enforce such promises. But of course it had the power to safeguard Kurdish interests if it wished. As it turns out, the Kurds might well thank Washington for its latest betrayal, for U.S. protection would not have come cheap. Without the TAL, the Kurds will not have to suffer Iraqi taxes or even the Iraqi flag. Their only reliable safeguard is thus activated: any attempt on Baghdad's part to further dilute their rights will mean secession.[45]

The "Democracy" Game

There is some irony in the fact that the United States has been democratically upstaged in both the Kurdish north and Shiite south. U.S. planners, if that is the right word, never expected legitimacy problems after Saddam's fall. Cheney had convinced his fatuous boss that the invaders would be cheered as liberators by crowds waving homemade American flags and chanting that democracy goes better with Coke. The Bush team intended to introduce its oily version of "democracy" once stability was achieved, and only belatedly learned that this was putting the cart before the horse: Stability itself would depend on democratic legitimacy.

As in Afghanistan, Bush's self-proclaimed victory turned out to be a mirage, or rather a whole series of them. As in Vietnam, victory was always just around the corner.[46] It was celebrated a second time with the capture of Saddam, which was followed by the April 2004 rising in Falluja. Again the victory band was cranked up for the sovereignty transfer, which was followed by the August 2004 rising in Najaf. Finally hope was vested in the reconstruction dollars that were expected to draw insurgents away to better paying jobs, but which mainly benefited corporations such as Halliburton.

At first the opposition had a hit-and-run character that made for anarchy but little concerted resistance. The real thing had its prelude in an unsuccessful but symbolically stunning attack on a convoy carrying the head of the U.S. Central Command, General John Abizaid. Two days later full rebellion erupted in Falluja. To the dismay of the Americans, Shiite militants under al-Sadr seized this opportunity to open a second front. Foolishly Allawi had closed Sadr's newspaper, prompting huge protests in Baghdad. Shiite and Sunni insurgents forged a startling alliance that took the fighting to numerous southern cities as well as to Sunni enclaves such as Ramadi.[47] If the American goal was to construct a single, trans-sectarian Iraq, the project was succeeding brilliantly.

The Coalition was forced to lift its siege on Falluja, but in August it was again mired in a politically strained battle with Sadr's Mahdi army in Najaf. To end that battle and avoid an even greater nationalist conflagration, Sistani had to be rushed back from heart surgery in London. Again his intercession spared the Americans a full revolt, but even he could not save them from their real enemy, which was themselves. While Najaf got world headlines, other urban areas were slipping away, leaving much of western Iraq under rebel control.[48] It was becoming obvious that Washington's strategy had a fatal flaw: The Iraqis that America now faced in the street were curiously unlike the ones they had listened to in modeling their occupation strategy. Unlike Chalabi and Allawi, they could not so easily be bought.[49] Hence they were "terrorists."

Finally the Americans awakened to the fact that some Shiites were worth courting. It was no accident that the Cold War between the Coalition and the Mahdi army went hot while Sistani was incapacitated.[50] The assumption that social order would follow automatically from Saddam's fall led Washington to place all its bets on a military solution, not only spurning local allies such as Sistani, but global ones as well. The whole principle of internationalism was jettisoned.[51]

In a desperate attempt to get the spotlight off the WMD issue, Bush declared his mission to be nothing less than the promotion of democracy throughout the Middle East. No doubt this was rather unsettling to the region's power elites, but it was hardly so radical a departure as American pundits assumed. It was common knowledge in policy circles that the tepid democratization on offer from Washington could easily be co-opted by ruling classes to buttress their legitimacy.[52] In short, Bush was playing the democracy game with loaded dice: Since all Arab OPEC nations are undemocratic, the president could gain political or commercial concessions simply by invoking the code word "democracy." This was a bargaining chip, not a mission, and refractory Arab oil states could of course fire back with the threat of price hikes. Their cooperation in keeping prices low would have to be won by reducing reform pressure. Both sides understood that "democracy" is a negotiable commodity.

In Iraq, however, the democracy game is complicated by spreading anarchy. Democracy can be negotiated away only when someone is in charge. No less a geopolitician than Robert McNamara avers that there is no way to topple a dictator like Saddam without taking on an obligation to fill his organizational shoes. Like it or not, filling that void is called nation building. The prime issue is whether it should be U.S.- or UN-directed.[53] Since preemptive action was beyond the bounds of the UN Charter, the United States had to act alone; and having done so, it was not about to surrender the crown jewels—the oil and the bases—to UN oversight. Nor could Washington sell its action back home without the appearance of some stupendous provocation. Just as Vietnam had been justified on the basis of a bogus story about torpedo attacks, Iraq had to be justified on the basis of imminent WMD peril.

In fact, the only WMD crisis in Iraq was planted there by the Americans themselves. Their "shock and awe" tactics involved weapons known to cause radiation illness and the host of maladies associated with the Gulf War syndrome. By mid-April 2003 the U.S. Air Force had fired more than 311,000 rounds of uranium A10 shells and 19,000 guided weapons of similar content in Iraq. Iraqi children now play on destroyed tanks which British survey teams felt safe to inspect only when wearing full-body radiation suits.[54]

This is reminiscent of the "rational irrationality" of the Vietnam War, whereby villages were "saved" by their literal destruction. Since Americans in Iraq reside in heavily fortified compounds and avoid "no go" zones, they are difficult targets. Much of the insurgency, therefore, is aimed at Iraqis who assist the occupation: police and security workers, local politicians and the judiciary. The result is the very unrest that the American presence was supposed to quell. Even Baghdad's "Green Zone"—the site of the Iraqi interim government and the U.S. central headquarters—is within reach of mortar attacks from the surrounding "Red Zone" that is coming to typify the whole country.

The government, moreover, is caught in a no-man's-land between Shiite resurgence and Sunni reaction, not to mention the ethnic divide between the Kurds and both. The United States would be wise not just to limit its exposure here, but to abbreviate its stay. With protests igniting all across Iraq over unemployment, petrol shortages, and chronic insecurity, and with militant resistance becoming more organized *after* Saddam's capture in December 2003, President Bush had difficulty maintaining his election-year pose as the man who brought democratic hope to Iraq and the whole Middle East. One of his biggest problems was the self-defeating nature of his ends and means. Counterinsurgency tactics that seemed necessary for securing minimal order enraged the general population whose support was essential. Democratization in Iraq is synonymous with Shiite power, which Washington fears more than it ever feared Saddam, and Sunni neighbors fear more than Osama.

Occupation forces were lucky the Shiites coalesced from the start around Sistani rather than radicals such as the cleric Mahmoud al-Hassani or the quasi-cleric al-Sadr, who could well have been involved in the April 2003 murder of the moderate cleric Abdel Majid al-Khoei.[55] Unfortunately, given the scandalous conduct of the occupying forces—unforgettably symbolized by the very name Abu Ghraib—there is plenty of grist for Sadr's mill. That became obvious as early as July 20, 2003, when Sadr mustered a huge demonstration at Najaf, denouncing Bush, Saddam, and Satan with equal fervor.[56] For those in the Bush administration who somehow failed to get the message, the August 2004 rising in Najaf left no doubt that Shiite compliance could no longer be taken for granted.

This is hardly to agree with Tariq Ali's barbed contention that most Iraqis were sorry to see Saddam toppled. In the early days of the occupation it would have been a task to find many non-Sunnis who even remotely felt this way. If Saddam had done nothing more than rob billions from the country while it was under crushing international sanctions, this would have earned him the lasting enmity of most Iraqis. And if the general public had been spiteful toward all Americans, as Ali alleges, U.S. forces would have suffered far more postwar casualties than they initially did in non-Sunni zones. Ali's "Iraq," as Johann Hari observes, is vintage New Left social fiction.[57]

What makes the present Iraqi meltdown all the more tragic is that many opportunities for a better outcome were squandered. Unbeknownst to Washington, the main shield against an anti-American cataclysm has been the civil Shiism that Sistani marshals. He is a protégé of the late Grand Ayatollah Abu al-Qassim al-Khoei, whose quietism stood in stark contrast to the flaming extremism of Khomeini.[58] In that spirit, Sistani is reputed to have advised the new government that in choosing the next leader, make sure he is not wearing a turban.

Had he wished to make serious trouble for the Americans, Sistani could have done so with a single fatwa, or simply by uttering the word *jihad*. Clearly he has no wish to imitate Iranian theocracy. By training and temperament he is an apolitical moderate who favors a substantial separation of religion and state. Another supporter of mosque/state dissociation is none other than Ayatollah Seyed Hussan Khomeini, the grandson of *the* Ayatollah Khomeini. The junior Khomeini's return to Iraq from Iran is emblematic of the more tempered Shia politics that Washington has tragically ignored.

With Najaf and Karala once again attracting thousands of pilgrims from across Asia and the Middle East, the Shiite wing of civil Islam could become an export commodity. Saddam did his best to crush all Islamism, but it was the senior Khomeini who came closest to snuffing out its civil component. The junior Khomeini is determined to reclaim that lost heritage. Turi Munthe points out the irony that Saddam's main political legacy, by way of reaction, is the very Islamism he tried to expunge.[59]

Unfortunately, many American "experts" view Islamism with equal suspicion. Daniel Pipes is not unusual in seeing it as the very antithesis of democracy.[60] This view fails to register a cardinal reality of the Iraqi "street": that, apart from Iraqi Kurdistan, the alternative to Islamist democracy will be anarchy or civil war. Hard economic and demographic realities (with 50 to 60 percent unemployment and half the population twenty or under) militate against Washington's secular development formula. What is urgently needed is the social cohesion that only Islamism can provide, and which only Sistani can generate in the post-Saddamist south. Sistani's moderation is reflected in the fact that the TAL took Islam only as "a source," not "*the* source," of future legislation. Even Pipes, who deplores any constitutional role for Islamic law, could imagine a far worse outcome than this.

Like the assassinated moderate Ayatollah Mohammad Bakr al-Hakim,[61] Sistani is somewhere near the middle on a Shiite political spectrum ranging from the elder Khomeini to Abdolkarim Soroush, an Iranian ex-theocrat who now mixes Koranic religious principles with generous portions of John Stuart Mill and John Rawls. Sistani's reason for promoting a healthy distinction (though not a Western-style barricade) between religion and the state is not so much to protect government from religious influence as to save religion from government corruption.[62] It should be stressed that the standards of freedom and tolerance that crept into the TAL were as much a product of Islamic tradition as of Western influence.[63]

The Anti-American Century

Washington glibly assumes that any democratic progress in the Middle East must be America's unilateral gift, yet the most promising democratic advocates in today's Iraq are the products of an East/West dialogue that is far older than American democracy. For Soroush these reformist roots reach back to the Hellenic-inspired rationalism of the Mu'tazilites in the Baghdad caliphate of the eighth and ninth centuries. The problem in most Islamic countries is not that the engineers and Western-educated specialists who increasingly manage society are too steeped in Islamic culture. As was pointed out by Indonesia's former president, Abdurrahman Wahid, the problem is that Muslim technocrats have at best a superficial grasp of Islam. They are prone to a literal and reductive religiosity that can be worse than none at all.[64]

A similar reductionism contributes to the common Western assumption that Islam and modernity are strictly at odds. Along with corporate greed and imperialist hubris, blanket anti-Islamism dooms U.S. policies in the Middle East. To no avail, the CIA and other U.S. agencies predicted the problems that surfaced after the "victory" in Iraq.[65] Cultural myopia acts as an empirical screen, making for the bad intelligence that dominated neocon war plans.

The invasion invited descriptions of the United States as a new Rome in its prime; but within six months that invincible image had given way to one of Rome in decline. Already the Bush Doctrine was showing signs of imperial overstretch, having spawned an anti-American rebound of global proportions. Walden Bello notes that the drubbing taken by the United States and other northern powers at the September 2003 WTO meeting in Cancun owed much to the Iraq quagmire. Likewise the growing confidence of the G20 draws upon the global climate of resistance that was seeded by the anti-war movement of early 2003.[66]

One year after the invasion, U.S. supporters such as Spain and Poland painfully recognized that they had been duped: Iraq's weapons threat had been fabricated. A former chief weapons inspector in Iraq, David Kay, issued a shocking report verifying that Saddam had destroyed most if not all of his WMD stockpile long before. Evidently he withheld evidence of this compliance in an effort to maintain an illusion of international stature.[67] This put him at ground zero of the Bush administration's guilty-until-proven-innocent hit list.

Ordinary Iraqis would pay the price for this curious blend of compliance and pugnacity. Civic, an NGO, conservatively estimated that 5,000 Iraqi civilians were killed between the outbreak of the war on March 20 and the end of major combat operations on May 1. But the death toll on innocent Iraqis continued to mount. Many died in noncombat "accidents" involving trigger-happy troops, as when a driver's bad muffler was mistaken for gunfire at a checkpoint. Amnesty International put the death count for the first year after hostilities commenced at over 10,000.[68] The standard army response was that civilians had been shot in accord with the proper "Rules of Engagement." But even this formality was often skipped. In one typical case a taxi was given the OK to pass an American convoy, but a machine gunner toward the front failed to get the message, and opened fire. The taxi driver was badly injured and his passengers, a mother and her six-year-old child, were killed. In violation of Article 27 of the Fourth Geneva Convention, the convoy continued without bothering to check if anyone was still alive. No report was filed, and later it proved impossible even to ascertain which convoy had been involved.[69]

It was obvious by 2004 that Iraq was a soft-power disaster packaged as a hard-power triumph. After $900 million had been spent looking for WMDs, none were found. Terrorist attacks were routine, electricity was an evanescent luxury, sectarian violence was on the rise, and humanitarian aid was so lacking that it would have been an international scandal had it been properly reported. With sewage backed up and drinking water contaminated, blood was in such short supply that doctors often had to donate their own blood to keep patients alive.[70] Even President Bush finally granted that he had "miscalculated" the postvictory trauma in Iraq.[71]

He declined to mention his regional miscalculation. For Arabs already seething over Washington's favoritism toward Israel, there was now a solid consensus that American hegemony was real and intolerable. Nor could it have been much more popular with Americans themselves had they comprehended the scope of its brutality, its duplicity, and (most especially) its costs. With the U.S. economy straining under the operation's $125 billion bill for the first year alone, the real war on terrorism was bound to suffer. Indeed, as an editorial in India's *Hindustan Times* noted, a new breeding ground for terrorism had been created in Iraq by ripping apart the country's social fabric and leaving dire problems to fester. This putative "war on terror" has given al Qaeda a new home.[72]

Meanwhile the major media have joined the military in whitewashing the human toll of the war. There has been a self-enforced ban on coverage of the largely nocturnal return of 14,000 medically evacuated soldiers, not to mention hundreds of returning coffins; and the only sustained coverage of Iraqi suffering has come from Arab sources such as *al Jazeera*. With good reason these alter-media depict the occupation and its proxies as agents of raw conquest. The final insult, however, is that this flagrantly imperialist operation has been rescripted as an exercise in democratization.

By no accident the CPA cut local ties that could have given particular constituencies a voice in Iraq's future, thus affording a degree of protection for minorities:

> So keen were the Americans to wash their hands of the awkward mosaic of Iraq's tribal, regional, and religious interests, that they couldn't even face drawing up constituency boundaries. As a result, Iraq is one seat, with 275 members of parliament to be elected by proportional representation. Iraqis will be asked to vote for national party lists, rather than to pick a local person representing the interests of their town. . . . [This] guarantees power will lie with big, organized, well-funded party machines that decide who tops the lists. The overall effect will be to polarize the debate, penalizing moderates or well-regarded local candidates or those without wealthy Iranian and Saudi backers.[73]

The Americans think they rather than the Iranians or Saudis will be pulling the strings. That of course would be a blueprint for nationalist resistance. It is telling that the United States is willing to accept this hazard rather than relinquish control of Iraqi politics (and oil). In effect they prefer the risk of mass insurrection to that of genuine democracy.

Ever since the end of the Cold War, the Arab world feared what would come of American unipolarity, and for its part the United States quickly replaced the ideological tilt of its anti-Soviet fixation with an anti-Islamic focus on civilizational clash. The original advice of the foremost "clash" theorists, Bernard Lewis and Samuel Huntington, was aimed primarily at conflict avoidance. But after 9/11 Lewis joined the neocon clamor for preemptive war and democratic imperialism.[74] Perhaps he now regrets this reversal, for the mess in Iraq provides ample support for his more cautious original position. Comparisons of America's Iraq and Vietnam debacles are inevitable. Jonathan Schell observes that when the United States

> arrived in Bagdad, there was no pre-existing popular resistance movement (or movements) in place. . . , as there had been when the Amercan military arrived in force in Vietnam. Neither was there any . . . imperial puppet government at hand like Ngo Dinh Diem's in Vietnam. Instead there was a double political vacuum. The consequence was anarchy. . . . Now that vacuum is being filled on one side. Movements of national resistance have arisen in both the Sunni north and the Shiite south. . . . On the American side, . . . Allawi . . . does the bidding of the United States without benefit of popular support. The contest has assumed a form distressingly familiar from other anti-imperial movements. The local resis-

tors are weak militarily but strong politically, the imperial masters are powerful militarily but nearly helpless politically.[75]

Schell's analysis is correct so far as it goes. There is indeed a proto-nationalist current flowing through "liberated" Iraq, but it is hardly the secular, Kemalist variety. Fortunately for the occupiers, the same sectarian and ethnic divisions that have plagued reconstruction efforts have also precluded the kind of cohesive resistance that upended U.S. strategy in Vietnam. Being as much a product of Islamism as of nationalism, Iraqi insurgency is a house divided—split not only along Sunni versus Shiite lines, but within the Shiite camp itself. Amidst this chaos, the occupation cuts both ways: spawning broad resistance but also forestalling civil war by providing the cardinal blessing of a common enemy. For that inadvertent gift, at least, President Bush deserves full credit. His policies have produced the miracle of cooperation between Sunni and Shiite adversaries.

On the world stage, likewise, Bush deserves credit for galvanizing the global revulsion that is putting a definitive end to the mythic "end of history." His neocons set out, by force of arms if necessary, to make this the American century. Instead they have inaugurated what could well be an anti-American century. For a world starved for oppositional direction, Bush has been a veritable guiding light, but toward what end? In the Muslim world—the only place where revulsion has so far been converted into effective resistance—no direction at all would have been a big improvement. Here the Bush Doctrine has given impetus to the worst kind of uncivil Islam. Not in his wildest dreams could Osama have hoped for more.

Notes

1. Thomas Powers, "The Vanishing Case for War," *New York Review of Books* 50, no. 19 (December 4, 2003), <www.nybooks.com/articles/16813>.

2. Thomas Powers, "How Bush Got It Wrong," *New York Review of Books* 51, no. 14 (September 23, 2004), <www.nybooks.com/articles/17413>. NIEs are prepared by an independent interagency group, the National Intelligence Council, which is highly regarded by the CIA. Its members later complained of administrative pressure on their WMD assessment, and of suppression of its important qualifiers. See Douglas Jehl and David E. Sangler, "Prewar Assessment on Iraq Saw Chance of Strong Division," *New York Times* (September 28, 2004), <www.nytimes.com/2004/09/28/politics/28intel.html>.

3. The "great communicator" himself habitually dozed off in cabinet meetings, and even slept through his historic meeting with the pope, yet he resisted the efforts of neocons like Richard Perle, Paul Wolfowitz, Donald Rumsfeld, and Dick Cheney to

ossify his Soviet policy. Appalled by Reagan's embrace of Gorbachev's perestroika and glasnost, these "B team" hawks wanted to transpose economic and military force into unilateral dictates. Reagan, however, simply wanted to negotiate with his enemies from a position of strength. See John Patrick Diggins, "How Reagan Beat the Neocons," *New York Times* (June 11, 2004), <www.nytimes.com/2004/06/11/opinion/11DIGG.html>.

4. David Barston, William J. Broad, and Jeff Gerth, "Skewed Intelligence Data in March to War in Iraq," *New York Times* (October 3, 2004), <www.nytimes.com/2004/10/03/international/middleeast/03tube.html>.

5. See Arthur Schlesinger Jr., "The Making of a Mess," *New York Review of Books* (September 23, 2004), <www.nybooks.com/articles/17397>.

6. James Fallows, "Proceed with Caution," *The Atlantic* (October 10, 2002), <www.theatlantic.com/unbound/interviews/int2002-10-10.htm>. Fallows also notes the strange dearth of criticism concerning the grounds for war from the *Democrats*, the supposed opposition party. Oddly, the only serious questioning on that level took place within the Republican Party.

7. Peter W. Galbraith, "Iraq: The Bungled Transition," *New York Review of Books* 51, no. 14 (September 23, 2004), <www.nybooks.com/articles/17406>.

8. Douglas McCollam, "How Chalabi Played the Press," *Columbia Journalism Review* (July/August 2004), <www.cjr.org/issues/2004/4/mccollam-list.asp>.

9. Mark Hosenball, Michael Isikoff, and Evan Thomas, "Cheney's Long Path to War," *Newsweek* (November 17, 2003), <www.truthout.org/docs_03/printer_111203D.shtml>.

10. At the time of the invasion the Bush administration had added this humanitarian rationale as a mere afterthought. See John Tirman, "The New Humanitarianism: How Military Intervention Came to Be the Norm," *Boston Review: A Political and Literary Forum* (December 2003/January 2004), <www.boston review.net/BR28.6/tirman.html>. The credibility of this motive is flatly denied by Human Rights Watch. See Ken Roth, "War in Iraq: Not a Humanitarian Intervention," *Human Rights Watch World Report 2004* (January 2004). The final nail in the coffin of Cheney's credibility was hammered by David Kay, on his January 2003 departure from his position as the head of the search effort for banned weapons in Iraq. Kay reached the conclusion that Iraq had no stockpiles of chemical and biographical weapons, and indeed had probably "got rid of" such weapons at the end of the Gulf War. See Richard W. Stevenson, "Iraq Illicit Arms Gone before War, Departing Inspector States," *New York Times* (January 24, 2004), <www.nytimes.com/2004/01/24/politics/24WEAP.html>. By early 2004 even Secretary of State Powell admitted that such evidence was lacking. See Christopher Marquis, "Powell Admits No Hard Proof in Linking Iraq to Al Qaeda," *New York Times* (January 9, 2004), <www.nytimes.com/2004/01/09/politics/09POWE.html>.

11. Lewis is not, however, an unqualified "orientalist," for he believes Arabs capable of implementing democracy and other modern institutions. True orientalists deny their aptitude for these tasks. Lewis views Iraqis as the heirs of a great civilization, but thinks they need "some guidance" at this stage. That is the connecting link between the Bush Doctrine and the Lewis Doctrine, for Bush sees himself as the perfect man to provide such guidance. See Peter Waldman, "A Historian's Take on Islam Steers U.S. in

Terrorism Fight," *The Wall Street Journal* (February 3, 2004), <wsj.com/article_email/print/0,SB1075760704849 18411-Ibje4Nklah3m5uvaH2GeKmEm4,00.html>.

12. See Paul Berman, Thomas Friedman, Christopher Hitchens, et al., "Liberal Hawks Reconsider the Iraq War," *Slate* (January 12, 2004), <slate.msn.com/toolbar.aspx?action=print&id=2093620>.

13. Moisés Naim, "Casualties of War," *Foreign Policy* (September/October 2004), <www.foreignpolicy.com/story/cms.php?story_id=2661&popup_delayed=1>.

14. See Gabriel Kolko, "Iraq, the United States, and the End of the European Coalition," *Journal of Contemporary Asia* 33, no. 3 (2003): 294 (291–98).

15. Kenneth M. Pollack, "Weapons of Misperception," *The Atlantic* (January 13, 2004), <www.theatlantic.com/unbound/interviews/int2004-01-13.htm>.

16. Michael Massing, "Now They Tell Us," *The New York Review of Books* 51, no. 3 (February 26, 2004), <www.nybooks.com/articles/16922>.

17. Matthew Rothschild, "Chalabi's Boondoggle," *The Progressive* (March 11, 2004), <www.progressive.org/webex04/wx031104.html>.

18. "Pentagon Pays Chalabi Group for Dubious Data," *HoustonChronicle.com* (March 11, 2004), <www.chron.com/cs/CDA/printstory.mpl/nation/2443637>.

19. "Iraq's Governing Council: A Dangerous Place between B and C," *The Economist* (February 19, 2004), <economist.com/world/africa/PrinterFriendly.cfm?Story_ID=2442073>.

20. Powell qtd. in Tariq Ali, "Re-Colonizing Iraq," *New Left Review* (May/June 2003): 9 (5–19).

21. Henry C. K. Liu, "Geopolitics in Iraq an Old Game," *Asia Times* (August 18, 2004), <www.atimes.com/atimes/Middle_East/FH18Ak02.html>.

22. "Frappée à Bagdad, l'Amérique tente d'impliquer les Nations unies," *Le Monde* (January 19, 2004), <www.lemond.fr/web/article/0,1-0@2-3220.36-349623,0.html>.

23. This tendentious interpretation ignores the deep complicity of Boutros-Ghali himself in the African tragedy, particularly in the case of Rwanda, as Linda Melvern amply documents. See, for example, her *A People Betrayed: The Role of the West in Rwanda's Genocide* (London: Zed Books, 2000).

24. Ali, "Re-Colonizing Iraq," 11–12.

25. The Northern Alliance, after all, had been mainly equipped and funded by Russia, Iran, and India. The UN extended that already broad international mandate, giving the interim government in Afghanistan a modicum of legitimacy. See James Dobbins, "Bringing the Afghan Experience to Iraq," *International Herald Tribune* (January 20, 2004), <www.iht.com/cgi-bin/generic/cgi?template=articleprint.tmplh& Article=125593>.

26. "Debating 9/11," *New York Times* (March 23, 2004), <www.nytimes.com/2004/03/23/opinion/23TUEE1.html>.

27. Judy Dempsey and Peter Spiegel, "Rumsfeld Attempts to Draw NATO in Iraq," *Financial Times* (February 6, 2004), <news.ft.com/servelet/Content?Server?pagename=FT.com/StoryFT/FullStory&c=StoryFT&cid=1075982364912>.

28. Galbraith, "Iraq: The Bungled Transition."

29. Fareed Zakaria, "An Absence of Legitimacy," *Washington Post* (January 20, 2004): A19; also published in *Newsweek* as "Bowing to the Mighty Ayatollah" (January 26, 2004), <www.msnbc.msn.com/Default.aspx?id=3990022&pl=0>.

30. Yitzhak Nakash, "The Shiites and the Future of Iraq," *Foreign Affairs* 82, no. 4 (July/August 2003): 21 (17–26).

31. Johann Hari, "Could Iraq's Democratic Future Depend on an Old Man Lying in a London Hospital Bed?" *Independent* (August 18, 2004), <argument.independent.co.uk/regular_columnists_hari/story. jsp?story=552548>.

32. "Iraqi Protests at US Political Plans Reveal Limitations of Resistance and Opposition," *Muslimedia.com* (February 2004), <www.muslimedia.com/editor170a.htm>.

33. Michael A. Weinstein, "Iraq's Slide toward Separation," *PINR: Power and Interest News Report* (August 11, 2004), <www.pinr.com/report.php?ac=view_report&report_id=195&language_id=1>.

34. Tim Judah, "In Iraqi Kurdistan," *New York Review of Books* (September 26, 2002), <www.nybooks.com/articles/15688>.

35. Simon Bromley, *Rethinking Middle East Politics: State Formation and Development* (Cambridge, U.K.: Polity Press, 1994), 137.

36. Khaled Salih, "Demonizing a Minority: The Case of the Kurds in Iraq," in Kirsten E. Schulze, Martin Stokes, and Colin Campbell, eds., *Nationalism, Minorities, and Diasporas: Identities and Rights in the Middle East* (London: Tauris Academic Studies, 1996), 87 (81–94).

37. Eliza Griswold, "With the Kurds," *The Nation* (April 14, 2003), <www.thenation.com/docprint.mhtml?i=20030414&s=griswold>.

38. Salih, "Demonizing a Minority," 83 and 92.

39. Mehrdad R. Izady, *The Kurds: A Concise Handbook* (Washington, DC: Taylor and Francis, 1992), 201.

40. Steven R. Weisman, "The Shape of a Future Iraq: U.S. Entangled in Disputes," *New York Times* (January 9, 2004), <www.nytimes.com/2004/01/09/politics/09DIPL.html>.

41. Adeed Dawisha, "Iraq: Setbacks, Advances, Prospects," *Journal of Democracy* 15, no. 1 (January 2004): 16 (5–20).

42. David Ignatius, "Compromise and Consequences in Iraq," *Washington Post* (March 5, 2004): A23.

43. See Galbraith, "Iraq: The Bungled Transition."

44. Peter W. Galbraith, "A Hole in the Heart of Kurdistan," *New York Times* (February 3, 2004), <www.nytimes.com/2004/02/03/opinion/03GALB.html>.

45. Galbraith, "Iraq: The Bungled Transition."

46. Larry Diamond, "What Went Wrong in Iraq," *Foreign Affairs* 83, no. 5 (September/October 2004): 36 (34–56).

47. Dan Murphy, "In Iraq, a 'Perfect Storm,'" *The Christian Science Monitor* (April 9, 2004), <www.csmonitor.com/2004/0409/p01s03-woiq.htm>.

48. Paul Krugman, "A No-Win Situation." *New York Times* (August 31, 2004), <www.nytimes.com/2004/08/31/opinion/31krugman.html>.

49. See Becky Tinsley, "America's Own Goal in Iraq," *New Statesman* (August 16, 2004), <www.newstatesman.com/site.php3?newTemplate=NSArticle_World&newDisplayURN=200408160015>.

50. Hari, "Could Iraq's."

51. Zakaria, "An Absence."

52. Thomas Carothers, "Is Gradualism Possible? Choosing a Strategy for Promoting Democracy in the Middle East," *Carnegie Working Papers: Democracy and Rule of Law Project/Middle East Series* 39 (June 2003), 6 (3–15).

53. Doug Saunders, "It's Just Wrong What We're Doing," *Globe and Mail* (January 24, 2004), <www.theglobeandmail.com/servlet/ArticleNews/TPPrint/LAC/20040124/MCNAMARA//?query=mcnamara>.

54. John Pilger, "American Terrorist," *OutlookIndia.com* (January 9, 2004), <www.outlookindia.com/full.asp?fodname=20040109&fname=pilger&sid=1>.

55. Paul Rogers, "America's Iraqi Dilemma," o*penDemocracy* (October 23, 2003), <www.opendemocracy.net/debates/article-2-89-1552.jsp#>.

56. "No to America, No to Saddam," *The Economist* (July 24, 2003), <economist.com/world/africa/PrinterFriendly.cfm?Story_ID=1944576>.

57. See Johann Hari, "USA: Bully or Beacon?" *The Independent* (November 21, 2003), <enjoyment.independent.co.uk/low_res/story.jsp?story=465921&host=5&dir=207>.

58. Edward Wong, "Iraq's Path Hinges on Words of Enigmatic Cleric," *New York Times* (January 25, 2004), <www.nytimes.com/2004/01/25/international/middleeast/25SIST.html>.

59. Turi Munthe, "Saddam's Islamist Legacy," o*penDemocracy* (October 6, 2003), <www.opendemocracy.net/articles/ViewPopUpArticle.jsp?id=2&articleId=1523>.

60. See, for example, Daniel Pipes, "Iraq Council Throws Hope for Democracy out the Window," *Chicago Sun-Times* (March 3, 2004), <www.suntimes.com/output/otherviews/cst-edt-pipes03.html>.

61. Al-Hakim's return with his 8,000 strong militia in May 2003 was widely compared to the Ayatollah's historic return to Iran from Iraq. See Firas Al-Atraqchi, "Iraqi Shiites' Quest for Elections," *IslamOnline.net* (February 15, 2004), <www.islamon-line.net/english/In_Depth/Iraq_Aftermath/2004/02/article_05.shtml>. Hakim once favored the Iranian theocratic model of religious statehood, but ended up approving a working relationship with the U.S. occupiers. Sistani, likewise, has helped to keep the lid on Shia resistance by endorsing both democracy and a Western-style separation of religion and state. See Scott Peterson, "In Iraq, Shiites Are Wild Card," *The Christian Science Monitor* (July 21, 2003), <www.csmonitor.com/2003/0721/p01s04-woiq.htm>.

62. Laura Secor, "The Democrat," *Boston.com* (March 14, 2004), <www.boston.com/news/globe/ideas/articles/2004/03/14/the_democrat?mode=PF>.

63. See Jim Hoagland, "Islam's Civil War," *Washington Post* (March 3, 2004): A27.

64. Abdurrahman Wahid, "How to Counter Islamic Extremism," *Diogenes* 50, no. 4 (2003): 124 (123–25).

65. James Fallows, "Blind into Bagdad," *The Atlantic* (January/February 2004), <www.theatlantic.com/issues/2004/01/fallows.htm>.

66. Walden Bello, "Global Civil Society Meets amidst Crisis of Empire," *Focus on the Global South* (January 17, 2004), <www.focusweb.org/administrator/popups/newswindow.php?id=146&print=print>.

67. Walter Pincus and Dana Milbank, "Kay Cites Evidence of Iraq Disarming," *Washington Post* (January 28, 2004): A01.

68. On Civic see Jeffrey Gettleman, "For Iraqis in Harm's Way, $5,000 and 'I'm Sorry,'" *New York Times* (March 17, 2004), <www.nytimes.com/2004/03/17/international/

middleeast/17CIVI.html>; and on Amnesty International see "10,000 civils tués en Irak depuis un an," *Nouvel Observateur* (March 19, 2004), <permanent.nouvelobs .com/etranger/20040318.OBS6150.html>.

69. Brian Cloughley, "Iron Hammers in Iraq: How to Destroy Democracy," *Counterpunch* (January 17/18, 2004), <wwwcounterpunch.org/cloughley01172004.html>.

70. Jeffrey Gettleman, "Chaos and War Leave Iraq's Hospitals in Ruins," *New York Times* (February 14, 2004), <www.nytimes.com/2004/02/14/international/middleeast/ 14HOSP.html>.

71. Rupert Cornwell, "Bush Admits He May Have Misjudged Post-War State of Iraq," *Independent* (August 28, 2004), <news.independent.co.uk/low_res/story .jsp?story=555907&host=3&dir=70>.

72. Tom Regan, "Global Opinion: World Is Not a Safer Place," *The Christian Science Monitor* (September 13, 2004), <www.csmonitor.com/2004/0913/dailyUpdate.html>.

73. Becky Tinsley, "America's Own Goal in Iraq," *New Statesman* (August 16, 2004), <www.newstatesman.com/site.php3?newTemplate=NSArticle_World&newDisplay URN=200408160015>.

74. Charles Glass, "Lewis of Arabia," *The Nation* (September 13, 2004), <www.thenation.com/docprint.mhtml?i=20040913&s=glass>.

75. Tom Englehart and Jonathan Schell, "The Empire That Fell As It Rose," *Mother Jones* (August 26, 2004), <www.motherjones.com/news/update/2004/08/08_404.html>.

8

Conclusion: All about Us

Us versus Them

T HE OMNIPRESENT QUESTION FOR AMERICANS after 9/11 was "why us?"[1] This question, however, bracketed "*us*" entirely. Since most agreed with President Bush that the United States had been a consistent "beacon of freedom" for the world,[2] little thought was given to the global impact of heinous U.S. policies. The answer to the 9/11 question had to lie, therefore, in the dark designs of rogue leaders such as Moumar Ghadaffi, Saddam Hussein, and Osama bin Laden, or in the atavistic nature of Islam itself. By this logic America was only at fault for having been too soft on its Islamic adversaries (or those of Israel, which comes to the same thing). Thus the *Wall Street Journal* wasted no time in blaming 9/11 on President Clinton's Munich-like appeasement of the Palestinians.

Seumas Milne aptly replied, in a *Guardian* piece of 9/13, that it boggles the mind to think what the *Journal* would consider a *Churchill*-like response.[3] To be fair to Churchill, his strategic acumen would be a considerable improvement over the Bush administration's hunt for one Islamic devil after another. The irony is that most of these demons were once abetted by American foreign policy. The Taliban, for example, was largely composed of veterans of the U.S.-funded Mujahedeen. Support was lavished on those groups which had the approval of Pakistan's Inter-Services Intelligence (ISI). It was in Pakistan's interest to cultivate fundamentalist leaders who lacked internal support and were therefore dependent on Pakistan for their political survival, much as President Hamid Karzai now depends on the United States.[4]

Lacking legitimacy, such a government could impose itself only by sheer force—hence the Taliban's reign of terror. Its one claim to legitimacy was its promise to end the country's chronic chaos. But as the late Abdul Haq admonished, Afghanistan could never be ruled strictly "by the gun."[5] By destroying every semblance of civil society—i.e., *civil Islam*—the Taliban set in motion a vicious cycle: less civil society requiring still more terror. Two weeks before 9/11, Ahmed Shah Massoud spelled out what that would soon mean for the United States.[6]

The more immediate U.S. contribution to the Taliban's rise could be described as negative complicity. America simply lost interest in Afghanistan after the Cold War (much as the current Bush administration—on the principle that military personnel should never act as "social workers"—has been a reluctant reconstructionist after ousting the Taliban).[7] This indifference left Washington's proxy, the ISI, free to combat progressive-minded Islamists such as Massoud (assassinated by the Taliban just two days before 9/11) and Haq (executed the next month). There were indications, however, that America's role in this horror story was moving beyond negative complicity. Shortly before 9/11, when President Bush still saw drugs as the root of global insecurity, the Taliban was being praised by Washington for stemming Afghanistan's opium trade; indeed it was rewarded with increasing American aid via the UN.[8] This made some sense so long as foreign policy could be reduced to drug enforcement. It is no surprise that the country's opium output rebounded with the good fortune of the Taliban's old foe, the Northern Alliance.

Embarrassing as that was, the White House had more pressing problems. With bin Laden on the loose, and with the president's Enron connection lurking in the shadows, the administration needed at all costs to divert attention from itself by turning the floodlights of its demonology on an accessible enemy. It is conveniently forgotten that a previous Republican administration maintained an alliance with Saddam Hussein in full knowledge of the fact that he had destroyed countless Kurdish villages in the late 1980s, killing between 100,000 to 150,000 helpless inhabitants.[9] After a cursory "investigation," then-Secretary of State George Schultz judged that these incidents did not warrant a ban on the sale of military equipment and strategic technology to Iraq.[10] Here, as in Afghanistan, the clean divide that Bush drew between "us and them" is a historical fiction. The White House case for geopolitical exorcism rests on public ignorance of (or indifference to) how for years the United States did its best to keep "them" in power.

Civil Islam

If simple demonology fails to explain 9/11, the idea that Islam itself is the culprit fares no better. One can forgive Salman Rushdie's contrary opinion,[11] but in fact Islam is a behavioral "mixed bag"—no more conducive to terrorism than is any other world religion. Even Samuel Huntington avers that "there is nothing inherently violent in Muslim theology. Islam, like any great religion, can be interpreted in a variety of ways. People like bin Laden can seize on things in the Koran as commands to go out and kill infidels. But the Pope did exactly the same thing when he launched the Crusades."[12] Much of what passes for hard-line Islamic tradition is of very recent *political* origin, or at least political exacerbation.

A graphic case in point is the rising power of Pakistani "tribal councils," which shroud themselves in a largely invented legal tradition. The "Islamic law" they practice owes much to the legacy of General Zia ul-Haq, who as president installed a draconian version of Islamic justice, including death by stoning,[13] from 1977 to 1988. The only available remedy for such judicial perversion is not secularization, which would further empower an already Westernized power elite, but better Islamic education. Presently 95 percent of Pakistan's population has no practical access to the centralized judicial system that is still conducted in English and is devoted to the same hegemonic ends as the colonial system it supplanted. This is a common predicament in today's Muslim world, and one that will only be magnified in years to come. Farish Noor points out how globalization has already engulfed nearly every Muslim state, commercializing the secular legal system at the expense of civil justice. By comparison, "traditional religious courts appear accessible, cheap, reliable and consistent. The beauty of sharia law—as seen by many ordinary Muslims—is that it at least offers some legal protection with clear verdicts."[14]

Pakistan's Imran Khan, former cricket champion and founder of the Justice Movement (Tehrik-e-Insaaf), makes a cogent case for Islamism as the best way out of this neocolonial rut.[15] His own conversion to serious public service followed his gravitation toward a deeply existential Islam. This spiritual passage into civil Islam was not, however, a categorically anti-Western passage. Khan remains dialogically open to the non-imperialistic aspects of Western culture. This should come as no surprise, for just as there has been a Tocquevillian awakening to the importance of civil society in the West, there is a growing recognition among Muslim reformists "that formal democracy cannot prevail unless government power is checked by strong civic associations"[16]—i.e., by civil Islam.

As the failure of modernist (non-civic) development schemes is laid bare, all Islamic regimes fall under the shadow of this reform dynamic.[17]

Some inoculate themselves by fostering a militant fundamentalism such as Saudi Wahhabism. Though President Suharto of Indonesia was always wary of Islamic politics, he too saw the need to defuse the Muslim pro-democracy movement of the 1990s through an eleventh hour alliance with ultraconservative Islamists.[18] Thus he cultivated the very elements that now pose a terrorist threat. Likewise, Pakistan is presently reverting to Zia-like Islamism. In such cases the real threat to democratization is not the chance that Islam will contaminate politics, but that an already corrupt and militaristic politics will contaminate Islam.

Beena Sarwar explains that "when the state declares some aspect of social power to be Islamic or traditional, it creates a political constituency in those who get that particular scrap of power. And once they have it they will defend it in the terms it came wrapped in, even if the 'tradition' is new and the 'Muslim law' even newer."[19] This was illustrated all too well by the recent order of a Pakistani jirga (tribal court) that a man's alleged crime—insulting the dignity of a higher-status tribe by having illicit sex with one of its members—be compensated by the legally administered gang-rape of his sister. Four men, including one of the jurists, took turns doing the court's bidding, after which the girl was made to walk home naked in full view of dozens of villagers. Although there is no precedent for this sentence, few in today's Pakistan dare resist such rulings.

Women's rights are especially at risk in the face of invented "traditions" that use Islam as a front. Educated Muslim women are fighting back by forming their own Koranic study groups.[20] This feminist wing of civil Islam—which does battle on two fronts, opposing both fundamentalist misogyny and Western sexism—made its global debut at the 1995 UN Conference on Women in Beijing. While chauvinistic interpretations of the Koran were given a drubbing, Western feminism was also targeted as an instrument of neocolonial globalization.[21] This double-edged contest typifies civil Islam's domestic and foreign stance.

Like most Islamic rulers, General Pervez Musharraf is fighting on those same fronts, but very much on the opposite side. His notorious constitutional revisionism includes a rule that only college graduates can run for high public office. That voided the candidacies of many leading political activists, such as the head of the Alliance for the Restoration of Democracy, Nawabzada Nasrulla Khan. There was also an attempt to disqualify Imran Khan for failing to file proof of his Oxford graduation. The ruling Pakistan Muslim League (PML) appeared to suffer a startling setback in the country's October 2002 elections, as voters registered their chagrin over Musharraf's Washington ties.

Qazi Hussein Ahmed—leader of the rising Muttahida Majlis-e-Amal (MMA), an alliance of six Islamic organizations—declared this a revolution against U.S. imperialism and Westernization. Paradoxically, however, nothing cements the PML's U.S. alliance so much as this MMA challenge. The October elections provided just the democratic gloss that Musharraf needed to paper over his constitutional ravages and to leverage Washington for still more support. The tactic worked: By mid-November U.S. Treasury Secretary Paul O'Neill was praising Musharraf for his anti-terrorist efforts and promising to forgive $1 billion of Pakistan's debt to the United States.

This lesson in political image control was not lost on Sheik Hamad bin Isa al-Khalifa, king of Bahrain, who decided to allow a parliamentary election for the first time in almost thirty years. America welcomed this move insofar as it stabilizes the political environment of a vital U.S. naval base. It was a risk-free venture, since the new house of Parliament could not act without the consent of the other house, which the Sunni king appoints. Shiite groups therefore organized an election boycott, but that did not prevent the arch-globalist Thomas Friedman from lauding the elections as a democratic beachhead in the Arab world.

Civil Islam must be prepared to fight the Musharrafs and the Friedmans alike. So, too, like Muslim feminists, it must combat both radical fundamentalism and blanket secularism. Bernard Lewis reduces modern Islam's field of choice to those fire-and-ice options, but in fact the traditions of Ataturk and Khomeini have struck a symbiotic bargain. While secular elites choke basic liberties, what remains of public discourse is shunted into fundamentalist mosques. America does its part by promoting some of the most repressive regimes on earth, and by withholding the modicum of support that civil Islamists need to function.

Nothing, not even radical Islamism, puts America's client regimes so much on edge as does civil Islam—hence the local and global ferment when Turkey's new Islamist-oriented Justice and Development Party (AKP) claimed a sweeping victory in the November 2002 elections. The AKP was forged out of the remnants of the Welfare Party that formed the first Islamist government in 1997, only to be ousted by the staunchly Kemalist military. With Turkey's EU application at issue, the military will have to exercise restraint this time, as the country's flagging economy badly needs that EU boost.

Thus the West finds itself in the curious position of securing the new Islamist government. Just ten days before the elections, Turkey's chief prosecutor tried to outlaw the AKP,[22] and the party's leader, Recep Tayyip Erdogan, had already been banned from public office; but the tide had turned both domestically and geopolitically against such anti-Islamism. Knowing its victory was less a religious endorsement than a vote against corruption, the AKP is in no position to spurn the West. Far more than the political establishment it displaced, this reform party promises full support for the human rights and democratic reforms mandated at Copenhagen for EU applicants.

An even better example of civil Islam's democratic propensity is the fledgling Kurdish government that emerged in northern Iraq after 1991 when a no-fly zone was put in place following the Gulf War. In an area 250 by 125 miles, bordered by Syria to the west, Turkey to the north, and Iran to the east, civil liberties took shape here as never before in Iraq, or any Arab country. The Bush administration boasted that its blueprint for a new Iraq would offer a democratic model for the Islamic world, but such a model already existed in the Kurdish zone.

While Saddam Hussein easily qualified as the antithesis of that model, it was his place in the global economy that enabled his petrol-driven regime to crush the median institutions that would normally buffer centrist oppression. Bryan Turner points out that standard orientalist depictions of Asian society have overlooked such mediating social structures in Asian society.[23] Ironically it is Western and especially American influence that has done the most to corrode these structures. Globalization has only accelerated this process, while Islamic resistance has been compelled to go global, setting the stage for the civilizational clash that Barber and Huntington warned of in the early 1990s.

Unlike its war on al Qaeda, which had all the marks of civilizational clash, America's two wars with Saddam amounted to disciplinary actions against a rogue puppet—a hired thug who decided to stake out his own turf. Despite their deep hatred of Saddam, Kurds were understandably slow to join this second war dance, since it could remove the protection they enjoyed in northern Iraq. They had not forgotten how the former President Bush left them in the lurch after encouraging their ill-considered revolt. Only after a million of them fled into Turkey and Iran did the UN establish the safe haven that became a regional prototype for civil Islam.

The U.S. Seal of Approval

Those who think Iraqi Kurds would be protected by an American engineered "regime change" in Baghdad should consider how little protection Turkish Kurds have received under America's Cold War aegis. Since 1984 there have been 40,000 Kurdish casualties in Turkey's undeclared ethnic war.[24] The end of the Cold War removed America's only excuse for not applying humanitarian pressure on Turkey. The only real pressure has come from the EU, which has induced the Turkish parliament to extend some rudimentary rights to the Kurds.[25] Television and radio stations, for example, are now allowed to broadcast up to forty-five minutes a day in Kurdish and other regional languages.

This limited but effective engagement stands in contrast to America's record of invasive but ethically nugatory "realism": roughly 200 military aggressions since World War II, plus countless economic machinations. Jeane Kirkpatrick defended such habits on the ground that authoritarian regimes, unlike "totalitarian" ones, would reform themselves in time. But as Stephen Kotkin points out in *Armageddon Averted* (2001), it was ultimately the Soviets who reformed themselves.

Today similar tactics keep the oil flowing but seldom result in significant reform apart from economic restructuration on globalist terms. Using the war on terrorism as its pretext, Bush foreign policy pushes the geopolitics of oil to new extremes. In the same week that Colin Powell arrived in Indonesia to fete the partial renewal of military aid to one of the world's most virulent military machines, the administration played its anti-terrorist card on the judiciary by attempting to block a lawsuit filed in the United States by the International Labor Rights Fund against Exxon Mobil on behalf of eleven Acehnese victims of assault, torture, and murder. The company claims it bears no responsibility for the actions of security forces guarding its facilities.[26]

Would Exxon have dared use that line if these facilities had been on U.S. soil and the victims had been Americans? The message this double standard sends to the global South raises the question of why it is only Muslim extremists who are effectively fighting globalization with more than words. Islamism is a categorical failure only for those, such as Daniel Pipes and Azar Nafisi, who see the New World Order as a categorical good.[27] Nothing personal here. The same judgment would come down on any serious resistance to globalization. Pushed to its logical conclusion, this globalist reflex leads to the apotheosis of order that Stanley Hoffmann deplores in Henry Kissinger and a new generation of realists.

Licensed by 9/11, these Empire builders are prepared to put human rights on permanent hold. Like Michael Ignatieff, Hoffmann laments that Clinton-era gains on the Palestinian issue have been sacrificed on the altar of anti-terrorism. Meanwhile the sympathy that the world showered on America after 9/11 has been answered with cold, unilateral contempt—this at a time when the United States, lacking the magnetic attraction of Cold War polarity, needs international support more than ever.[28]

Unable to depend on unconditional Cold War allies, America looks all the more to its client states for loyalty. These correctly take Bush administration policies as an American seal of approval for hard-line tactics. Thus Egypt feels secure in its "republonarchy" ("Gomloukiya"), as Saad Eddin Ibrahim dubs it. Ibrahim's Cairo University professorship and joint Egyptian-U.S. citizenship did not shield him in his pro-democratic activism. He was arrested on bogus charges of embezzling funds from the European Union, receiving donations without government permission, and harming Egypt's international reputation. Although the EU insisted that no embezzlement took place, the sixty-three-year-old reformist was convicted and sentenced to seven years at hard labor, which could have been a death sentence for a man of his age and poor health. His only real "crime" was encouraging voter registration and assisting the EU in monitoring elections.

At first the U.S. State Department simply went on record as being "deeply disappointed" by the court's ruling.[29] Thomas Friedman's response was well stated, if more than a little naïve: "'Disappointed?' I'm disappointed when the Baltimore Orioles lose. When an Egyptian president we give $2 billion a year to jails a pro-American democracy advocate, I'm *outraged* and expect America to do something about it. I'm also frightened because if there is no space in Egypt for democratic voices for changes, then Egyptians will only be left with the mosque. . . ."[30]

True enough. But this show of outrage hinges on a degree of surprise that is inconceivable in view of America's stance toward Islamic states since the early Cold War era. Washington still keeps its silence concerning the fact that not one of the twenty-two members of the Arab League is a democracy. Was it beyond Friedman's globalist imagination that Bush was calling the shots with Mubarak, even as Mubarak called the shots with the Egyptian courts? And could his fellow neoliberals-turned-hawks be unaware that part of the current leadership crisis in Iraq stems from the absence of suitable replacements for Saddam, given the fact that most of the country's best intellectuals had been liquidated long before, and with Washington's tacit blessing, for having been affiliated with the Left?[31]

Had the United States shown half as much concern over the plight of women within its spheres of influence as it did over Left ideology, the condition of 50 percent of the Saudi population could have been much ameliorated. The sordid truth is that even under Saddam Iraqi women enjoyed more privileges and opportunities than their Saudi counterparts. This is one of many reasons why Saddam's regime was no friend of al Qaeda. While Bush propaganda depicted Saddam as a rabid Islamist, jihadists more realistically took him for a secularist. So did the CIA, which for many years helped him to keep his U.S. stamp of approval.

America's animus against Islamic politics is even more pronounced in Central Asia, where Islamism functions to destabilize present regimes. When it is considered that these ruling structures were left over from Soviet days, and in Central Asia did not undergo the reforms associated with glasnost, it becomes obvious that a destabilizing force is not necessarily a bad thing. To snuff out Islamic oppositionalism is to reinforce the residual Stalinism that plagues the region to this day, and ironically is more ingrained here than in present-day

Russia, where apparatchik kleptocracy has been more a problem than old-style despotism.

Human Rights Watch reports Uzbek president Islam Karimov, having repeatedly extended his term of office, now publicly questions the efficacy of democracy, human rights, and freedom of the press. He signed a memorandum promising reforms during his trip to Washington in 2002, but returned home to launch another crackdown, targeting not only "Islamic extremists" but all Muslim opponents.[32] In 2003 Congress passed legislation to keep him at his word, and under pressure from Congress the administration nominally cut the $18 million in military and economic aid that Uzbekistan was getting. A spokesman for the Uzbek foreign ministry, however, stated that as they understood it, the change only meant that the aid would have to be dispersed on a project-by-project basis; and in February 2004 Secretary of Defense Rumsfeld was in Uzbekistan reassuring Karimov that human rights are not America's prime concern. An administrative power shift in favor of the State Department (subsequent to recent scandals and revelations regarding Iraq) alters these priorities somewhat, but not enough to upset Uzbek officials.

The situation in Turkmenistan is hardly better, but at least it provides comic relief from the usual banality of evil. Saparmurat Niyazov is better known as Akbar Turkmenbashi, or the Great Leader of all Turkmen. Streets, factories, airports, all kinds of public works, and even one city have been named for this de facto president for life. Not satisfied, the Great Leader has arranged to have the month of January renamed Turkmenbashi.

A more cosmopolitan veneer is laid over repression by Kazakhstan's Nursultan Nazarbayev, who shares something of the Bush family commitment to privitization: According to his own prime minister he put away $1 billion of a payment from Chevron into a secret Swiss bank account, while his daughter owns most of the country's news media. Most importantly he holds the winning cards on terrorism and oil, the two most pressing concerns of American power politics. Nazarbayev has been an ardent supporter of the pro-West Eurasian Economic Community (EurAsEC), which formerly held the line against Russia's ambition to cultivate a "Big Brother" unilateralism in the region, even to the point of resurrecting the limited sovereignty principle of the Brezhnev Doctrine.[33] Confident of solid U.S. support, but recently moving closer to Russia as well, Nazarbayev is now intensifying his crackdown on independent media (thus serving his daughter's media interests) and on opposition groups such as the Democratic Choice of Kazakhstan (DCK).

There was one grand exception to this pattern, or so it seemed in better times, before the Americans arrived. After its independence in 1991, Kyrgyzstan stood apart from its neighbors by virtue of its relative tolerance for a free press and political opposition. This was because the Kyrgyz Republic (to use its formal name) did not follow other former Soviet republics in making an ex-first secretary of the Communist Party its new president. Rather it chose a respected scientist, Askar Akayev, whom Al Gore once described as "a democrat to the bone."[34] This made for good press, but it was the country's assiduous compliance with IMF directives that in 1998 made Kyrgyzstan the first former Soviet republic admitted to the World Trade Organization. Akayev collected still more points by providing a base for 2,000 Allied troops when the United States took the West to war in Afghanistan. In a recent speech at Harvard, Akayev stressed his economic achievements and dismissed any "universal formula" by which his democratic performance might be found wanting. Democratization, he argued, must be defined in terms of the "historical practice" of a given country.[35]

What that bodes for Kyrgyz reformism is not hard to guess. American backing made Akayev feel secure enough to move up the realist food chain: arresting his leading political critic, Azimbek Beknazarov, and cracking down on independent news media. When this shocking reversal ignited demonstrations, the police opened fire, killing several protesters and provoking even larger demonstrations. Thanks to that surge of popular resistance, and no thanks to America's growing influence, charges were dropped against Beknazarov, who returned triumphant to parliament as of June 2002. Protesters are now turning to the more formidable task of ridding the country of its aspirant czar. A crucial test for Central Asian reformism will be whether Akayev further violates the Kyrgyz constitution by running once more for president in late 2005.

Akayev himself is assisting the protesters by flaunting his nepotism and crony capitalism at a time when most of the country is in deep depression. Living standards have collapsed since the Soviet era, especially in the south, since most of the country's $2 billion in foreign loans have been corralled by a few families, businesses, and bureaucrats near Bishkek in the north. While Akayev's wife cornered the market on government appointments, his son-in-law emerged as a business mogul, pushing out the less privileged competition. At this critical moment, President Bush decided to invite Akayev to Washington, presumably as a reward for playing host to Coalition forces, but also putting a U.S. stamp of approval on Akayev's reactionary turn.

Getting Past Fukuyama and Huntington

While few Americans registered these events, it was harder for the average CNN viewer not to notice when in August 2002 President Musharraf, as discussed before, posted his infamous constitutional amendments. Henceforth he could dissolve the parliament at will and personally appoint the prime minister, supreme court justices, cabinet, military chiefs, and all top bureaucrats. To test the water, he made these plans known in advance, but predictably there was no comment from the U.S. State Department.

Musharraf had convinced Washington that peace in Kashmir and the permanent de-Talibanization of Afghanistan were almost exclusively in his hands. Only he could rein in the Muslim terrorists that operate with impunity out of Pakistan. To prove his seriousness he made sure his court rendered a prompt death sentence to Omar Saeed Sheikh for the murder of *Wall Street Journal* reporter Daniel Pearl. It was of small importance that domestic support for Musharraf had plummeted, for the army would now decide most matters, including who could run for elections. That is to say that no serious opponents, such as the former prime ministers Benazir Bhutto and Nawaz Sharif, would be on the ballot. But pro-Taliban fundamentalists were welcome.

A human rights activist, Hina Jilani, asks why the country even bothers to hold elections. The obvious answer is that it pleases Washington by keeping up appearances. Ahmed Rashid points out how the army and the ISI adroitly sponsored their nominal adversaries, the mullahs, in the general elections of October 10, 2002. This sent Washington the message that the alternative to Musharraf would be the Talibanization of Pakistan and the re-Talibanization of Afghanistan. This oppositional façade prompted the Bush administration to declare the election "a milestone for democracy," even as the EU called it "seriously flawed."[36] Thus the American public can go on believing the United States is doing a fine job of promoting democracy by holding Islamic politics at bay. Like a weed killer that kills all living things, current anti-terrorist policies root out both civil and uncivil Islamism.

On the surface these adventures in armed democratization radically depart from the professed doctrines of post–Cold War globalism. With the Cold War safely behind, neoliberals concluded that commerce alone would best advance their interests. The cure for bad geopolitics would be *no* geopolitics. Obviously that notion is hard to sustain after 9/11, but the ensuing "war on terrorism" is informed by strategies cut from an equally totalistic mold. Fukuyama *et al.* believe that the appropriate cure for extremist Islamic politics is *no* Islamic politics—complete political secularization.[37] It follows that the war on terrorism should not be directed against terrorists alone, nor even against radical Islamists alone, but against all Islamists, which is to say all Muslims "for whom religious identity overrides all other political values."[38]

For any devout Christian, no less than a devout Muslim, religious identity trumps other values. This is seldom regarded as a democratic defect in the West, and likewise Islamic identity has often proved a formidable force of democratic reform. One civil Islamic model took shape in Iran in the early 1960s under the banner of the Freedom Movement, which fervently opposed the Shah. It was this version of Islamic governance—aimed at a republic run by Shiite experts, not a theocracy run by clerics—which the 1979 revolution first realized. That was before Khomeini declared all supporters of democracy the enemies of Islam.[39] The movement's broad base of support, especially among students, ensured that "safavid" mullahs would ban it and do their best to crush it.

Now it is back, however, and the mullahs are restless. It is no comfort to them that Iran has the youngest population in the world, three-quarters of which is under twenty-five. Attending Friday prayers is not the younger generation's idea of fun. For that they look to the West, and especially to America.[40] President Bush unwittingly came to the aid of the mullahs with his State of the Union message of January 2002. By casting Iran as an "Axis of Evil" nation, Bush put pro-Western reformists on the defensive. President Khatami, as Whit Mason notes, can at best pass for an Iranian Gorbachev, but never a Yeltsin. Mason nonetheless senses in Iranian cities a republican spirit reminiscent of Barcelona on the eve of the Spanish Civil War.[41] He fails to mention, however, one crucial difference: the Spanish republicans were not just anticlerical, but strictly anti-religious. By contrast, Iranian reformism is very much a civil *religious* phenomenon. It is arguable that such religious reformism could have helped Spanish republicans win the loyalty of the general population, just as civil Islam is the best bridge between traditional Islamic politics and modern democracy.

To some degree this holds for Pakistan as well. Even such an uncompromising critic of Western culture as the late Sayyid Mawdudi, founder of the Jamaat-i Islami (JI), granted that there is no essential disagreement between Islamism and Western democratism on issues such as legal equality and freedom from oppression. JI has long stood in defense of civil liberties and as a bastion of pro-democratic dissent.[42] Like the Egyptian fundamentalist Yusaf al-Qardawi, most Islamists resist only the blanket import of Western culture.[43] They recoil from Western consumerism and its political appendage, the bread-and-circus "democracy" that thrives under corporate auspices. To that extent civil and uncivil Islam stand as one. But they are profoundly at odds where cultural dialogics is concerned—a vantage advanced by President Khatami of Iran and by Anwar Ibrahim, the ill-fated former deputy prime minister of Malaysia, in the days before Mahathir's full crackdown on Islamic reformism.[44]

Nowhere, however, is that civil Islamic difference so pronounced as in Indonesia. When the Islamic extremist Abu Bakar Bashir, founder of the al Qaeda–linked Jemaah Islamiyah, pressed the Indonesian legislature for a constitutional amendment to make Islamic sharia the law of the land, it was the country's two major Islamic parties which most forcefully blocked the proposition. So, too, most Muslim leaders were fast to endorse tough security laws following the terrorist bombing of October 12, 2002, in Bali. Nor do Muslim moderates think much of Bashir's goal of a pan-Islamic state uniting Malaysia, Indonesia, and the southern Philippines. If Bashir's brand of Islamism gains popularity, it will be because the government failed to tap the moral resources of civil Islam. That is the view of Azymardi Azra, rector of the Syarif Hidayat-ullah Islamic State University. In his opinion ex-President Megawati needed to marshal the support of moderate Muslims while toughening her opposition to terrorists. Up until the Bali tragedy her government had done neither.[45] Jihadic Islamism will be the winner if Jakarta now yields to Washington's push for a general war on Islamism.

As Azra attests, terrorism must be fought within rather than against Islamic politics. Even in Aceh, Indonesia's most intensely Islamic province, religious leaders oppose the cruel and unusual punishments associated with some forms of sharia.[46] It was to forestall political development that Suharto's New Order disempowered the country's ulema (traditional religious teachers); and it is political corruption, not democracy, that is threatened by the resurgence of the ulema. By the same token, the best means of combating Islamic terrorism is not, as Washington has insisted after 9/11, intense remilitarization and re-Pentagonization.

Any effective anti-terrorist strategy, Sidney Jones argues, must remove the conditions that fostered Islamic extremism in the first place.[47] And in Indonesia civil Islam is the only mechanism capable of expunging the corruption and repression that fuel extremism. The real enemy is the politics of resentment that cloaks itself in the trappings of Islam. The choice, therefore, is not between Islamism and secularism, but civil and uncivil Islam. If the former treats the state, in effect, as "one nation under Allah," that is no more anti-democratic than the principle "one nation under God."

Fukuyama just doesn't get it. He fails to see that maligning the politics of Islamic identity does a favor for the terrorist cause by blowing the bridge between "us and them";[48] and although Huntington avoids such neoliberal hubris, the gap between the two is not so wide as has been supposed. Their contest can better be described as a fraternal tug-of-war between Eurocentric optimism and pessimism. Both would offer the West as a model for global emulation wherever possible. They differ greatly, however, as to the scope of that possibility. Huntington is grimly reconciled to the West's cultural insularity, given what he considers the incorrigibility and very real danger of the cultural Other, and especially the Islamic Other, whereas Fukuyama holds out hope for an ever widening zone of posthistorical agreement. His brand of neoliberalism is always glad to lend a hand in liberating the Other from itself. Such globalism is just another name for neocolonialism.

Initially the Bush administration sustained Clinton's economic globalization while embracing isolation in other respects. It struck a balance, that is, between Fukuyama and Huntington. That changed on 9/11, when the Islamic Other paid its epochal visit on the symbolic centers of globalist trade and security. This was not a good day for Fukuyama's end-of-history teleology, but neither was it a good day for Huntington's cultural isolationism. As Karen Armstrong puts it, the inescapable lesson of that fateful day was that we now live in one world. If, like the Bush administration, we try to escape this fact, the world will have the last word.[49]

Conclusion: The Core Problem

These new terrors render old lines of defense obsolete or woefully inadequate, and old lines of foreign policy undecidable. One tragic error of twentieth-century international relations was its rigid bifurcation of realist and idealist strategies. Our current crisis demands that the two be brought into a workable relationship—my term for this merger being "moral realism."[50] This affords a geopolitical alternative to isolationism and imperialism alike. Moral realism rejects the ends and means of corporate globalization, on the one side, and Bush/Rumsfeld militancy on the other. It starts with a dialogic encounter with the cultural Other, in this case the civil Islamic Other. With Amartya Sen it recognizes that respect for basic freedom is hardly the monopoly of the West; and it observes that Islamic tolerance is an especially fertile field for democratic development.[51]

The very opposite view is taken by the Bush administration, which imposes cultural norms with the same unilateral fiat it applies to military decisions. Islamic militants are among the beneficiaries. When Bush, mirroring the theocrats' "Great Satan" view of America, vilified the entire Iranian nation, he gave the clerics temporary respite from their demographic dilemma in the face of the 70 percent of Iranians who are under age thirty and on the edge of revolt. This put at risk five years of arduous diplomatic bridge building with Khatami's moderate Islamism. Similar dialogic opportunities are being wasted throughout the Muslim world.

Civil Islam is the missing dialogic link between America and that world. Though it hardly registers in Western media coverage, Muslim civility is a growing force of change at the grassroots level in such diverse cultural climates as Indonesia and Egypt. The most popular Islamic preacher in Indonesia, Abdullah Gymnastiar, talks mainly about practical and personal issues to his rapt television audience. Even in Egypt, where Islamic extremism has competed with the government in its hostility toward moderate reformism, there are similar signs of transition. Many young Egyptians are turning away from the revolutionary Islamism of the 1980s towards a more personal and ethical faith, closely akin to the call of the Arab poet Adonis for an Islamic subjectivist revolution. There is a growing consensus that violence in general, and terrorism in particular, are very un-Islamic. Many former Egyptian militants have publicly renounced their prior activities and condemned Osama bin Laden's tactics, especially after 9/11.[52]

Promising as these developments are, the Egyptian case presages a reverse danger: the untimely forfeiture of modern Islam's political nature, and hence its oppositional resolve.[53] Political extremism, unfortunately, is giving way to a programmatically apolitical politics. Not surprisingly the personalization of Islam that is sweeping Egypt—pushing cassette sales of the country's leading televangelist, Amr Khaled, over those of the hottest pop stars—has been most entrenched within the affluent classes.[54] This privatization leaves the most explosive public issues to fester unattended. It is a safe bet that less privileged classes will not reach out to Amr Khaled for guidance. And the moderate political leaders they might have turned to, such as Professor Ibraham, will have been silenced.[55]

Indonesian Islam is less inclined toward this pendulum swing into apolitical civility. Even the affable and business-mined Gymnastiar is political enough to condemn American Middle East policies, and to underscore his disaffection by refusing all invitations to visit the United States. When he met Secretary of State Colin Powell he took the occasion to brief him on the axial principle of civil Islam: while Christians ground their faith in love, Muslims center theirs around fairness. That, he stressed, is America's core problem in dealing with the Islamic world. Washington's manifest unfairness is a veritable factory for blowback.

This is producing, in terms of culture clash, the equivalent of a new Cold War. Yet despite events such as the *Cole* attack and 9/11, radical Islamism is still a basically defensive reflex. In the view of Adonis, author of the shockingly prophetic poem, "The Funeral of New York," the geocultural battle lines of this war are internal to the West. They are drawn, that is, in terms of a different kind of civilizational clash: the widening gap between the richness and breadth of American culture, on the one side, and the poverty and narrowness of American foreign policy on the other. This rift traces largely to America's bad listening skills, such that only Islamic terrorism gets a hearing. The real enemy is not so much Islamism as our own cultural closure. More even than the first Cold War, this one is all about us.

Notes

1. Ladan Boroumand and Roya Boroumand, "Terror, Islam, and Democracy," *Journal of Democracy* 13, no. 2 (April 2002): 5 (5–20).

2. John F. Burns, "America Inspires Both Longing and Loathing in Arab World," *New York Times* (September 16, 2001), <www.nytimes.com/2001/09/16/international/16AMER.html>.

3. Seumas Milne, "They Can't See Why They Are Hated," *Guardian Unlimited* (September 13, 2001), <www.guardian.co.uk/comment/story/0,3604,551036,00.html>. The *Journal's* line of argument is part of an Orwellian rewrite of the Palestinian crisis whereby the recent spate of terrorism is thought to "balance the books" of over three decades of Israeli occupation and oppression. See David Crossman, "Fictions Embraced by an Israel at War," *New York Times* (October 1, 2002), <www.nytimes.com/2202/10/01/opinion/ 01GROS.html>.

4. See Admed Rashid, "Pakistan on the Edge," *The New York Review of Books* (October 10, 2002), <www.nybooks.com/articles/15740>.

5. Abdul Haq, interviewed by Anatol Lieven, "Voices from the Region: Interview with Commander Abdul Haq," *Carnegie Endowment Publications* (interviewed of October 11, 2001), <www.ceip.org/files/publications/lievendispatch-haq.asp>.

6. "Commander Admad Shah," *Afghan-Info.com* (last update January 14, 2002), <www.afghan-info.com/Politics/Massoud/AhmadShahMassoud_Page.htm>.

7. See Ahmed Rashid, "Afghanistan Imperiled," *The Nation* (October 4, 2002), <www.thenation.com/docprint.mhtml?I=2002=1014&rashid>.

8. This is all the more astonishing in view of the fact that since 1998 American intelligence had received a barrage of warnings concerning an impending attack on U.S. targets, including the World Trade Center, by al Qaeda operatives. See James Risen, "U.S. Was Aware of bin Laden Threat before Sept. 11 Attacks," *New York Times* (September 19, 2002), <www.nytimes.com/2002/09/19/politics/19CND-INTE.html>.

9. Micha Odenheimer, "Vicious Circles Closing In" [interviewed with Thomas von der Osten-Sacken], *Ha'aretz English Edition* (October 4, 2002), <www.haaretzdaily.com/hasenpages/ ShArt.jhtml?item No=215930>; and Tim Judah, "In Iraqi Kurdistan," *The New York Review of Books* (September 26, 2002), <www.nybooks.com/article/15688>.

10. Dilip Hiro, "When US Turned a Blind Eye to Poison Gas," *The Observer* (September 1, 2002), <www.observer.co.uk/Print/0,3858,4492363,00.html>.

11. Salman Rushdie, "Yes, This Is about Islam," *New York Times* (November 2, 2001), <www.nytimes.com/2001/11/02/opinion/02RUSH.html>.

12. Samuel Huntington, "So Are Civilizations at War?" [interview], *The Observer* (October 21, 2001), <www.observer.co.uk/Print/0,3858,4281700,00.html>.

13. There is no mention of death by stoning in the Koran, but the Old Testament repeatedly recommends it, and today's Christian Reconstructionists advocate it for crimes such as adultery and heresy. Meanwhile the 70,000 to 80,000 strong World Church of the Creator, centered in East Peoria, Illinois, promotes random brutality to blacks and other racial "enemies." See Nicholas D. Kristof, "Hate, American Style," *New York Times* (August 30, 2002), <www.nytimes.com/2002/08/30/opinion.30KRIShtml>.

14. Farish A. Noor, "Negotiating Islamic Law," *The Far Eastern Economic Review* (September 19, 2002), <www.feer.com/articles/2002/0209-19/p023fcol.html>.

15. Imran Khan, "Politics in Pakistan" [interview by Satish Kumar], *Resurgence* (downloaded September 19, 2002), <resurgence.gn.apc.org/articles/khan.htm>.

16. Robert W. Hefner, *Civil Islam: Muslims and Democratization in Indonesia* (Princeton, NJ: Princeton University Press, 2000), 13.

17. See John L. Esposito, "Introduction," in John L. Esposito, ed., *Political Islam: Revolution, Radicalism, or Reform?* (Boulder, CO: Lynne Rienner, 1997), 2–3 (1–14). Negatively understood, this dynamic can be seen as the complete abnegation of development theories, both liberal and Marxist, which construed modernization as a singular, world-historical phenomenon. See Leonard Binder, *Islamic Liberalism: A Critique of Development Ideologies* (Chicago: University of Chicago Press, 1988), 207.

18. Robert W. Hefner, "Islam and Nation in the Post-Suharto Era," in Adam Schwarz and Jonathan Paris, eds., *The Politics of Post-Suharto Indonesia* (New York: Council on Foreign Relations Press, 1990), 48. Suharto's turn can be traced to December 1990, when he shocked Western admirers of his anti-Islamism by authorizing the formation of the Association of Indonesian Muslim Intellectuals (ICMI). See Robert W. Hefner, "Islamization and Democratization in Indonesia," in Robert Hefner and Patricia Horvatich, eds., *Islam in an Era of Nation-States* (Honolulu: University of Hawai'i Press, 1997), 75 (75–127).

19. Beena Sarwar, "Brutality Cloaked as Tradition," *New York Times* (August 6, 2002), <www.nytimes.com/2002/08/06/opinion/06SARW.html>.

20. John L. Esposito, *Islam: The Straight Path*, expanded ed. (New York: Oxford University Press, 1991), 206–7.

21. Jacqueline Aquino Siapno, *Gender, Islam, Nationalism and the State in Aceh: The Paradox of Power, Co-optation and Resistance* (London: Routledge Curzon, 2002), 65.

22. Ian Fisher, "Turkish Government Takes Steps to Shut Popular Islamist Party," *New York Times* (October 24, 2002), <www.nytimes.com/2002/10/24/international/middleeast/24TURK.html>.

23. Bryan Turner, *Orientalism, Postmodernism and Globalism* (London: Routledge, 1994), 23.

24. Ian Urbina, "Poetic Injustice: U.S. War Interests in Turkey Hinder Democracy," *In These Times* (November 8, 2002), <www.inthesetimes.com/issue/27/01/news1.shtml>.

25. "Turkish Parliament, Looking to Europe, Passes Reforms," Associated Press report in *New York Times* (August 4, 2002), <www.nytimes.com/2002/08/04/international/europe/04TURK.html>. To be sure, these tactics can cut both ways. For decades Turkey played its Cold War card to stanch criticism of its domestic policies, and in 2000, when an American congressman pushed for a resolution condemning Turkey's 1915 slaughter of Armenians, Turkey killed the motion by threatening to close NATO bases and to seek a rapprochement with Iraq and Iran. See Mark Mazower, "The G-World," *London Review of Books* 23, no. 3 (February 8, 2001), <www.lrb.co.uk/v23/n03/mazo01.html>.

26. "Oil Diplomacy," *New York Times* (August 19, 2002), <www.nytimes.com/2002/8/19/opinion/19MON3.html>.

27. See Daniel Pipes and Azar Nafisi, "The Future of Islamism in the Muslim World," *Policywatch* (February 10, 1999), <www.danielpipes.org/pf.php?id=304>.

28. Stanley Hoffmann, "America Alone in the World," *The American Prospect* 13, no. 17 (September 23, 2002), <www.prospect.org/print-friendly/print/V13/17/hoffmann-s .html>.

29. Later, under rising media pressure, Washington announced a freeze on *additional* U.S. assistance to Egypt in protest of Ibrahim's treatment. Note that this freeze has no effect on the $2 billion in aid that Egypt already gets annually, making it the Arab world's biggest welfare recipient. The *New York Times* calls this action "commendable," but clearly it is tantamount to an assurance that the present $2 billion is not in jeopardy so long as Egypt continues to rubber-stamp U.S. policies. See "The Right Message to Egypt," *New York Times* (August 20, 2002), <www.nytimes.com/ 2002/08/20/opinion/20TUES3.html>. It is telling that Western diplomats, far from promoting democratic processes, tend to place their bets on Egypt's heir apparent, Gamal Mubarak, the president's son. See Jane Perlez, "Egyptians See U.S. as Meddling in Their Politics," *New York Times* (October 3, 2002), <www.nytimes.com/2002/10/03/ international/middleeast/03EGYP.html>.

30. Thomas L. Friedman, "Bush's Shame," *New York Times* (August 4, 2002), <www.nytimes.com/2002/0804/opinion/04FRIE.html>.

31. "Tariq Ali on 9/11" [interview by Doug Henwood on September 20, 2001], *Left Business Observer* 98 (October 2001), <www.leftbusinessobserver.com/Ali.html>.

32. See "Profile of the President Islam Karimov," *Human Rights News* (March 7, 2002), <www.hrw.org/press/2002/karimovprof.html>.

33. See Sergei Blagov, "Russia Mulls a New Unilateralism," *Eurasianet.org* (July 27, 2002), <www.eurasianet.org/department/insight/articles/eav071602.shtml>.

34. Robert G. Kaiser, "Difficult Times for a Key Ally in Terror War: Kyrgyzstan's Politics, Economy in Turmoil," *Washington Post* (August 5, 2002): A09.

35. Erdin Beshimov, "Akayev: We Do Democracy the Kyrgyz Way," *Yale Global* (October 18, 2004), <yaleglobal.yale.edu/article.print?id=4707>.

36. Ahmed Rashid, "A Fine Fix," *Far Eastern Economic Review* (October 24, 2002), <www.feer.com/cgi-bin/prog/printeasy?id=23162.981091599>.

37. This strategy is premised on the popular notion that Islam is inherently stultifying and undemocratic. Few in the West know anything about civil Islam, which does not make the evening news. Few would have heard of the ninth-century "Mutazilism" that interpreted the Koran as a metaphorical and historical body of literature rather than a literal and static dead end. Almost everyone, however, knows about the fatwa on Salman Rushdie. For a useful corrective to Fukuyama see Sage Stossel, "Life, Liberty, and the Pursuit of Islam," *The Atlantic Online* (December 12, 2001), <www .unbound/flashbks/democislam.htm>.

38. Francis Fukuyama, "Has History Started Again?" *Policy* (winter 2002), <www.cis.org.au/Policy/winter02/polwin02-1.htm>. Not surprisingly Fukuyama cites consumerism as one of the values most threatened by this deplorable religious reaction. Graham Fuller less tendentiously defines Islamism, or political Islam, "as the belief that the Koran and the Hadith (Traditions of the Prophet's Life) have something important to say about the way society and governance should be ordered. . . ." See

Fuller's "The Future of Political Islam," *Foreign Affairs* 81, no. 2 (March/April 2002): 49 (°48–60).

39. Whit Mason, "Iran's Simmering Discontent," *World Policy Journal* 29, no. 1 (spring 2002): 77 (71–80).

40. Helena Smith, "Generation Ex-Communicated," *The Guardian* (September 3, 2002), <www.guardian.co.uk/Print/0,3858,4493754,00.html>.

41. Mason, "Iran's Simmering Discontent," 72, 73, and 79.

42. V. R. Nasr, "Islamic Opposition in the Political Process: Lessons from Pakistan," in John L. Esposito, ed., *Political Islam: Revolution, Radicalism, or Reform?* (Boulder, CO: Lynne Rienner Publishers, 1997), 137 (135–56).

43. Shukri B. Abed, "Islam and Democracy," in David Garnham and Mark Tessler, eds., *Democracy, War and Peace in the Middle East* (Bloomington and Indianapolis: Indiana University Press, 1995), 122–25 (116–32). On Egyptian centrism, see Raymond William Baker, "Invidious Comparisons: Realism, Postmodern Globalism, and Centrist Islamic Movements in Egypt," in John L. Esposito, ed., *Political Islam: Revolution, Radicalism, or Reform?* (Boulder, CO: Lynne Rienner Publishers, 1997), 115 (115–33).

44. See Mona Abaza, *Shifting Worlds: Debates on Islam and Knowledge in Malaysia and Egypt* (London: Routledge Curzon, 2002), 7; and Osman Bakar, "Inter-Civilizational Dialogue: Theory and Practice in Islam," in Nakamura Mitsuo, Sharon Siddique, and Omar Farouk Bajunid, eds., *Islam and Civil Society in Southeast Asia* (Singapore: Institute of Southeast Asian Studies, 2001), 165 (164–76).

45. John McBeth, "Weak Link in the Anti-Terror Chain," *Far Eastern Economic Review* (October 24, 2002), <www.feer.com/cgi-bin/prog/printeasy?id=50248.486043802>.

46. See John McBeth and Banda Aceh, "The Case for Islamic Law," *The Far Eastern Economic Review* (August 22, 2002), <www.feer.com/articles/2002/0208_22/p012 region.html>. In Malaysia, however, the situation is quite the opposite. Here the Islamic PAS Party seeks to enforce a hard-line version of hudad, the Islamic criminal code, in the two states where PAS dominates. This would undermine the moderate sharia that now applies to personal matters such as divorce. Again it is the local particulars of political culture rather than Islam as such which render Islamic justice reformist or repressive. Regarding PAS, see S. Jayasankaran, "A Malaysian Duel over Islam," *The Far Eastern Economic Review* (August 22, 2002), <www.feer.com/cgi-bin/prog/printeasy>.

47. Until recently the Asia director of Human Rights Watch, Sidney Jones is now the director of the International Crisis Group, which has just released a report by her on the terrorist threat in Indonesia. Her conclusion is that the worst threat lies in the extremism that repressive anti-terrorist action would generate. See Jane Perlez, "Indonesia Preacher Is behind Radical Network, Report Says," *New York Times* (August 11, 2002), <www.nytimes.com/2002/08/11/international/asia/11WEB.INDO.html>.

48. Fukuyama is hardly unique in this error. Western leaders and media pundits typically understate the terrorist's political motivations while overstating their religious determination. See Eric Rouleau, "Politics in the Name of the Prophet," *Le Monde diplomatique* (November 2001), <www.en.monde-diplomatique.fr/2001/11/09prophet>.

49. Karen Armstrong, "The West Has to Understand the Causes of Muslim Rage," *The Independent* (August 7, 2002), <enjoyment.independent.co.uk/books/reviews/story.jsp?story=321984>.

50. William H. Thornton, *Fire on the Rim: The Cultural Dynamics of East/West Power Politics* (Lanham, MD: Rowman & Littlefield, 2002), chapter 8.

51. Amartya Sen, *Development as Freedom* (New York: Alfred A. Knopf, 1999), 238–40.

52. "Kinder, Gentler Islam," *The Economist* (June 29, 2002), 44 and 46. A similar critical drift in Saudi Arabia has been far less effective, but there is hope that the shocking fall of the average Saudi income from $24,000 to $7,000 will rectify that. See "Palpitations at the Kingdom's Heart," *The Economist* (August 24, 2002), <economist.com/world/africa/index.cfm?Story_ID=1291310>.

53. Putting aside the deeper theological question of Islam's core principles, it is sufficient to note the oppositional turn that Islam took during its anti-colonial and post-colonial resurgence. Clifford Geertz points out how Islam, in its cultural and political rebound, also gravitated toward a scripturally centered identity. See Clifford Geertz, *Islam Observed: Religious Development in Morocco and Indonesia* (Chicago: University of Chicago Press, 1968), 64–65.

54. Geertz, *Islam Observed*, 44.

55. Update: Fortunately Ibrahim has been released. While Washington focused its attention on Iraq, President Mubarak laid the diplomatic foundation for a smooth transfer of power to his son, Gamal Mubarak, by sending him as the leader of an official delegation to the White House. Since Gamal is being packaged as a progressive, Cairo found it efficacious to stage Ibrahim's release as a sample of the essential goodness of the Mubarak dynasty. See Jackson Diehl, "Gorbachev on the Nile?" *Washington Post* (February 10, 2003): A21.

Index

Abu Ghraib, 52
Abu Sayyaf, 79–80
Aceh, 64, 69, 75, 88n35, 207, 213
Acre Popular Front, 28
Adonis, 215
Afghanistan: continued disorder in, 11n17; current poppy boom, 146n34; interim government gets legitimacy from UN presence, 197n25; invasion of, 3; as Islamic Republic, 127; lack of American interest in Afghan nation-building, 202; ongoing trauma in, 125; pipeline politics in, 121; refugees, 146n33; state terrorism under the Taliban, 122; U.S. contribution to insecurity, 124; U.S. support of known terrorists in, 63; U.S. wants Afghanistan weak and dependent, 119
Ajami, Fouad: anti-Islamism of, 178n77
Akayev, Askar, 131; Bush puts a U.S. stamp of approval on his reactionary turn, 210; as globalist, 136
AKP (Justice and Development Party), 149n84; squeezed between Turkey's secular establishment and the Islamic

old guard of the Welfare Party, 138, 140; sweeping victory in November 2002, 205
Albright, Madeleine, 29, 47
Algeria, 27, 35n57; democratic Islamism of, 28
Ali, Tariq, 95; weakness of his picture of Iraq at the time of Saddam's overthrow, 190
Aliyev, Heidar, 130
Aliyev, Ilham, 130; as new U.S. and EU crony, 130–31
Allawi, Ayad, 182; his INA (Iraqi National Accord) versus Chalabi's INC, 180; as neocolonial agent, 155
al Qaeda, geopolitics of, 4; nuclear dealings, 108
Annan, Kofi: not a U.S. rubber stamp, 183
antiwar movement, 25, 36n60
Anwar Ibrahim, 62–63, 75, 76n51, 212
APEC (Asia-Pacific Economic Cooperation): antiterrorism of, 66; compared to ASEAN, 87n18; "open regionalism" of, 64
Aquino, Corazon, 77, 80

About the Author

William H. Thornton is professor of cultural studies and globalization at National Cheng Kung University in Tainan, Taiwan. His previous books were *Cultural Prosaics: The Second Postmodern Turn* (1998) and *Fire on the Rim: The Cultural Dynamics of East/West Power Politics* (2002).